Southern Living®
OUR READERS
Top-Rated
RECIPES

*Pear Salad with
Raspberry Cream, page 41*

Southern Living

OUR READERS
Top-Rated
RECIPES

Compiled and Edited by
Jane E. Gentry

Oxmoor House

© 2005 by Oxmoor House, Inc.
Book Division of Southern Progress Corporation
P. O. Box 2262, Birmingham, Alabama 35201-2262

Southern Living® is a federally registered trademark belonging to
Southern Living, Inc.

ISBN: 0-8487-3054-2
Library of Congress Control Number: 2005922033
Printed in the United States of America
Third Printing 2006

Editor in Chief: Nancy Fitzpatrick Wyatt
Executive Editor: Susan Carlisle Payne
Art Director: Cynthia Rose Cooper
Copy Chief: Allison Long Lowery

Southern Living®
Our Readers' Top-Rated Recipes

Editor: Jane E. Gentry
Nutrition Editor: Holley Contri Johnson, M.S., R.D.
Copy Editor: Diane Rose
Editorial Assistant: Shannon Friedmann
Senior Photographer: Jim Bathie
Senior Photo Stylist: Kay E. Clarke
Director, Test Kitchens: Elizabeth Tyler Luckett
Assistant Director, Test Kitchens: Julie Christopher
Test Kitchens Staff: Kristi Carter, Nicole Lee Faber,
Kathleen Royal Phillips, Elise Weis, Kelley Self Wilton
Publishing Systems Administrator: Rick Tucker
Director of Production: Phillip Lee
Production Manager: Greg A. Amason
Production Assistant: Faye Porter Bonner

Contributors:
Designer: Nancy Johnson
Indexer: Mary Ann Laurens
Interns: Leighton Batte, Julie Boston, Marian Cairns, Sheila Egts

Cover: Blackberry-Raspberry Truffle Cake, page 335
Back Cover: Peppery Chicken Fried Chicken, page 208; Two-Cheese Squash Casserole, page 314;
Creole Jambalaya, page 10; White Chocolate Chip-Oatmeal Cookies, page 361

To order additional publications, call 1-800-765-6400.

For more books to enrich your life, visit **oxmoorhouse.com**

Top-rated recipes and reader comments from AOL Food and **SouthernLiving.com**. For thousands more
recipes tested and rated by the AOL Food community, AOL members can access AOL Food using AOL Keyword: *Food*,
or Southern Living® subscribers can go to **SouthernLiving.com** and click on *Food*.

contents

Hello, Neighbor!

We discovered that *Southern Living* readers are using the Internet to do what neighbors have loved doing for years—chatting over the backyard fence. They share pot roast victories, turkey surprises, culinary accomplishments, and even a little dating advice! Over 5,000 *Southern Living* recipes are available on AOL Food and **SouthernLiving.com,** where readers share stories about testing the recipes and rate their favorites. In *Southern Living® Our Readers' Top-Rated Recipes,* we've compiled over 550 surefire recipes that our readers rated 5 stars—along with tips, substitution suggestions, and menu pairing ideas straight from *Southern Living* readers.

- "My roasts are usually as tender as an old shoe. Every time I use this recipe, my roast comes out fall-apart tender!"
    —*Tenderhearted for* **Aunt Mary's Pot Roast** (page 52)

- "This turkey recipe deserves more stars than I can give. My family complained about not having enough leftovers because it was just so good."
    —*Left with No Leftovers by* **Sugar-and-Spice Cured Turkey** (page 62)

- "Every bite was devoured amidst oohing and aaahing! This recipe made me look like a gourmet chef!"
    —*Made Famous Thanks to* **Sweet Potato Crème Brûlée** (page 73)

- "This is quick, easy, and sure to impress that special lady! That's right, this is a great recipe for guys to try."
    —*In Love with* **Green Bean Alfredo with Cheese Ravioli** (page 58)

We've put our recipes to the true test, and they've received our readers' seals of approval! Home cooks everywhere have shared their secrets and favorites with each other online—and now you're in on the scoop. So turn the page and find out what the chat is all about.

The Editors

top 10
reader-rated
favorites

★★★★★

Nibble on one of these top 10 recipes that our readers most frequently added to their personal online cookbooks.

Linzer Cookies, page 16

Cooks Chat

"This is a favorite! I made this last week, and I'm making it again tonight. My husband loves it, and my parents do, too. The corn tortillas add a delicious and different flavor. I did add fresh sliced mushrooms to the onion and pepper mixture. This recipe is very easy if you don't want to spend all night in the kitchen. I can't tell you how the leftovers were—we didn't have any."

"My entire family loved this. Very tasty and satisfying. It's not too often that I please everyone!"

"My family was tired of the same old dinners. I tried this recipe, and it's now requested at least once a week. Very easy to make before or after work. Delicious!"

FOR THE HOLIDAYS

★ ★ ★ ★ ★

Cooks Chat

"These cookies are so good! I divided the dough and rolled half in crushed pecans. For the rest, I dipped the baked cookies halfway in chocolate. I liked the ones with the pecans so much that I ate them all, so be careful!"

#1 King Ranch Chicken Casserole

Reader Favorite

Prep: 35 min.   **Cook:** 35 min.

1 large onion, chopped
1 large green bell pepper, chopped
2 tablespoons vegetable oil
2 cups chopped cooked chicken
1 (10¾-ounce) can cream of chicken soup, undiluted
1 (10¾-ounce) can cream of mushroom soup, undiluted

1 (10-ounce) can diced tomatoes and green chiles
1 teaspoon chili powder
¼ teaspoon salt
¼ teaspoon garlic powder
¼ teaspoon pepper
12 (6-inch) corn tortillas
2 cups (8 ounces) shredded Cheddar cheese, divided

• Sauté onion and bell pepper in hot oil in a large skillet over medium-high heat 5 minutes or until tender. Stir in chicken and next 7 ingredients; remove from heat.
• Tear tortillas into 1-inch pieces, and layer one-third of tortilla pieces in bottom of a lightly greased 13- x 9-inch baking dish. Top with one-third of chicken mixture and ⅔ cup cheese. Repeat layers twice.
• Bake at 350° for 30 to 35 minutes. Yield: 6 to 8 servings.

Note: Freeze casserole up to 1 month, if desired. Thaw in refrigerator overnight, and bake as directed.

#2 Santa's Shortbread Cookies

Reader Favorite

Prep: 15 min.   **Cook:** 12 min. per batch   **Other:** 8 hrs.

1 cup butter, softened
¾ cup powdered sugar
2 teaspoons vanilla extract

2 cups all-purpose flour
¼ teaspoon baking powder
⅛ teaspoon salt

• Beat butter at medium speed with an electric mixer until creamy; gradually add powdered sugar, beating well. Add vanilla, beating until blended.
• Combine flour, baking powder, and salt; add to butter mixture, beating at low speed until blended.

• Divide cookie dough in half; shape each portion into a 10-inch log. Wrap in wax paper, and chill 8 hours; or freeze up to 6 weeks, and thaw in refrigerator.
• Cut each roll into ⅓-inch-thick slices; place on lightly greased baking sheets.
• Bake at 350° for 10 to 12 minutes or until lightly browned. Transfer to wire racks to cool. Yield: 5 dozen.

Chocolate-Dipped Shortbread Cookies: Microwave ½ cup (3 ounces) semisweet chocolate morsels in a glass bowl at HIGH 1 minute. Stir until smooth. Dip half of each cooled cookie into chocolate. Place on wax paper to set.

Peanut Butter-and-Jelly Shortbread Cookies: Stir ½ cup peanut butter into dough after adding flour mixture. Make an indentation in center of each cookie slice before baking. Fill each indentation with ¼ teaspoon jelly. Bake as directed.

Chocolate-Mint Shortbread Cookies: Stir 1 (4.67-ounce) package chocolate mints, chopped, into dough after adding flour mixture. Proceed as directed.

Toffee Shortbread Cookies: Stir 1 cup toffee bits into dough after adding flour mixture. Proceed as directed. (For testing purposes only, we used Heath Bits O' Brickle Toffee Bits, found near chocolate morsels in the grocery store.)

Pecan-Crusted Shortbread Cookies: Coat 10-inch logs with ¾ cup finely chopped pecans. Proceed as directed.

Red Cinnamon Candy Shortbread Cookies: Stir ½ cup red cinnamon candies into dough after adding flour mixture. Proceed as directed.

Snowman Shortbread Cookies: Chill dough 2 hours after adding flour mixture. Shape dough into 16 (¾-inch) balls, 16 (½-inch) balls, and 16 (¼-inch) balls. Use 1 ball of each size to make snowman shapes, leaving no space between balls. Bake as directed. For eyes, use black gel frosting after cookies cool, or press chocolate mini-morsels onto warm cookies. Make scarves using red decorator frosting after cookies cool.

★★★★★

Cooks Chat

"I served this to my family, and everyone had seconds. I made fresh rolls, coleslaw, and peach cobbler to go with it. This is a great dish because most of the ingredients are on hand, and it takes no time to cook the rice. I will certainly serve this again."

"This was my first taste of Creole jambalaya, and I was delighted with it. I changed a couple of things around in the recipe by omitting the green onions and adding a 24-ounce can of diced tomatoes. We had it for leftovers the next day, and it tasted even better!"

#3 *Reader Favorite*

Creole Jambalaya

Prep: 25 min.   **Cook:** 1 hr.

2 tablespoons butter or
    margarine
1 large onion, chopped
1 green bell pepper, chopped
8 green onions, chopped
2 celery ribs, chopped
3 cups cubed cooked ham
    (1 pound)
1 pound Cajun-flavored or
    smoked sausage, sliced

1 (8-ounce) can tomato sauce
½ teaspoon salt
½ teaspoon ground black
    pepper
¼ teaspoon ground red pepper
5 cups cooked rice
Garnishes: fresh parsley sprig,
    chopped fresh parsley

• Melt butter in a large skillet over medium heat. Add onion and next 3 ingredients; sauté until tender. Add ham, sausage, and next 4 ingredients. Cook, stirring occasionally, 20 minutes.
• Stir in rice, cover, and cook, stirring occasionally, 30 minutes over low heat. Garnish, if desired. Yield: 8 servings.

Hearty Potato Soup

Prep: 8 min.   **Cook:** 3 hrs., 30 min.

6 potatoes, peeled and cut into
⅓-inch cubes (2½ pounds)
2 medium onions, diced
2 carrots, thinly sliced
2 celery ribs, thinly sliced
2 (14-ounce) cans low-sodium
fat-free chicken broth

1 teaspoon dried basil
1 teaspoon salt
½ teaspoon pepper
¼ cup all-purpose flour
1½ cups fat-free half-and-half
Italian Bread Bowls
Garnish: fresh celery leaves

• Combine first 8 ingredients in a 4½-quart slow cooker.
• Cook, covered, at HIGH 3 hours or until vegetables are tender.
• Stir together flour and half-and-half; stir into soup. Cover and cook 30 minutes or until thoroughly heated. Serve in Italian Bread Bowls. Garnish, if desired. Yield: 8½ cups.

Italian Bread Bowls

Prep: 15 min.   **Cook:** 30 min.   **Other:** 1 hr., 15 min.

2½ cups warm water (100°
to 110°)
2 (¼-ounce) envelopes active
dry yeast
2 teaspoons salt

2 tablespoons vegetable oil
7 cups all-purpose flour
1 tablespoon cornmeal
1 egg white
1 tablespoon water

• Stir together 2½ cups water and yeast in a large bowl; let stand 5 minutes. Stir in salt and oil.
• Add flour gradually, beating at medium speed with an electric mixer until a soft dough forms.
• Turn dough out onto a floured surface; knead until smooth and elastic (4 to 6 minutes). Place in a lightly greased bowl, turning to grease top. Cover and let rise in a warm place (85°), free from drafts, 35 minutes or until doubled in bulk.
• Punch dough down, and divide into 8 equal portions. Shape each portion into a 4-inch round loaf. Place loaves on lightly greased baking sheets sprinkled with cornmeal. Cover and let rise in a warm place, free from drafts, 35 minutes or until doubled in bulk.
• Stir together egg white and 1 tablespoon water; brush over loaves.
• Bake at 400° for 15 minutes. Brush with remaining egg mixture, and bake 10 to 15 more minutes or until golden. Cool on wire racks. Freeze up to 1 month, if desired.
• Cut a ½-inch-thick slice from top of each loaf; scoop out centers, leaving ¾-inch-thick shells. (Reserve centers for other uses.) Fill bread bowls with hot soup, and serve immediately. Yield: 8 servings.

KITCHEN COMFORT
★ ★ ★ ★ ★

Cooks Chat

"This is the best potato soup recipe; it's my new favorite! I served it with barbecued beef sandwiches for a small dinner for friends. They loved it. Fixing it in the slow cooker was a breeze."

"This was so good—even my children ate it! I will definitely prepare this again."

#5 Low-and-Slow Baby Back Ribs

Reader Favorite

Prep: 20 min.   **Cook:** 6 hrs., 20 min.   **Other:** 8 hrs., 10 min.

3 slabs baby back pork ribs
Barbecue Rub
Hickory chips

Apple juice
Vinegar Sauce

• Rinse and pat ribs dry. Remove thin membrane from back of ribs by slicing into it with a knife and then pulling. (This will make ribs more tender and allow meat to absorb smoke and rub.)
• Sprinkle meat generously with Barbecue Rub. Massage rub into meat. Wrap tightly with plastic wrap, and chill 8 hours.
• Prepare a hot fire by piling charcoal on 1 side of grill, leaving other side empty. (For gas grills, light only 1 side.) Place cooking grate on grill. Arrange ribs over unlit side.
• Grill 2 hours, covered with grill lid, adding 5 to 7 charcoal pieces every 45 minutes to 1 hour, and keeping temperature between 225° and 250°. Add a handful of hickory chips to the charcoal every 20 to 30 minutes. Spritz ribs with apple juice from a squeeze-trigger sprayer each time you add wood chips.
• Reposition rib slabs occasionally, placing the slab closest to the heat source in the back and adding hickory chips and coals as needed to maintain the low temperature. Grill 2 more hours. Remove ribs from grill, and place on heavy-duty aluminum foil. Spritz ribs generously with apple juice; tightly seal. Place foil-wrapped ribs back on the grill; cook 2 more hours.
• Remove ribs from foil, place flat on grill, and baste generously with Vinegar Sauce. Grill 20 more minutes. Remove from grill, and let stand 10 minutes. Cut ribs into 3-rib sections, slicing between bones. Yield: 6 servings.

Barbecue Rub

Prep: 10 min.

1 cup firmly packed dark
   brown sugar
½ cup garlic powder
½ cup kosher salt
½ cup paprika
2 tablespoons onion powder
1 tablespoon dry mustard

1 tablespoon Creole seasoning
1 tablespoon chili powder
1 tablespoon ground red pepper
1 tablespoon ground cumin
1 tablespoon ground black
   pepper

• Stir together all ingredients in a bowl. Store in an airtight container. Yield: about 3 cups.

Vinegar Sauce

Prep: 5 min.   **Cook:** 15 min.

2 cups apple cider vinegar
½ cup white vinegar
½ cup apple juice
¼ cup firmly packed brown
    sugar
1 tablespoon kosher salt

½ tablespoon freshly ground
    black pepper
½ teaspoon ground red
    pepper
½ teaspoon paprika

• Place all ingredients in a saucepan, and bring to a boil; reduce heat, and simmer 15 minutes. Chill until ready to use. Reheat, if desired. Yield: about 4½ cups.

Reader Favorite #6

Chicken Fajita Pizza

Prep: 15 min.   **Cook:** 22 min.

½ (24-ounce) package
    refrigerated pizza crusts
2 skinned and boned chicken
    breasts, cut into strips
1 tablespoon vegetable oil
2 teaspoons chili powder
1 teaspoon salt
½ teaspoon garlic powder
1 small onion, sliced

1 small green bell pepper,
    chopped
1 cup salsa
1 (8-ounce) package shredded
    Monterey Jack cheese
Toppings: diced tomatoes,
    shredded lettuce, sour
    cream

• Place crust on a lightly greased baking sheet.
• Sauté chicken in hot oil in a skillet over medium-high heat 5 minutes or until tender. Stir in chili powder, salt, and garlic powder. Remove from skillet, and set aside.
• Add onion and bell pepper to skillet; sauté 5 minutes or until tender.
• Spread crust with salsa; top with chicken, onion mixture, and cheese.
• Bake at 425° for 10 to 12 minutes or until cheese melts. Serve with desired toppings. Yield: 4 to 6 servings.

Note: For testing purposes only, we used Mama Mary's Gourmet Pizza Crusts.

PARTY PLEASER
★★★★★

Cooks Chat

"I will keep this recipe in my favorite cookbook so I can make this again. This could be used for both special occasions and everyday meals. It's big enough to serve all by itself."

"This was a big success with my family and friends. No one could quit eating it! Everyone loves Mexican food, so I served it with Spanish rice and guacamole. What a great pizza!"

Cooks Chat

"This was a real hit at my party, and it even worked as a nonalcoholic drink for the kids' dinner! Instead of using star fruit, I used 3 golden kiwifruit for garnishing. Terrific!"

"This punch went over really well with all my friends. To garnish the punch, I threaded strawberries, pineapple, and kiwifruit onto skewers."

Cooks Chat

"I have made many breakfast casseroles, and this one is a keeper. The Hawaiian bread makes this sweet, and the texture is very plump. I added the whole pack of bacon instead of just 8 slices. It's just as good the next morning if you have any leftovers."

"Excellent! A wonderful change from the same old breakfast casserole. The salsa was a huge hit. I will definitely make this again."

#7 Fruit Punch

Reader Favorite

Prep: 5 min.

This refreshing recipe tastes just as good without the rum.

3 cups cranberry juice cocktail
2 cups pineapple juice
2 cups orange juice
1 (1-liter) bottle ginger ale, chilled

¾ to 1 cup light rum
Garnish: 1 star fruit, cut into ¼-inch slices

• Combine first 3 ingredients in a large bowl, and chill up to 8 hours, if desired. Stir ginger ale and rum into juice mixture just before serving. Serve over ice. Garnish, if desired. Yield: 12 cups.

#8 Bacon-and-Egg Casserole

Reader Favorite

Prep: 25 min.　**Cook:** 35 min.　**Other:** 8 hrs., 30 min.

Assemble this hearty dish the night before, and bake the next morning.

1 (16-ounce) Hawaiian bread loaf, cut into ¾-inch cubes
2 cups (8 ounces) finely shredded Mexican four-cheese blend
½ pound bacon, cooked and crumbled (8 slices)
8 large eggs

2½ cups milk
½ teaspoon salt
½ teaspoon pepper
1 teaspoon dried mustard
½ teaspoon Worcestershire sauce
Salsa or sliced fresh tomatoes

• Arrange bread cubes in a lightly greased 13- x 9-inch baking dish. Sprinkle with shredded cheese and crumbled bacon.
• Whisk together eggs, milk, salt, pepper, mustard, and Worcestershire sauce. Pour over prepared dish; press down bread cubes with a spoon to allow bread to soak up liquid. Cover and chill 8 hours. Let stand 30 minutes before baking.
• Bake at 350° for 35 minutes or until set and golden. Serve with salsa or sliced fresh tomatoes. Yield: 8 to 10 servings.

Note: Hawaiian bread may be found in the deli section of the supermarket. Substitute 10 to 12 white bread slices, cubed, for Hawaiian bread, if desired.

Fruit Punch

#9 Reader Favorite Baked Sweet 'n' Savory Mashed Potatoes

Prep: 20 min.   **Cook:** 50 min.

3½ pounds baking potatoes, peeled and cut into 1-inch pieces
1 tablespoon salt, divided
1 (29-ounce) can sweet potatoes in syrup, drained and mashed

1 (8-ounce) package ⅓-less-fat cream cheese, softened
6 bacon slices, cooked and crumbled
¾ cup light sour cream
⅔ cup chicken broth
½ teaspoon pepper

• Bring potatoes, 1 teaspoon salt, and water to cover to a boil in a Dutch oven; cook 30 minutes or until tender. Drain.
• Return potatoes to Dutch oven. Add sweet potatoes and cream cheese; mash until smooth with a potato masher. Stir in bacon, next 3 ingredients, and remaining 2 teaspoons salt. Spoon mixture into a lightly greased 11- x 7-inch baking dish. Bake, uncovered, at 350° for 20 minutes. Yield: 6 to 8 servings.

#10 Reader Favorite Linzer Cookies

Prep: 25 min.   **Cook:** 15 min. per batch   **Other:** 1 hr.

(shown on page 7)

1¼ cups butter, softened
1 cup powdered sugar, sifted
2½ cups all-purpose flour
½ cup finely chopped pecans, toasted
¼ teaspoon salt

¼ teaspoon ground cloves
¼ teaspoon ground cinnamon
1 teaspoon grated lemon rind
¼ cup seedless raspberry jam
Powdered sugar

• Beat butter at medium speed with an electric mixer; gradually add 1 cup powdered sugar, beating until light and fluffy.
• Combine flour and next 5 ingredients; gradually add to butter mixture, beating just until blended.
• Divide dough into 2 equal portions. Cover and chill 1 hour.
• Roll each portion to ⅛-inch thickness on a lightly floured surface; cut with a 3-inch star-shaped cutter. Cut centers out of half of cookies with a 1½ inch star shaped cutter. Place all stars on lightly greased baking sheets.
• Bake at 325° for 15 minutes; cool on wire racks. Spread solid cookies with jam; sprinkle remaining stars with powdered sugar. Top each solid cookie with a hollow star. Yield: about 3 dozen.

menus

★★★★★

Gather family and friends and cozy up to a home-cooked meal with these 5-star menus.

Aunt Mary's Pot Roast,
page 52

Company's Coming

serves 8

Chili-Rubbed Salmon*   *Cheesy Scalloped Potatoes*   *Steamed zucchini*

Bakery rolls   *Garden Sangría*   *Ultimate Cheesecake*

*Double recipe to serve 8.

Cooks Chat

"This recipe is great. I didn't have dillseed, so I used a dash of garlic powder and dillweed instead. Next time, I will serve it on a bed of Caesar salad!"

"I don't even like salmon, but this was delicious! Quick, easy, and packed with flavor."

Chili-Rubbed Salmon

Prep: 5 min.   **Cook:** 10 min.

1 tablespoon chili powder
2 teaspoons dillseeds
1 teaspoon lemon pepper
½ teaspoon ground cumin

4 (4- to 6-ounce) salmon steaks
¼ cup butter or margarine
Garnishes: fresh thyme sprigs,
  lemon zest, edible flowers

• Combine first 4 ingredients; press evenly over steaks.
• Melt butter in a large nonstick skillet over medium heat; add steaks, and cook 5 minutes on each side or until fish flakes with a fork. Garnish, if desired. Yield: 4 servings.

Cheesy Scalloped Potatoes

Prep: 10 min.　**Cook:** 1 hr., 2 min.　**Other:** 15 min.

2½ pounds red potatoes,
　unpeeled
3 tablespoons butter or
　margarine
⅓ cup chopped green onions
⅓ cup chopped red bell pepper
1 garlic clove, minced
¼ teaspoon ground red pepper

2 cups whipping cream
¾ cup milk
¾ teaspoon salt
¼ teaspoon freshly ground
　pepper
1 cup (4 ounces) shredded
　Swiss cheese
¼ cup grated Parmesan cheese

• Cut potatoes into ⅛-inch-thick slices; set aside.
• Melt butter in a Dutch oven over medium-high heat; add green onions and next 3 ingredients. Cook, stirring constantly, 2 minutes. Add whipping cream and next 3 ingredients, stirring well.
• Add potato slices; bring to a boil over medium heat, and cook, stirring gently, 15 minutes or until potato slices are tender. Spoon into a lightly greased 11- x 7-inch baking dish; sprinkle with cheeses.
• Bake at 350° for 45 minutes or until bubbly and golden brown. Let stand 15 minutes before serving. Yield: 8 servings.

Cooks Chat

"Yum, yum! I am still talking about these potatoes today after serving them at a dinner party last night. Everyone loved them. These potatoes are going in my file under 'favorites.'"

"These scalloped potatoes are to die for; they're the best I've ever tasted. I made a few changes: I used russet potatoes, a yellow bell pepper (that was what I had on hand), 4 cloves of garlic, 1 teaspoon of ground red pepper, and no salt. I covered the dish for the first half hour and then uncovered for another half hour. I made this for the first time a few days ago when I had company for dinner. Everyone loved it! I had to give them a copy of the recipe."

Garden Sangría

Prep: 10 min.　**Other:** 8 hrs.

1 gallon dry white wine
2 cups brandy
1 cup orange liqueur
4 oranges, sliced
1 bunch fresh mint leaves
1 (1-liter) bottle club soda,
　chilled*

1 quart whole strawberries
2 lemons, thinly sliced
2 limes, thinly sliced
Garnishes: fresh mint sprigs,
　strawberries, red seedless
　grapes, orange and lime
　wedges

• Combine first 5 ingredients in a large container; cover and chill 8 hours.
• Add club soda and next 3 ingredients just before serving; serve sangría over ice, if desired. Garnish, if desired. Yield: 1½ gallons.

*Substitute ginger ale for club soda, if desired.

Cooks Chat

"This is a BEAUTIFUL presentation! I always get raves! I have used white grape juice with splashes of lemon and orange juice in the place of wine and liquor for a nonalcoholic version."

"This recipe is very adaptable. For a party, I used a wine I knew all my guests would like (blush), and it was perfect. It is very strong in its uncut state, and I used several liters of ginger ale to turn it into a sparkling wine cooler."

Cooks Chat

"Excellent recipe. I haven't found a better one. This cheesecake is requested every holiday, and my family actually judges cheesecakes at restaurants based on this one."

"This cheesecake is delicious. I have given this recipe to a few friends already. It was a big hit at the Cub Scout picnic."

"Love it! I make it with Splenda (it measures cup for cup the same as sugar), and no one can tell. For the crust, I use 2 cups of ground pecans for the graham cracker crumbs and ½ cup melted butter (with no sugar or Splenda). The perfect low-carb dessert. The sour cream topping is optional for me. I use a fresh fruit topping, sweetened with Splenda."

Ultimate Cheesecake

Prep: 15 min.   **Cook:** 1 hr., 22 min.   **Other:** 12 hrs., 10 min.

2 cups graham cracker crumbs
¼ cup sugar
½ cup butter or margarine, melted
7 large eggs
4 (8-ounce) packages cream cheese, softened
1¾ cups sugar

2 teaspoons vanilla extract
1 (16-ounce) container sour cream
½ cup sugar
⅛ teaspoon vanilla extract
Apricot Glaze
Garnish: strawberry halves

• Stir together first 3 ingredients; press into bottom and 1 inch up sides of a 10-inch springform pan. Chill 1 hour.
• Beat eggs at medium speed with an electric mixer. Add cream cheese, and beat until blended. Gradually add 1¾ cups sugar, beating well. Stir in 2 teaspoons vanilla extract. Pour batter into chilled crust.
• Bake at 350° for 1 hour and 15 minutes. Cool on a wire rack 10 minutes. Increase oven temperature to 425°.
• Stir together sour cream, ½ cup sugar, and ⅛ teaspoon vanilla; spread over cheesecake.
• Bake at 425° for 5 to 7 minutes. Cool on a wire rack 1 hour. Cover and chill at least 10 hours. Remove sides of pan. Serve with Apricot Glaze, and garnish, if desired. Yield: 12 to 14 servings.

Apricot Glaze

Prep: 5 min.   **Cook:** 15 min.

1 (10-ounce) jar apricot jam
¼ cup sugar

¼ cup water
1 tablespoon rum or brandy

• Combine first 3 ingredients in a small saucepan over low heat; cook, stirring occasionally, until consistency of syrup. Remove from heat. Stir in rum; pour through a fine wire-mesh strainer. Cool and serve over cheesecake slices. Yield: 1½ cups.

Cherry Glaze: Substitute cherry preserves for apricot jam; do not strain before serving.

Vegetarian Night

serves 6

Spinach-Black Bean Lasagna   Greek Caesar Salad

Key Lime Cheesecake with Strawberry Sauce

Spinach-Black Bean Lasagna

Prep: 25 min.   **Cook:** 1 hr., 5 min.

2 large eggs, lightly beaten
1 (15-ounce) container ricotta
   cheese
1 (10-ounce) package frozen
   chopped spinach, thawed
   and well drained
¼ cup chopped fresh cilantro
½ teaspoon salt
4 cups (16 ounces) shredded
   Monterey Jack cheese with
   peppers, divided

2 (16-ounce) cans black beans,
   rinsed and drained
1 (2-pound, 13-ounce) jar pasta
   sauce
½ teaspoon ground cumin
9 precooked lasagna noodles
Garnish: chopped fresh cilantro

• Stir together first 5 ingredients and 1 cup Monterey Jack cheese; set aside.

• Mash beans with a potato masher or fork in a large bowl; stir in pasta sauce and cumin. Spread one-third of bean mixture on bottom of a lightly greased 13- x 9-inch baking dish.

• Layer with 3 noodles, half of spinach mixture, and 1 cup Monterey Jack cheese; repeat layers. Spread with one-third bean mixture; top with remaining 3 noodles and remaining bean mixture.

• Bake, covered, at 350° for 1 hour; uncover and top with remaining Monterey Jack cheese. Bake 5 more minutes or until cheese melts. Garnish, if desired. Yield: 6 servings.

KITCHEN COMFORT

Cooks Chat

"A friend made this for our first annual 'guinea pig brunch,' where we try recipes for the first time and determine if they're keepers or not. This was a hit! It will definitely become a favorite to make for family and friends!"

"This is very easy to make, but it tastes like you spent hours in the kitchen. Your nonvegetarian friends won't even know it's meatless unless you tell them!"

"This was a wonderful dish. Even my husband loved it, which totally surprised me, since he doesn't usually like dishes without meat. We like to use fresh spinach rather than frozen."

Greek Caesar Salad

Prep: 10 min.

¾ cup olive oil
¼ cup lemon juice
¼ cup egg substitute
2 garlic cloves, pressed
1 teaspoon dried oregano
¼ teaspoon salt

⅛ teaspoon pepper
1 head romaine lettuce, torn
¾ cup kalamata olives
1 small red onion, thinly sliced
½ cup crumbled feta cheese
Pita Croutons

• Combine olive oil and next 6 ingredients in a small bowl, stirring with a wire whisk. Cover olive oil mixture, and chill until ready to serve.
• Combine lettuce and next 3 ingredients in a large bowl; gradually add enough olive oil mixture to coat leaves, tossing gently. Sprinkle with Pita Croutons, and serve with remaining olive oil mixture. Yield: 6 servings.

Pita Croutons

Prep: 5 min.   **Cook:** 7 min.

2 tablespoons olive oil
1 teaspoon dried oregano
¼ teaspoon crushed garlic

Dash of salt
1 (8-inch) pita bread round, split into 2 circles

• Combine olive oil and next 3 ingredients, and brush olive oil mixture over the inside of each pita bread circle.
• Cut each pita bread circle into bite-size pieces, and place on a baking sheet.
• Bake at 400° for 5 to 7 minutes or until croutons are golden brown. Yield: 1⅓ cups.

Key Lime Cheesecake with Strawberry Sauce

Prep: 20 min.   **Cook:** 1 hr., 13 min.   **Other:** 8 hrs., 15 min.

2 cups graham cracker crumbs
¼ cup sugar
½ cup butter, melted
3 (8-ounce) packages cream cheese, softened
1¼ cups sugar
3 large eggs

1 (8-ounce) container sour cream
1½ teaspoons grated lime rind
½ cup Key lime juice
Garnishes: strawberry halves, lime slice, lime zest
Strawberry Sauce

• Stir together first 3 ingredients; press on bottom and 1 inch up sides of a greased 9-inch springform pan. Bake at 350° for 8 minutes; cool.

• Beat cream cheese at medium speed with an electric mixer until fluffy; gradually add 1¼ cups sugar, beating until blended. Add eggs, 1 at a time, beating well after each addition. Stir in sour cream, rind, and juice. Pour batter into crust.

• Bake at 325° for 1 hour and 5 minutes; turn oven off. Partially open oven door; let stand in oven 15 minutes. Remove from oven, and immediately run a knife around edge of pan, releasing sides.

• Cool completely in pan on a wire rack; cover and chill 8 hours. Garnish, if desired, and serve with sauce. Yield: 10 to 12 servings.

Strawberry Sauce

Prep: 5 min.

1¼ cups fresh strawberries   1½ teaspoons grated lime rind
¼ cup sugar

• Process all ingredients in a food processor until smooth, stopping to scrape down sides. Yield: 1 cup.

Cooks Chat

"I am not a cheesecake fan; however, I made one of these over the Christmas holidays and was told it was the best cheesecake the guests had ever had. I am not an experienced cook, and I found this recipe fairly easy."

Autumn Harvest

serves 6

Grilled Maple Chipotle Pork Chops on Smoked Gouda Grits   *Steamed broccoli*

Sweet Potato Biscuits   *Caramel-Applesauce Cobbler with Bourbon-Pecan Ice Cream*

Cooks Chat

"We had a cookout, and I wanted to do something a little different. The maple chipotle sauce would be good on anything—chicken, steak, or veggies. The grits were wonderful. In fact, one friend called the next morning and said she wanted them for breakfast."

"My husband and I love this recipe. It is easy and quick enough to make during the week, but it tastes like it took much longer. This would be great for a cookout with friends. I recommend trying it. Don't skip the grits. They make the meal complete."

Grilled Maple Chipotle Pork Chops on Smoked Gouda Grits

Prep: 10 min.   **Cook:** 20 min.

½ cup barbecue sauce
½ cup maple syrup
2 chipotle peppers in adobo sauce, seeded and minced
1 teaspoon adobo sauce from can

6 (1¼-inch-thick) bone-in pork loin chops
1 teaspoon salt
1 teaspoon pepper
Smoked Gouda Grits

- Whisk together first 4 ingredients, and set aside.
- Sprinkle pork chops evenly with salt and pepper.
- Grill, covered with grill lid, over medium-high heat (350° to 400°) 20 minutes or until a meat thermometer inserted into thickest portion registers 155°, turning once. Baste with half of sauce mixture the last 5 minutes of cooking or when meat thermometer registers 145°. Let pork stand until thermometer registers 160°.
- Spoon Smoked Gouda Grits evenly onto 6 serving plates; top each with a pork chop, and drizzle evenly with remaining barbecue sauce mixture. Yield: 6 servings.

Smoked Gouda Grits

Prep: 5 min.   **Cook:** 10 min.

6 cups low-sodium chicken broth or water
2 cups milk
1 teaspoon salt
½ teaspoon white pepper

2 cups uncooked quick-cooking grits
1⅔ cups shredded smoked Gouda cheese
3 tablespoons unsalted butter

- Bring first 4 ingredients to a boil in a medium saucepan, and gradually whisk in grits. Cover, reduce heat, and simmer, stirring occasionally, 5 minutes or until thickened. Add cheese and butter, stirring until melted. Yield: 6 to 8 servings.

Sweet Potato Biscuits

Prep: 25 min.   **Cook:** 12 min.   **Other:** 4 hrs., 30 min.

1 (¼-ounce) envelope active
   dry yeast
¼ cup warm water (100° to
   110°)
1 (15-ounce) can sweet
   potatoes in syrup, drained
   and mashed

½ cup butter or margarine,
   softened
½ cup sugar
1 teaspoon salt
2½ cups all-purpose flour
1 teaspoon baking powder
Melted butter

• Combine yeast and ¼ cup warm water; let stand 5 minutes.
• Stir together sweet potatoes and butter, blending well. Stir in
sugar and salt; add yeast mixture, stirring until smooth.
• Combine flour and baking powder; gradually stir into potato
mixture until blended. Lightly knead until dough holds together.
• Shape dough into a ball; place in a buttered mixing bowl. Brush
top with melted butter. Cover and let rise in a warm place (85°),
free from drafts, 2½ hours or until doubled in bulk.
• Punch dough down, and turn out onto a floured surface. Roll
dough to a ½-inch thickness; cut with a 2-inch round cutter, and
place on greased baking sheets. Cover and let rise in a warm place,
free from drafts, 2 hours or until doubled in bulk.
• Bake at 400° for 12 minutes or until golden. Yield: 34 biscuits.

SOUTHERN CLASSIC

Cooks Chat

*"This recipe is delicious. These are
some of the best biscuits I have
made. When you serve them to
guests, make sure you have enough
for seconds and thirds. They are
hard to stop eating! Much more
flavorful than regular biscuits."*

Caramel-Applesauce Cobbler with Bourbon-Pecan Ice Cream

Prep: 45 min.   **Cook:** 35 min.

½ cup butter or margarine
12 large Granny Smith apples, peeled and sliced
2 cups sugar

2 tablespoons lemon juice
1 (15-ounce) package refrigerated piecrusts
Bourbon-Pecan Ice Cream

• Melt butter in a large Dutch oven over medium-high heat. Add apple, sugar, and lemon juice; cook, stirring often, 20 to 25 minutes or until apple is caramel-colored. Spoon into a shallow, greased 2-quart baking dish.
• Unroll each piecrust, and cut into ½-inch strips. Arrange strips in a lattice design over filling; fold edges under. Place remaining strips on a baking sheet.
• Bake remaining strips at 425° for 8 to 10 minutes or until golden. Set aside to serve with cobbler. Bake cobbler at 425° for 20 to 25 minutes or until crust is golden. Serve warm with pastry strips and Bourbon-Pecan Ice Cream. Yield: 8 servings.

Bourbon-Pecan Ice Cream

Prep: 5 min.   **Other:** 4 hrs.

2 pints homemade-style vanilla ice cream, softened

1 cup chopped toasted pecans
¼ cup bourbon

• Stir together all ingredients; freeze 4 hours. Yield: 2 pints.

Easy Tropical Luau

serves 12

Tropical Spinach Salad with Grilled Shrimp∗   *Southern Breeze*   *Tropical Rum Trifle*

∗*Double recipe to serve 12.*

Tropical Spinach Salad with Grilled Shrimp

Prep: 30 min.   **Cook:** 4 min.   **Other:** 1 hr.

2 pounds unpeeled, large fresh shrimp
Citrus Marinade (page 28)
8 (12-inch) wooden skewers
2 (6-ounce) packages fresh baby spinach
2 mangoes, peeled and sliced
1 medium-size red onion, sliced
1 (3-ounce) package goat cheese, crumbled
1 cup fresh raspberries
½ cup chopped pistachio nuts
Fresh Basil Vinaigrette (page 28)

• Peel shrimp; devein, if desired. Place shrimp in a large zip-top freezer bag, and add Citrus Marinade. Seal and shake to coat. Chill 1 hour.
• Soak skewers in water to cover for 30 minutes.
• Remove shrimp from marinade, discarding marinade. Thread shrimp onto skewers.
• Grill, covered with grill lid, over medium-high heat (350° to 400°) 2 minutes on each side or just until shrimp turn pink. Remove shrimp from skewers.
• Arrange baby spinach on a large serving platter. Top evenly with mango slices, onion slices, and grilled shrimp. Sprinkle with crumbled goat cheese, raspberries, and chopped pistachio nuts. Serve with Fresh Basil Vinaigrette. Yield: 6 servings.

Tropical Spinach Salad with Grilled Pork Tenderloin: Substitute 2 (1-pound) pork tenderloins for shrimp. Grill, covered with grill lid, over medium-high heat (350° to 400°) 10 to 12 minutes on each side or until a meat thermometer inserted into thickest portion registers 155°. Let stand 10 minutes or until thermometer registers 160°. Slice and serve as directed.

Tropical Spinach Salad with Grilled Chicken: Substitute 6 skinned and boned chicken breasts for shrimp. Grill, covered with grill lid, over medium-high heat (350° to 400°) 4 minutes on each side or until done. Let stand 10 minutes. Slice and serve as directed.

GRILLIN' GREAT
★★★★★

Cooks Chat

"A gorgeous salad full of colors, textures, and flavor. It was a hands-down hit at my Easter dinner party. It's a little labor-intensive for an everyday dish, but the results are well worth the work. I served this with a nice French Chablis and fresh crusty bread."

Citrus Marinade

Prep: 5 min.

¾ cup fresh orange juice
2 tablespoons chopped fresh
 basil
2 tablespoons lime juice
2 tablespoons extra-virgin
 olive oil

1 garlic clove, crushed
½ teaspoon dried crushed red
 pepper
¼ teaspoon salt

• Whisk together all ingredients. Yield: 1 cup.

Fresh Basil Vinaigrette

Prep: 5 min.

¼ cup chopped fresh basil
¼ cup raspberry vinegar
1 teaspoon Dijon mustard
1 garlic clove, chopped

¼ teaspoon salt
¼ teaspoon pepper
¾ cup extra-virgin olive oil

• Process first 6 ingredients in a blender until smooth. With blender running, gradually add oil in a slow, steady stream; process until smooth. Yield: 1 cup.

Cooks Chat

"I just had this delightful punch last night at a Southern Living at HOME® *party that I consulted. It was simple for the hostess to prepare, yet it was so refreshing! The blue ice cubes make it fun, and the punch had just the right blend of flavors."*

"I made this recipe for a family get-together, and it was delicious! The kids and the adults loved it. The contrast of the ice and the pineapple juice was very nice."

Southern Breeze

Prep: 10 min.   **Other:** 8 hrs.

1 cup sugar
1 (0.22-ounce) envelope
 unsweetened blue
 raspberry lemonade mix
7 cups water
1 (6-ounce) can frozen
 lemonade concentrate,
 thawed

1 (46-ounce) can unsweetened
 pineapple juice, chilled
1 (2-liter) bottle ginger ale,
 chilled

• Stir together first 4 ingredients in a 2-quart pitcher; pour evenly into 5 ice cube trays, and freeze at least 8 hours.
• Combine pineapple juice and ginger ale; serve over raspberry ice cubes. Yield: 12 servings.

Note: For testing purposes only, we used Kool-Aid Twists Ice Blue Raspberry Lemonade Unsweetened Soft Drink Mix.

Tropical Rum Trifle

Prep: 45 min.   **Other:** 1hr., 50 min.

Make the Coconut Cream Custard first;
while it's chilling, prepare the remaining ingredients.

2 mangoes, peeled and cut into
⅓-inch cubes*
1 (20-ounce) can pineapple
chunks in syrup, undrained
⅓ cup coconut-flavored rum
1 (10.75-ounce) frozen pound
cake, thawed and thinly
sliced
2 bananas, sliced
Coconut Cream Custard

1⅓ cups sweetened flaked
coconut, toasted
⅔ cup chopped macadamia
nuts, toasted
1 cup whipping cream
¼ cup powdered sugar
¼ teaspoon vanilla extract
Garnishes: mango, star fruit,
toasted coconut, toasted
macadamia nuts

• Stir together first 3 ingredients in a bowl. Cover and chill
20 minutes.
• Remove fruit from bowl with a slotted spoon, reserving syrup
mixture.
• Brush pound cake slices with syrup mixture. Arrange half of slices
in bottom of 4-quart bowl or trifle bowl. Top with half each of
mango mixture, banana slices, Coconut Cream Custard, coconut,
and macadamia nuts. Repeat layers.
• Beat whipping cream until foamy; gradually add sugar, beating
until soft peaks form. Add vanilla; beat until blended. Spread evenly
over top of trifle. Cover and chill 1½ hours. Garnish, if desired.
Yield: 10 to 12 servings.

*Substitute 1 (24-ounce) jar refrigerated mango, drained and cut
into ½-inch cubes, for fresh, if desired.

Note: For testing purposes only, we used Malibu Caribbean Rum
with Coconut Flavor.

Coconut Cream Custard

Prep: 10 min.   **Cook:** 3 min.   **Other:** 1 hr.

1 cup sugar
⅓ cup cornstarch
2 cups milk

1 (14-ounce) can coconut milk
6 egg yolks

• Whisk together all ingredients in a heavy saucepan. Bring to a
boil over medium heat, whisking constantly; boil, whisking constantly, 1 minute or until thickened. Remove from heat. Place pan
in ice water; whisk custard occasionally until cool.
• Cover and chill 1 hour. Yield: 4 cups.

Cooks Chat

*"This recipe was easy to put together.
I took it to a dinner party, and
everyone raved about the combination of flavors. The comment heard
most often was what a perfect light
summer dessert it was!"*

Homestyle Comfort

serves 8

Chicken-Fried Steak*   *Mashed potatoes*

Easy Peach Cobbler   *Southern Sweetened Tea*

*Double recipe to serve 8.

Cooks Chat

"This is the best recipe I've tried for chicken fried steak. So crispy and full of flavor—just plain yummy! It looked just like the picture, and my guests were impressed."

"This has become a family favorite. It's reliable, easy to follow, and does not require unusual ingredients. I had tried many different recipes for Chicken-Fried Steak and was always disappointed."

"Awesome. Being from south Texas, I know chicken-fried steak, and this is a really authentic recipe. It has that Southern, down-home taste. Make sure you use peanut oil—it gets hotter without smoking."

Chicken-Fried Steak

Prep: 10 min.   **Cook:** 30 min.

¼ teaspoon salt
¼ teaspoon ground black pepper
4 (4-ounce) cubed steaks
38 saltine crackers, crushed (about 1 sleeve)
1¼ cups all-purpose flour, divided
½ teaspoon baking powder

2 teaspoons salt, divided
1½ teaspoons ground black pepper, divided
½ teaspoon ground red pepper
4¾ cups milk, divided
2 large eggs
3½ cups peanut oil
Garnish: chopped parsley

• Sprinkle salt and ¼ teaspoon black pepper evenly over steaks. Set aside.
• Combine cracker crumbs, 1 cup flour, baking powder, 1 teaspoon salt, ½ teaspoon black pepper, and red pepper.
• Whisk together ¾ cup milk and eggs. Dredge steaks in cracker crumb mixture; dip in milk mixture, and dredge again in cracker mixture.
• Pour oil into a 12-inch skillet; heat to 360° (do not use a non-stick skillet). Fry steaks 10 minutes. Turn and fry 4 to 5 minutes or until golden. Remove steaks to a wire rack in a jellyroll pan. Keep steaks warm in a 225° oven. Carefully drain hot oil, reserving cooked bits and 1 tablespoon drippings in skillet.
• Whisk together remaining 4 cups milk, ¼ cup flour, 1 teaspoon salt, and 1 teaspoon black pepper. Add to reserved drippings in skillet; cook, whisking constantly, over medium-high heat, 10 to 12 minutes or until thickened. Serve gravy over steaks and mashed potatoes. Garnish, if desired. Yield: 4 servings.

Chicken-Fried Steak

Easy Peach Cobbler

Prep: 15 min.   **Cook:** 45 min.

½ cup unsalted butter
1 cup all-purpose flour
2 cups sugar, divided
1 tablespoon baking powder
Pinch of salt

1 cup milk
4 cups fresh peach slices
1 tablespoon lemon juice
Ground cinnamon or nutmeg
    (optional)

• Melt butter in a 13- x 9-inch baking dish.
• Combine flour, 1 cup sugar, baking powder, and salt; add milk, stirring just until dry ingredients are moistened. Pour batter over butter (do not stir).
• Bring remaining 1 cup sugar, peach slices, and lemon juice to a boil over high heat, stirring constantly; pour over batter (do not stir). Sprinkle with cinnamon, if desired.
• Bake at 375° for 40 to 45 minutes or until golden brown. Serve cobbler warm or cool. Yield: 10 servings.

SOUTHERN CLASSIC
★ ★ ★ ★ ★

Cooks Chat

"This is the best peach cobbler recipe I've found. It tastes more like the cobblers my grandmother made. It's simple to make, and the ingredients are readily available. If friends are coming by, I can prepare this dessert, pop it in the oven, and wait for the oohs and aahs as my guests are welcomed by the aroma of freshly-baked peach cobbler."

Southern Sweetened Tea

Prep: 2 min.   **Cook:** 5 min.   **Other:** 10 min.

Cooks Chat

"My kids discovered sweet tea while visiting Mississippi and got hooked. When we returned home to Alaska, our first issue of Southern Living *included this recipe. It works, it's easy, and it's great. Thanks!"*

6 cups water

4 family-size tea bags

1 to 1¾ cups sugar

• Bring 6 cups water to a boil in a saucepan; add tea bags. Boil 1 minute; remove from heat. Cover and steep 10 minutes. Remove tea bags, squeezing gently.

• Add sugar, stirring until dissolved. Pour into a 1-gallon pitcher, and add enough water to fill pitcher. Serve over ice. Yield: 1 gallon.

A Texas-Style Cookout

serves 8

Traditional Brisket   Deli coleslaw or potato salad   Best Pinto Beans

Texas White Sangría   Two-Step Pound Cake

Traditional Brisket

Prep: 40 min.   **Cook:** 6 hrs., 30 min.   **Other:** 9 hrs.

The rule of thumb is to smoke brisket 1 hour and 15 minutes per pound at 225° to 250° until the internal temperature reaches 190°. The meat is safe to eat at a lower temperature but isn't tender yet.

1 (5¾-pound) trimmed beef
   brisket flat
Brisket Rub (page 34)
Hickory smoking chips
Basting mop*

Brisket Mopping Sauce
   (page 34)
Brisket Red Sauce (page 34)
   (optional)

• Sprinkle each side of beef with ¼ cup Brisket Rub; rub thoroughly into meat. Wrap brisket in plastic wrap, and chill 8 hours.
• Soak hickory chips in water for 8 hours. Drain.
• Prepare smoker according to manufacturer's directions, regulating temperature with a thermometer to 225°; allow it to maintain that temperature for 1 hour before adding beef.
• Remove beef from refrigerator, and let stand 30 minutes.
• Place brisket on smoker rack, fat side up. Insert thermometer horizontally into thickest portion of beef. Maintain smoker temperature between 225° and 250°.
• Add a handful (about ¼ cup) of hickory chips about every hour.
• With basting mop, brush beef liberally with Brisket Mopping Sauce when beef starts to look dry. (Internal temperature will be about 156°.) Mop top of brisket every hour. When internal temperature reaches 170°, place brisket on a sheet of heavy-duty aluminum foil; mop liberally with Brisket Mopping Sauce. Wrap tightly, and return to smoker.
• Remove brisket from smoker when internal temperature reaches 190° with an instant-read thermometer. Let stand 1 hour. Cut into very thin (⅛- to ¼-inch thick) slices. Serve with Brisket Red Sauce, if desired. Yield: 8 servings.

*Basting mops may be found in the grilling-supply section of supermarkets, restaurant-supply stores, and sporting goods stores.

SOUTHERN CLASSIC

Cooks Chat

"Fifteen years ago, I spent a summer in Houston, Texas, and fell in love with barbecued beef brisket. Oddly enough, this is just like the recipe I brought back home with me to Tennessee. It's great."

"This recipe is awesome! The brisket was very tender and full of flavor. We will definitely use it as our standard brisket recipe. The only complaint is that the red sauce has too much vinegar and was a little thin. I will adjust that to personal taste."

Brisket Rub

Prep: 5 min.

This makes enough for about three briskets.

¼ cup kosher salt
¼ cup sugar
¼ cup black pepper
¾ cup paprika
2 tablespoons garlic powder

2 tablespoons garlic salt
2 tablespoons onion powder
2 tablespoons chili powder
2 teaspoons ground red pepper

• Combine all ingredients. Store in an airtight container. Yield: 2 cups.

Brisket Mopping Sauce

Prep: 10 min.

This makes enough sauce for about two briskets, so halve the recipe if you're preparing just one.

1 (12-ounce) bottle beer
1 cup apple cider vinegar
1 onion, minced
4 garlic cloves, minced

½ cup water
½ cup Worcestershire sauce
¼ cup vegetable oil
2 tablespoons Brisket Rub

• Stir together all ingredients until blended. Yield: 4 cups.

Brisket Red Sauce

Prep: 10 min.

1½ cups apple cider vinegar
1 cup ketchup
½ teaspoon ground red pepper
¼ cup Worcestershire sauce
1 teaspoon salt
½ teaspoon black pepper
½ teaspoon onion powder

½ tablespoon garlic powder
½ tablespoon ground cumin
2 tablespoons unsalted butter, melted
½ cup firmly packed brown sugar

• Stir together all ingredients until blended. Serve sauce heated or at room temperature. Yield: 3½ cups.

Best Pinto Beans

Prep: 15 min.   **Cook:** 1 hr., 25 min.

1 pound fresh pinto beans,
    sorted and rinsed*
1 smoked ham hock
1 (10-ounce) can diced
    tomatoes and green chiles
1 (32-ounce) container chicken
    broth
1 green bell pepper, chopped
1 celery rib, chopped

½ onion, chopped
Dash of hot sauce
1 teaspoon salt
1 teaspoon garlic powder
1 teaspoon dried oregano
½ teaspoon dried thyme
½ teaspoon pepper
1 teaspoon Worcestershire sauce
Hot cooked rice

• Place beans in a large Dutch oven, and add water to cover. Bring to a boil, and cook, uncovered, 30 minutes. Drain.
• Add ham hock, tomatoes, broth, and next 10 ingredients to Dutch oven with beans; cook 55 minutes or until beans are tender. Serve over rice. Yield: 8 servings.

*Substitute dried pinto beans for fresh, if desired.

KITCHEN COMFORT
★ ★ ★ ★ ★

Cooks Chat

"Excellent and easy recipe! I get requests to make this from family and friends. It's spicy, so adjust seasonings to your taste."

Texas White Sangría

Prep: 15 min.   **Cook:** 8 min.

1⅓ cups water
½ cup sugar
4 (3-inch) cinnamon sticks
1 cup fresh mint leaves, divided
1 (750-milliliter) bottle dry
    white wine

2 lemons, sliced
2 oranges, sliced
2 peaches, peeled and sliced
2 cups club soda, chilled

• Bring first 3 ingredients and ½ cup mint leaves to a boil in a saucepan over medium heat. Reduce heat, and simmer 5 minutes. Remove from heat, and cool. Cover and let stand 8 hours, if desired. Remove cinnamon sticks and mint leaves with a slotted spoon.
• Combine sugar mixture, remaining ½ cup mint leaves, wine, and next 3 ingredients in a large pitcher; chill overnight, if desired. Stir in club soda before serving. Serve over ice. Yield: 10 to 12 servings.

MAKE AHEAD
★ ★ ★ ★ ★

Cooks Chat

"This is a very tasty sangría and is great to serve to a crowd. I doubled the recipe and served it in a big glass barrel. It's wonderful because you can make it ahead of time."

"I used fresh mint leaves from my garden instead of store-bought mint. My guests were very impressed. This recipe is a permanent addition to my summer entertaining menu!"

Two-Step Pound Cake

Prep: 10 min.   **Cook:** 1 hr., 30 min.

This cake requires a heavy-duty stand mixer with a 4-quart bowl and a paddle attachment.

4 cups all-purpose flour	¾ cup milk
3 cups sugar	6 eggs
1 pound butter, softened	2 teaspoons vanilla extract

• Place flour, sugar, butter, milk, eggs, and vanilla (in that order) in a 4-quart bowl. Beat at low speed with a heavy-duty electric mixer 1 minute, stopping to scrape down sides. Beat at medium speed 2 minutes. Pour into a greased and floured 10-inch tube pan.
• Bake at 325° for 1 hour and 30 minutes or until a long wooden pick inserted in center comes out clean. Cool in pan on a wire rack 10 minutes. Remove from pan; cool completely on wire rack. Yield: 1 (10-inch) cake.

Note: For testing purposes only, we used a KitchenAid Mixer.

Traditional Method:
• Beat butter at medium speed with an electric mixer 2 minutes or until creamy. Gradually add sugar, beating until light and fluffy. Add eggs, 1 at a time, beating after each addition.
• Add flour to butter mixture alternately with milk, beginning and ending with flour. Beat at low speed just until blended after each addition. Stir in vanilla.
• Pour batter into a greased and floured 10-inch tube pan. Bake as directed in two-step method.

Soup and Sandwich Night

serves 4

Creamy Onion-and-Potato Soup

Italian BLT Sandwiches

Creamy Onion-and-Potato Soup

Prep: 10 min.   **Cook:** 22 min.

For thicker soup, puree half of soup in a blender or food processor.

2 tablespoons butter or
  margarine
2 tablespoons all-purpose flour
1 large onion, chopped
1 garlic clove, pressed
2 (14-ounce) cans chicken
  broth
1 bunch green onions, sliced

3 large potatoes, peeled and
  cubed or 2 (14½-ounce)
  cans whole new potatoes,
  drained
⅛ teaspoon salt
¼ teaspoon pepper
1 cup milk

• Melt butter in a Dutch oven over low heat, and whisk in flour until smooth. Cook, whisking constantly, 1 minute.
• Whisk in chopped onion and pressed garlic, and cook 1 minute. Gradually whisk in chicken broth until blended.
• Add green onions and next 3 ingredients. Bring mixture to a boil; cover, reduce heat, and simmer, stirring often, 15 minutes or until cubed potato is tender. Stir in milk, and cook until soup is thoroughly heated. Yield: 7 cups.

Italian BLT Sandwiches

Prep: 25 min.   **Cook:** 6 min.

Looking for a way to turn an old standby sandwich into something special? Try using Italian bread and a blend of Mediterranean flavors for a new twist.

½ (16-ounce) Italian bread loaf
¼ cup Italian dressing
⅓ cup shredded Parmesan cheese
½ cup mayonnaise
½ cup mustard
½ pound thinly sliced Genoa salami
½ pound thinly sliced mortadella or bologna

4 (1-ounce) provolone cheese slices
Romaine lettuce leaves
3 plum tomatoes, sliced
8 bacon slices, cooked and cut in half
Garnish: pimiento-stuffed green olives

• Cut bread diagonally into 8 slices; arrange on a baking sheet. Brush slices evenly with Italian dressing, and sprinkle with Parmesan cheese.
• Bake at 375° for 5 to 6 minutes or until lightly toasted. Stir together mayonnaise and mustard; spread untoasted side of bread evenly with mayonnaise mixture.
• Layer 4 bread slices, mayonnaise mixture side up, with salami and next 5 ingredients. Top with remaining 4 bread slices, mayonnaise side down. Secure with wooden picks. Garnish, if desired. Yield: 4 servings.

QUICK & EASY

Cooks Chat

"This is an excellent sandwich! Great for company! The edges of the bread seemed to get a bit hard in the oven, making it a little challenging to eat, but my company felt the 'crustiness' added to the sandwich's appeal!"

"What a great sandwich! I am so tired of the same ol', same ol', so I tried this recipe and am so glad I did. It was wonderful, and my husband loved it as well."

Fancy Fixin's

serves 8

Beef Fillets with Stilton-Portobello Sauce   *Garlic Mashed Potatoes*

Pear Salad with Raspberry Cream*   *Warm Fudge-Filled Cheesecake*

*Double recipe to serve 8.

QUICK & EASY

Cooks Chat

"OUT OF THIS WORLD! I made this for Christmas Eve, along with roasted potatoes and fresh green beans steamed with tomatoes, basil, and olive oil. I used blue cheese instead of Stilton and cooked with an aged Cabernet that also accompanied our dinner. WOW!"

"This recipe is so incredibly easy to prepare and is absolutely delicious. It's my new tradition for Christmas Eve dinner!"

Beef Fillets with Stilton-Portobello Sauce

Prep: 10 min.   **Cook:** 25 min.

8 (6-ounce) beef tenderloin fillets
1 tablespoon chopped fresh thyme
¾ teaspoon pepper
½ cup butter, divided
2 (6-ounce) packages portobello mushroom caps, sliced

½ cup dry red wine or beef broth
¾ cup sour cream
4½ ounces Stilton cheese, crumbled and divided

• Rub fillets evenly with thyme and pepper. Melt ¼ cup butter in a large skillet over medium-high heat. Add fillets; cook 5 minutes on each side or to desired doneness. Remove from skillet, and keep warm.
• Melt remaining ¼ cup butter in skillet. Add mushrooms, and sauté 3 to 4 minutes or until tender. Add wine, and cook 1 to 2 minutes, stirring to loosen particles from bottom of skillet. Stir in sour cream and ¼ cup cheese until melted. Drizzle sauce over fillets; sprinkle with remaining cheese. Yield: 8 servings.

KITCHEN COMFORT
★★★★★

Cooks Chat

"These are great with holiday meals, and they even make everyday meals special. My family asks for them all the time."

Garlic Mashed Potatoes

Prep: 20 min.   **Cook:** 30 min.

8 baking potatoes, peeled and quartered (about 4 pounds)
1¾ teaspoons salt, divided
½ cup butter, softened

¾ cup half-and-half
3 large garlic cloves, pressed
½ teaspoon white pepper
¼ cup chopped fresh parsley

• Bring potatoes, 1 teaspoon salt, and water to cover to a boil in a Dutch oven; cover, reduce heat, and simmer 30 minutes or until tender. Drain. Beat potatoes, remaining ¾ teaspoon salt, butter, half-and-half, garlic, and pepper at medium speed with an electric mixer until smooth. Stir in parsley. Yield: 8 servings.

Pear Salad with Raspberry Cream

Prep: 20 min.

¾ cup sour cream
¼ cup raspberry preserves
3 tablespoons red wine vinegar
⅛ teaspoon Dijon mustard
4 firm, ripe pears
2 tablespoons lemon juice
1 head Bibb lettuce, torn

1 small head romaine lettuce, torn
½ cup (2 ounces) freshly grated Parmesan cheese
6 bacon slices, cooked and crumbled
½ cup fresh raspberries

• Whisk together first 4 ingredients. Set dressing aside.
• Peel pears, if desired; quarter pears. Brush with lemon juice.
• Arrange lettuce on 4 plates. Arrange pear quarters over lettuce. Drizzle with dressing; sprinkle with cheese, bacon, and raspberries. Yield: 4 servings.

QUICK & EASY

Cooks Chat

"I made this salad for a Christmas luncheon, and the presentation was beautiful. But I can't stop there. It was a delicious combination of flavors, and everyone enjoyed it to the last bite. This is a keeper!"

"Very different. This is great for a luncheon."

Warm Fudge-Filled Cheesecake

Prep: 20 min.   **Cook:** 1 hr., 15 min.   **Other:** 1 hr.

½ cup butter or margarine, softened
⅓ cup sugar
1 cup all-purpose flour
1 tablespoon vanilla, divided
⅔ cup chopped pistachios
4 (8-ounce) packages cream cheese, softened
1½ cups sugar
4 large eggs
2 cups (12-ounce package) semisweet chocolate mini-morsels
Sweetened whipped cream (optional)
Garnish: chocolate shavings

• Beat butter at medium speed with an electric mixer until creamy; add ⅓ cup sugar, beating well. Gradually add flour, beating at low speed until blended. Stir in 1 teaspoon vanilla and pistachios. Press into bottom and 1½ inches up sides of a 9-inch springform pan.
• Bake at 350° for 12 to 15 minutes or until golden. Cool on a wire rack.
• Beat cream cheese at medium speed with an electric mixer until light and fluffy; gradually add 1½ cups sugar, beating well. Add eggs, 1 at a time, beating just until yellow disappears. Stir in remaining 2 teaspoons vanilla (do not overmix).
• Pour half of batter into crust, and sprinkle with chocolate morsels to within ¾ inch of edge. Pour in remaining batter, starting at outer edge and working toward center. Place cheesecake on a baking sheet.
• Bake at 350° for 1 hour or until set. Cool on a wire rack 1 hour. Serve slightly warm with sweetened whipped cream, if desired. Garnish, if desired. Yield: 12 servings.

Mexican Fiesta

serves 4

Rio Grande Limeade   Black Bean Salsa   Chips

Chicken Enchiladas   Mexican rice

Molletes   Vanilla-Cinnamon Ice Cream

Rio Grande Limeade

Prep: 10 min.   **Other:** 8 hrs.

2 (12-ounce) cans frozen
    limeade concentrate,
    thawed
3 cups tequila

3 cups water
2 cups orange liqueur
1 cup fresh lime juice
Garnish: lime slices

• Stir together first 5 ingredients. Chill 8 hours. Serve over ice. Garnish, if desired. Yield: 3 quarts.

Black Bean Salsa

Prep: 20 min.

1 (15-ounce) can black beans,
    rinsed and drained
½ cup frozen corn, thawed
2 plum tomatoes, seeded and
    chopped

1 green onion, chopped
2 tablespoons fresh lime juice
1 tablespoon fresh cilantro
1 garlic clove, pressed
½ teaspoon Creole seasoning

• Stir together all ingredients. Cover and chill until ready to serve. Yield: about 3 cups.

Cooks Chat

"OH MAN! I cannot say it enough—this dish is wonderful. I doubled the recipe to feed six people, and we had enough leftovers for lunch the next day. The kids gobbled this up. Serve with refried beans."

"Excellent and very easy to make. The cilantro really made the dish. The first time I made this, my boyfriend ate three enchiladas! The sauce also adds to it. This will be a regular in our house! I served it with a side of refried beans. I boiled the chicken breasts and shredded the meat using two forks."

Chicken Enchiladas

Prep: 15 min. **Cook:** 40 min.

3 cups chopped cooked chicken
2 cups (8 ounces) shredded Monterey Jack cheese with peppers
½ cup sour cream
1 (4.5-ounce) can chopped green chiles, drained
⅓ cup chopped fresh cilantro

8 (8-inch) flour tortillas
1 (8-ounce) container sour cream
1 (8-ounce) jar tomatillo salsa
Toppings: diced tomatoes, chopped avocado, chopped green onions, sliced ripe olives, chopped cilantro

• Stir together first 5 ingredients. Spoon chicken mixture evenly down center of each tortilla, and roll up. Arrange, seam side down, in a lightly greased 13- x 9-inch baking dish. Coat tortillas with cooking spray.
• Bake at 350° for 35 to 40 minutes or until golden brown.
• Stir together 8-ounce container sour cream and salsa. Spoon over hot enchiladas; sprinkle with desired toppings. Yield: 4 servings.

Molletes

Prep: 20 min.　**Cook:** 10 min.　**Other:** 2 hrs., 5 min.

1 (¼-ounce) envelope active
　dry yeast
1 cup warm water (100° to
　110°)
⅔ cup sugar, divided

5 cups bread flour
½ cup shortening, divided
2 large eggs
¼ teaspoon salt
⅓ cup all-purpose flour

• Stir together yeast, 1 cup warm water, and 2 tablespoons sugar in a 2-cup liquid measuring cup; let stand 5 minutes.
• Stir together 6 tablespoons sugar, bread flour, ⅓ cup shortening, eggs, and salt in bowl of a heavy-duty electric stand mixer. Add yeast mixture to flour mixture, and beat at medium speed with mixer, using dough hook attachment, 6 minutes.
• Combine remaining sugar and all-purpose flour in a bowl; cut in remaining shortening with a fork until blended to form a paste.
• Divide dough into 12 equal portions; shape into balls, and place on 2 lightly greased baking sheets (6 balls per baking sheet). Spread 2 teaspoons flour paste on top of each ball. Slightly flatten each ball using a dulce marker dipped in flour or a kaiser roll stamp dipped in flour. Cover dough with wax paper or plastic wrap.
• Preheat oven to 170° to 200°; turn oven off, leaving oven door open 1 minute. Place dough, covered, in oven; let rise, with oven door closed, 2 hours or until doubled in bulk. Remove dough, and preheat oven to 425°. Bake molletes, uncovered, at 425° for 8 to 10 minutes or until golden brown. Cool molletes on baking sheets on wire racks. Yield: 1 dozen.

Chocolate Molletes: Stir 2 tablespoons unsweetened cocoa into paste mixture.
Pink Molletes: Stir 3 drops red liquid food coloring into paste mixture.
Red Molletes: Stir 6 drops red liquid food coloring into paste mixture.

Vanilla-Cinnamon Ice Cream

Prep: 10 min.　**Other:** 1 hr.

1 quart vanilla ice cream,
　softened
¼ cup milk

2 tablespoons brown sugar
¼ teaspoon ground cinnamon

• Stir together all ingredients. Freeze 1 hour. Yield: about 4 cups.

KIDS LOVE IT

Cooks Chat

"I spent an entire summer in Mexico eating these almost daily. I was very anxious to make my own. I thought they came out very close to the original, but I would double the recipe for the topping."

"This recipe was easy and wonderful. I am from Brownsville, Texas, and my parents used to buy molletes on Saturday mornings. Sometimes they were in the shape of turtles. I felt as if I were back in the Rio."

MAKE AHEAD

Cooks Chat

"I loved this and so did my family. It's a very simple recipe and doesn't take long. I would use this for birthday parties as well as for everyday menus."

Easy Italian Night

serves 6

Extra-Easy Lasagna   *Italian House Salad*

Tiramisu

Cooks Chat

"My family really loves lasagna, but I rarely make the dish because I don't want to cook the noodles. This is the answer! It's quick and delicious!"

"Excellent taste and easy preparation. It took me about half an hour to prepare, but I reckon it won't be more than a quarter of an hour next time."

Extra-Easy Lasagna

Prep: 15 min.   **Cook:** 55 min.   **Other:** 10 min.

1 pound lean ground beef
4 cups tomato-basil pasta sauce
6 uncooked lasagna noodles
1 (15-ounce) container ricotta cheese
2½ cups (10 ounces) shredded mozzarella cheese
¼ cup hot water

• Cook beef in a large skillet over medium heat, stirring until it crumbles and is no longer pink; drain. Stir in pasta sauce.
• Spread one-third of meat sauce in a lightly greased 11- x 7-inch baking dish; layer with 3 uncooked noodles and half each of ricotta cheese and mozzarella cheese. (The ricotta cheese layer will be thin.) Repeat procedure; spread remaining one-third of meat sauce over mozzarella cheese. Slowly pour ¼ cup hot water around inside edge of dish. Tightly cover baking dish with 2 layers of heavy-duty aluminum foil.
• Bake at 375° for 45 minutes; uncover and bake 10 more minutes. Let stand 10 minutes before serving. Yield: 6 to 8 servings.

Note: For testing purposes only, we used Classico Tomato & Basil pasta sauce.

Italian House Salad

Prep: 20 min.

⅓ cup shredded Parmesan
    cheese
⅔ cup vegetable oil
⅓ cup red wine vinegar
1 teaspoon dried Italian
    seasoning
1 teaspoon dried parsley flakes
¼ teaspoon garlic powder
¼ teaspoon pepper
⅛ teaspoon salt
1 large head Red Leaf lettuce,
    torn

1 (14-ounce) can quartered
    artichoke hearts, drained
1 (6-ounce) can pitted ripe
    olives, drained
4 plum tomatoes, coarsely
    chopped
1 small red onion, thinly sliced
½ pound provolone cheese,
    shredded

• Whisk together first 8 ingredients.
• Place lettuce and next 5 ingredients in a large bowl. Drizzle with vinaigrette, and toss gently to coat. Yield: 6 servings.

Cooks Chat

"I served this at a dinner party for 15 people (I doubled recipe), and I received compliments from all. Thanks!"

Tiramisu

Prep: 30 min.   **Other:** 2 hrs.

½ (16-ounce) package
    mascarpone cheese*
½ cup sugar
2½ cups whipping cream,
    divided
1 cup hot water

1 tablespoon instant coffee
    granules
¼ cup coffee liqueur
24 ladyfingers (2 [3-ounce]
    packages)
1 teaspoon unsweetened cocoa

• Beat cheese, sugar, and ½ cup whipping cream at medium speed with an electric mixer until creamy.
• Beat remaining 2 cups whipping cream at medium speed with an electric mixer until soft peaks form. Fold into cheese mixture.
• Stir together 1 cup hot water and coffee granules until granules dissolve. Stir in liqueur.
• Split ladyfingers in half, and brush cut sides of ladyfingers evenly with coffee mixture.
• Arrange one-fourth of ladyfingers in bottom of a 4-quart trifle bowl. Top with one-fourth of cheese mixture. Repeat layers 3 times. Sprinkle with cocoa. Chill tiramisu at least 2 hours. Yield: 8 servings.

*Substitute cream cheese for mascarpone cheese, if desired.

Cooks Chat

"Excellent recipe for company. It's easy to prepare, yet looks like you spent a lot of time on it. Absolutely delicious! Not too filling after a big meal."

"This was a big hit at Christmas and looks like you spent more time on it than you did. It's a nice change from cheesecake—lighter and very yummy."

"This recipe is my secret weapon. I use a little more booze than it calls for. I also add cinnamon and nutmeg to the cocoa and sprinkle it between layers as well. It's fantastic!"

Summer Splendor

serves 6

Macadamia-Mango Chicken   *Homemade Lemonade*   *Jumbleberry Trifle*

Macadamia-Mango Chicken

Prep: 15 min.   **Cook:** 12 min.   **Other:** 1 hr.

½ cup soy sauce
2 garlic cloves, minced
1 tablespoon brown sugar
1 tablespoon olive oil
1 teaspoon grated fresh
 ginger

6 skinned and boned chicken
 breasts
Mustard Sauce
3 tablespoons chopped
 macadamia nuts
Mango Salsa

• Combine first 5 ingredients in a shallow dish or zip-top freezer bag; add chicken. Cover or seal, and chill 1 hour, turning once.
• Remove chicken from marinade, discarding marinade. Grill, covered with lid, over medium-high heat (350° to 400°) 6 minutes on each side or until done. Drizzle with Mustard Sauce; sprinkle with nuts. Serve with Mango Salsa and, if desired, saffron rice. Yield: 6 servings.

Mustard Sauce

Prep: 5 min.

½ cup Dijon mustard
2 tablespoons light brown sugar

2 tablespoons pineapple juice
⅛ to ¼ teaspoon red pepper

• Stir together all ingredients; cover and chill, if desired. Yield: ⅔ cup.

Mango Salsa

Prep: 25 min.   **Other:** 2 hrs.

2 ripe mangoes (about 1
 pound), peeled and diced
1 red bell pepper, diced
1 jalapeño pepper, seeded and
 diced
3 tablespoons chopped fresh
 cilantro

2 tablespoons chopped fresh
 mint
1 small red onion, chopped
2 tablespoons honey
1 tablespoon fresh lime juice
¼ teaspoon red pepper
¼ teaspoon salt

• Stir together all ingredients; cover and chill 2 hours. Yield: 2 cups.

Homemade Lemonade

Prep: 20 min.　**Other:** 8 hrs.

1½ cups sugar
½ cup boiling water
2 teaspoons grated lemon rind

1½ cups fresh lemon juice
5 cups cold water

• Stir together sugar and ½ cup boiling water until sugar dissolves.
• Stir in rind, juice, and cold water. Chill 8 hours. Yield: 8 cups.

Cooks Chat

"A delicious summertime drink!"

Jumbleberry Trifle

Prep: 45 min.　**Other:** 50 min.

1 (10-ounce) package frozen
　unsweetened raspberries,
　thawed
1 (18-ounce) jar seedless
　blackberry jam or
　preserves, divided
1 (10.75-ounce) frozen pound
　cake, thawed

2 tablespoons cream sherry
1½ cups whipping cream
1 (10-ounce) jar lemon curd
Garnishes: whipped cream,
　fresh raspberries and
　blackberries, fresh mint
　sprigs, lemon rind strips

Cooks Chat

"I have made this recipe several times for gatherings. It gets rave reviews every time. It's perfect for spring get-togethers, such as Easter or a baby shower."

• Stir together raspberries and 1 cup jam. Press mixture through a wire-mesh strainer using the back of a spoon into a bowl; discard seeds. Cover sauce; chill 20 minutes.
• Cut pound cake into ¼-inch-thick slices. Spread remaining jam on 1 side of half of slices; top with remaining slices. Cut sandwiches into ½-inch cubes; drizzle with sherry, and set aside.
• Beat whipping cream and lemon curd at low speed with an electric mixer until blended. Gradually increase mixer speed, beating until medium peaks form. Cover and chill 30 minutes.
• Spoon 1 tablespoon berry sauce into 8 large wine glasses; top with about ¼ cup each of cake cubes and lemon curd mixture. Repeat layers once, ending with berry sauce. Serve immediately, or chill until ready to serve. Garnish, if desired. Yield: 8 servings.

Make-Ahead Brunch

serves 8

Bloody Mary Punch   Christmas Morning Sticky Buns

Brie-and-Sausage Breakfast Casserole

Cooks Chat

"Great! The Old Bay seasoning really makes it different. I served this at a brunch and used pickled asparagus as 'stirrers' and placed a boiled shrimp on the rim of each glass. I have also used Clamato juice in place of the vegetable juice. Great presentation! I'll make it again and again and again!"

Bloody Mary Punch

Prep: 10 min.

1 (46-ounce) can vegetable juice, chilled
¾ cup vodka, chilled
1 tablespoon freshly ground pepper
3 tablespoons fresh lime juice

1 to 2 tablespoons hot sauce
2 tablespoons Worcestershire sauce
1 teaspoon Old Bay seasoning
Celery sticks (optional)
Cooked shrimp (optional)

• Combine first 7 ingredients in a punch bowl or a pitcher. Serve over ice in glasses. Serve with celery and shrimp, if desired. Yield: about 1½ quarts.

Cooks Chat

"This is one of the best pull-apart roll recipes that I have ever tried."

Christmas Morning Sticky Buns

Prep: 5 min.   **Cook:** 30 min.   **Other:** 8 hrs.

½ cup chopped pecans or walnuts
1 (25-ounce) package frozen roll dough, thawed
1 (3.4-ounce) package butterscotch instant pudding mix

½ cup butter or margarine, melted
½ cup firmly packed brown sugar
¾ teaspoon ground cinnamon

• Sprinkle pecans in bottom of a buttered 12-cup Bundt pan.
• Arrange dough in pan; sprinkle with dry pudding mix.
• Stir together butter, brown sugar, and cinnamon; pour over rolls. Cover and chill 8 hours.
• Bake at 350° for 30 minutes or until golden brown. Invert onto a serving plate, and serve immediately. Yield: 8 servings.

Brie-and-Sausage Breakfast Casserole

Prep: 20 min.   **Cook:** 1 hr.   **Other:** 8 hrs.

1 (8-ounce) round Brie*
1 pound ground hot pork
    sausage
6 white bread slices
1 cup grated Parmesan cheese
7 large eggs, divided
3 cups whipping cream, divided
2 cups fat-free milk

1 tablespoon chopped fresh or
    1 teaspoon dried rubbed
    sage
1 teaspoon seasoned salt
1 teaspoon dry mustard
Garnishes: chopped green
    onions, shaved Parmesan
    cheese

• Trim and discard rind from Brie. Cut cheese into cubes; set aside.
• Cook sausage in a large skillet over medium-high heat, stirring until crumbled and no longer pink; drain well.
• Cut crusts from bread slices, and place crusts evenly in bottom of a lightly greased 13- x 9-inch baking dish. Layer evenly with bread slices, sausage, Brie, and Parmesan cheese.
• Whisk together 5 eggs, 2 cups whipping cream, and next 4 ingredients; pour evenly over cheeses. Cover and chill 8 hours.
• Whisk together remaining 2 eggs and 1 cup whipping cream; pour evenly over chilled mixture.
• Bake at 350° for 1 hour or until set. Garnish, if desired. Yield: 8 to 10 servings.

*Substitute 2 cups (8 ounces) shredded Swiss cheese for Brie, if desired.

Cooks Chat

"I made this breakfast casserole for my Sunday school class, and they loved it. The men especially enjoyed it. Some people said that they normally wouldn't eat a breakfast casserole, but this one was good. The Brie cheese really makes it."

"This casserole is fantastic. I've made it twice—once with Brie and once with Swiss. I think Swiss is my favorite, but it's hard to choose!"

All-American Fare

serves 6

Aunt Mary's Pot Roast   Buttery Herb-Cheese Muffins

Chocolate-Oatmeal Chunk Cookies

Cooks Chat

"This was too easy to produce such a delicious dinner. If more people discover how easy this is, those of us who have a reputation of being an excellent cook (as I have) will lose our reputation."

"My roasts are usually as tender as an old shoe. Every time I use this recipe, my roast comes out fall-apart tender! I cook mine a little longer than the recipe calls for—more like 4 to 5 hours. Excellent recipe!"

"Truly an old-fashioned favorite. The meat was very tender and tasty. I added the roasted vegetables to the pot roast the last 15 minutes. A tossed salad and some French bread are all you need to complete the meal. There is no doubt that this will become a favorite at our table."

Aunt Mary's Pot Roast

Prep: 10 min.   **Cook:** 3 hrs., 10 min.

Long before the advent of electricity, pioneers were using cast-iron Dutch ovens (as called for in this recipe) as "slow cookers."

1 (3- to 4-pound) boneless chuck roast, trimmed*
1 (12-ounce) can beer
1 (0.6-ounce) envelope Italian dressing mix
Roasted Vegetables (optional)

• Brown roast on all sides in a lightly oiled 5-quart cast-iron Dutch oven over high heat. Remove from heat; add beer and dressing mix.
• Bake, covered, at 300° for 3 hours or until tender, turning once. Serve with Roasted Vegetables, if desired. Yield: 6 servings.

*To reduce the fat in this recipe, substitute an eye of round roast for the chuck roast. Both cuts of meat become fall-apart tender when cooked with slow, moist heat.

Roasted Vegetables

Prep: 10 min.   **Cook:** 45 min.

Slow roasting in a cast-iron skillet accentuates the natural sweetness of these root vegetables. If desired, you may omit the olive oil and add vegetables to the Dutch oven with the pot roast during the last hour of baking.

1½ pounds new potatoes, cut in half
1 (1-pound) package baby carrots
2 medium onions, quartered
1 tablespoon olive oil
Salt and pepper to taste

• Toss potatoes, baby carrots, and onions with olive oil, and season to taste with salt and pepper.
• Bake at 300° in a large cast-iron skillet for 45 minutes, stirring once. Yield: 6 servings.

Buttery Herb-Cheese Muffins

Prep: 10 min.   **Cook:** 25 min.

2 cups self-rising flour
1 cup butter, melted
½ cup sour cream

1 (6.5-ounce) package garlic-and-herb spreadable cheese, softened

• Stir together all ingredients just until blended.
• Spoon muffin batter into lightly greased miniature muffin pans, filling to the top.
• Bake at 350° for 25 minutes or until lightly browned. Yield: 2½ dozen.

Note: For testing purposes only, we used Alouette Garlic and Herbs Gourmet Spreadable Cheese.

Chocolate-Oatmeal Chunk Cookies

Prep: 15 min.   **Cook:** 9 min. per batch

1 cup butter or margarine, softened
1 cup firmly packed brown sugar
½ cup granulated sugar
2 large eggs
2 teaspoons vanilla extract
2 cups all-purpose flour

¾ teaspoon baking soda
1 teaspoon salt
3 cups uncooked regular oats
1 (11.5-ounce) package semisweet chocolate chunks
1 cup pecan pieces

• Beat butter and sugars at medium speed with an electric mixer until creamy. Add eggs and vanilla, beating well.
• Combine flour, baking soda, and salt; add to butter mixture, mixing well. Stir in oats, chocolate chunks, and pecans. Drop by rounded tablespoonfuls unto ungreased baking sheets.
• Bake at 350° for 9 minutes or until golden. Cool slightly on baking sheets; transfer to wire racks to cool completely. Yield: 5 dozen.

Game-Day Plan

serves 8 to 10

Game-Day Chili   Beer Bread   Chocolate-Glazed Brownies

Game-Day Chili

Prep: 25 min.   **Cook:** 3 hrs.

2 pounds ground chuck
1 medium onion, chopped
3 to 4 garlic cloves, minced
2 (15-ounce) cans pinto beans,
    rinsed and drained
3 (8-ounce) cans tomato sauce
1 (12-ounce) bottle dark beer
1 (14-ounce) can beef broth
1 (6-ounce) can tomato paste
1 (4.5-ounce) can chopped
    green chiles

2 tablespoons chili powder
1 tablespoon Worcestershire
    sauce
2 teaspoons ground cumin
1 to 2 teaspoons ground red
    pepper
1 teaspoon paprika
1 teaspoon hot sauce
Garnish: pickled jalapeño
    pepper slices

• Cook first 3 ingredients in a Dutch oven over medium heat, stirring until meat crumbles and is no longer pink. Drain well.
• Combine meat mixture, beans, and next 11 ingredients in Dutch oven; bring to a boil. Reduce heat, and simmer 3 hours or until thickened. Garnish, if desired. Yield: 13 cups.

Note: For testing purposes only, we used Sierra Nevada Pale Ale.

PARTY PLEASER

Cooks Chat

"This chili is very tasty. We had friends over, and everyone loved it. Children may find it too spicy, but I think it's great!"

"Excellent! I have made this numerous times since this recipe came out in Southern Living. *My family loves it, even my kids. I make mine in the slow cooker and cook it all day."*

"We substituted kidney beans for pinto beans, and it came out great. This is the only chili recipe I have found in a long time that wasn't too spicy."

Cooks Chat

"This recipe is wonderful, and it goes great with Game-Day Chili! Everyone loved it, even the children."

"This bread is so easy, and it tastes great! Everyone wants the recipe when I serve it. Great with soups and stews."

Beer Bread

Prep: 5 min. **Cook:** 1 hr.

3 cups self-rising flour
¼ cup sugar

1 (12-ounce) bottle light or dark beer

• Stir together all ingredients; spoon dough into a lightly greased 8½- x 4½-inch loafpan.
• Bake at 375° for 55 to 60 minutes or until golden brown. Cool in pan on a wire rack 5 minutes. Remove from pan, and cool on wire rack. Yield: 1 loaf.

Note: For testing purposes only, we used Honey Brown beer.

Cooks Chat

"Everyone loved these! They were gone by the second day. I added extra morsels for an especially chocolaty flavor. Great recipe! It was simple and quick, and it made a lot. I have replaced my usual time-consuming recipe with this one."

"I am only 12 years old. I found this recipe—I'm not a big cooker (to tell you the truth, I can't even crack an egg well)—and it turned out AWESOME! It was also really easy to make! I highly recommend it. It tastes better than that stuff in a box! ;-)"

"I love to bake and have tried many brownies-from-scratch recipes; these are the best ones I have ever made. They are just as good without the frosting."

Chocolate-Glazed Brownies

Prep: 30 min. **Cook:** 30 min. **Other:** 20 min.

1 cup sugar
⅔ cup butter or margarine
¼ cup water
4 cups (24 ounces) semisweet chocolate morsels, divided
1 teaspoon vanilla extract

1½ cups all-purpose flour
½ teaspoon baking soda
½ teaspoon salt
4 large eggs
1 cup chopped pecans, toasted

• Cook first 3 ingredients in a large saucepan over high heat, stirring constantly, until sugar melts. Add 2 cups chocolate morsels and vanilla, stirring until mixture is smooth. Let cool 15 minutes.
• Add flour, baking soda, and salt to cooled chocolate mixture, stirring until blended; stir in eggs and chopped pecans until blended. Spread brownie batter into a greased and floured 13- x 9-inch pan.
• Bake at 325° for 30 minutes. Sprinkle remaining 2 cups chocolate morsels evenly over warm brownies, and let stand 5 minutes to soften. Spread over top. Cool on a wire rack. Yield: 18 brownies.

You're Special

serves 6

Herb-Roasted Pork Tenderloin *Green Bean Alfredo with Cheese Ravioli*

Tossed salad *Bakery rolls* *Hot Fudge Cake*

Herb-Roasted Pork Tenderloin

Prep: 8 min. **Cook:** 40 min. **Other:** 30 min.

¼ cup soy sauce
¼ cup Worcestershire sauce
¼ cup vegetable oil
1 teaspoon dried thyme
1 teaspoon dried marjoram
1 teaspoon rubbed sage
1 teaspoon garlic powder

1 teaspoon onion powder
1 teaspoon ground ginger
1 teaspoon salt
1 teaspoon pepper
1 (1½-pound) package pork
 tenderloins

• Stir together first 11 ingredients in a shallow dish or zip-top freezer bag. Prick pork with a fork, and place in marinade, turning to coat. Cover or seal; let stand at room temperature 30 minutes, or chill 2 hours. Remove from marinade, discarding marinade. Place pork on a rack in a roasting pan.

• Bake at 350° for 40 minutes or until a meat thermometer inserted into thickest portion registers 160°. Yield: 6 servings.

KITCHEN COMFORT
★ ★ ★ ★ ★

Cooks Chat

"Wow! This is really delicious and supereasy. I've made this for dinner parties as well as casual family meals, and it's always been a hit."

"Delicious! We put this on the grill, and the wonderful smell drove the neighbors crazy. It's a keeper."

"This was great and really easy, too. We cooked it on the grill, and it turned out great!"

Cooks Chat

"Outstanding date food! This is quick, easy, and sure to impress that special lady! That's right, this is a great recipe for guys to try. It worked for me. Serve it with red wine and a pork loin."

Green Bean Alfredo with Cheese Ravioli

Prep: 20 min.   **Cook:** 23 min.

1 (1-pound) package frozen cheese-filled ravioli
3 tablespoons butter or margarine
1 pound fresh green beans
2 garlic cloves, pressed
½ teaspoon chopped fresh rosemary

1½ cups whipping cream
¾ cup dry white wine or chicken broth
¾ teaspoon freshly ground pepper
¼ cup (1 ounce) shredded Parmesan cheese
Garnish: fresh rosemary sprigs

• Cook pasta according to package directions; keep warm.
• Melt butter in a large nonstick skillet over medium-high heat; add green beans, garlic, and rosemary, and sauté 6 minutes or until beans are crisp-tender. Remove mixture, and set aside.
• Add whipping cream to skillet, and bring to a boil, stirring constantly. Cook, stirring constantly, 10 minutes.
• Return green bean mixture to skillet; add wine and pepper, and cook 5 minutes. Stir in 2 tablespoons cheese. Serve over ravioli, and sprinkle evenly with remaining 2 tablespoons cheese. Garnish, if desired. Yield: 6 servings.

Cooks Chat

"My cake mix called for 1⅓ cups water. I used ⅔ cup of Kahlúa and water to equal 1⅓ cups liquid. This is a wonderful recipe! We serve it with ice cream and whipped cream. The sauce is not as thick as I would like, but if I waited longer to dig into it, it might set more. It reheats well in the microwave."

"I modified this recipe just a little. Instead of pecans, I used chopped black walnuts and black walnut ice cream. Either way, this is delicious."

Hot Fudge Cake

Prep: 8 min.   **Cook:** 45 min.   **Other:** 10 min.

1 (18.25-ounce) package devil's food cake mix without pudding
1 cup sugar
¼ cup cocoa

2 cups hot water
1 teaspoon vanilla extract
Vanilla ice cream
Toasted chopped pecans

• Prepare cake batter according to package directions. Pour into a lightly greased 13- x 9-inch pan.
• Stir together sugar and next 3 ingredients; pour over batter (it will sink to bottom of pan). Do not stir.
• Bake at 350° for 45 minutes. Let stand 10 minutes. Serve with vanilla ice cream and chopped pecans. Yield: 12 to 15 servings.

Ladies Lunch for a Bunch

serves 12

Green Chile-Pimiento Cheese Sandwiches   Okra pickles

Strawberries with Fluffy Cream Cheese Dip   Cranberry-Pineapple Punch

Mocha-Chocolate Shortbread   Coffee

Green Chile-Pimiento Cheese

QUICK & EASY
★ ★ ★ ★ ★

Prep: 15 min.

2 (8-ounce) blocks extra-sharp
  Cheddar cheese, shredded
1 (8-ounce) block Monterey
  Jack cheese with peppers,
  shredded
1 cup mayonnaise
1 (4.5-ounce) can chopped
  green chiles

1 (4-ounce) jar diced pimiento,
  drained
1 medium poblano chile
  pepper, seeded and minced
¼ small sweet onion, minced
2 teaspoons Worcestershire
  sauce

• Stir together all ingredients in a large bowl. Yield: 6 cups.

Green Chile-Pimiento Cheese Sandwiches: Spread ½ cup
cheese mixture on 6 to 8 whole-grain bread slices; top with bread
slices. Trim crusts, and cut sandwiches lengthwise into thirds.
Reserve remaining cheese for other uses.

Cooks Chat

"I tasted this at a Southern Living
at HOME® *party. It's positively delicious—pimiento cheese with a kick!
Everyone loved it. I will definitely
be making this for my family."*

*"I have made this many times for
my family. This is one of those
special recipes that you don't want
to share."*

*"I love making this. To simplify it a
bit, I omit the poblano chile and
onion. It's still delicious and has a
wonderful flavor people rave
about!"*

Cooks Chat

"I made this one time for a potluck at my work; now I can't get it off my coworkers' minds. They don't let me bring anything other than this dip. It's requested every time: 'Oh, please bring that fantastic fruit dip.' It's a winner."

"Awesome! I tried the dip with other fruits, and it was just as good."

"This is so good! I made it for a baby shower when I needed an easy dish to whip up. It looked luxurious, and everyone loved it!"

Strawberries with Fluffy Cream Cheese Dip

Prep: 10 min.

1 (8-ounce) package cream
   cheese, softened
2 cups powdered sugar

2 teaspoons vanilla extract
1 cup whipped cream
Fresh whole strawberries

• Beat cream cheese, powdered sugar, and vanilla at medium speed with an electric mixer until fluffy. Fold in whipped cream; serve with berries. Yield: 3 cups.

Citrus-Cream Cheese Dip: Add 1 tablespoon grated lime, lemon, or orange rind to cream cheese mixture. Proceed with recipe as directed.

Orange-Flavored Cream Cheese Dip: Add ¼ cup orange liqueur to cream cheese mixture. Proceed with recipe as directed.

Orange Marmalade-Cream Cheese Dip: Add ½ cup orange marmalade to cream cheese mixture. Proceed with recipe as directed.

Cooks Chat

"This has just enough sweetness and tartness. I had a party for 75, and all loved it!"

Cranberry-Pineapple Punch

Prep: 10 min.   **Other:** 8 hrs.

1 (48-ounce) bottle cranberry
   juice drink
1 (46-ounce) can pineapple
   juice

½ cup sugar
2 teaspoons almond extract
1 (2-liter) bottle ginger ale,
   chilled

• Stir together first 4 ingredients until sugar dissolves. Cover and chill 8 hours.
• Stir in ginger ale just before serving. Yield: 6½ quarts (26 cups).

Mocha-Chocolate Shortbread

Prep: 15 min.   **Cook:** 20 min.   **Other:** 30 min.

1¼ cups all-purpose flour
½ cup powdered sugar
2 teaspoons instant coffee
   granules
⅔ cup butter or margarine,
   softened

½ teaspoon vanilla extract
2 cups (12 ounces) semisweet
   chocolate morsels, divided
Vanilla or coffee ice cream
   (optional)

• Combine first 3 ingredients in a medium bowl; add butter and vanilla, and beat at low speed with an electric mixer until blended.
• Stir in 1 cup chocolate morsels.
• Press dough into an ungreased 9-inch square pan; prick dough with a fork.
• Bake at 325° for 20 minutes or until lightly browned. Sprinkle remaining 1 cup morsels over top, and spread to cover. Cut short-bread into 25 (about 1¾-inch) squares; cut each square into 2 triangles. Let cool 30 minutes in pan before removing. Serve with ice cream, if desired. Yield: 50 triangles.

PARTY PLEASER

Cooks Chat

"I give this recipe 5 stars. It's incredibly easy and delicious. This is a great quick dessert for company because it's fancier than chocolate chip cookies and goes very well with coffee. Be careful of overcooking this one—it's moist and delicious if you take it out when lightly browned. Enjoy!"

"The serving size is very small if cut like the recipe suggests—perfect for a bite with coffee!"

"Easy to make! You can use flavored coffees to fit your mood."

An Occasion of Thanksgiving

serves 6 to 8

Sugar-and-Spice Cured Turkey   Cornbread Dressing   Cranberry Salsa

Squash Casserole   Brussels Sprouts with Apples   Praline Coffee

Stuffed Pumpkin with Cranberry-Raisin Bread Pudding

Cooks Chat

"I am a traditionalist and have always done the buttering and basting. Never again! This turkey recipe deserves more stars than I can give. My family complained about not having enough leftovers because it was just so good. So moist, it actually drips. The best!"

"Absolutely the best turkey I've ever roasted! I prepared this last Thanksgiving and then, much to my dismay, lost the recipe. When my family started asking if I'd be doing the turkey like last year's winner, I panicked. Hooray for the Web site!"

"Made this for Thanksgiving. Won't be frying turkey anymore—this was the best any of us had ever had. It was easy to make, very tender, and very juicy. No dryness whatsoever."

Sugar-and-Spice Cured Turkey

Prep: 10 min.   **Cook:** 3 hrs., 5 min.   **Other:** 8 hrs., 15 min.

1 (12-pound) whole turkey
¼ cup firmly packed light
    brown sugar
2 tablespoons kosher or
    coarse-grain sea salt
1 teaspoon onion powder
½ teaspoon garlic powder
½ teaspoon ground allspice
½ teaspoon ground cloves
½ teaspoon ground mace
1 large onion, quartered
2 (14-ounce) cans low-sodium
    chicken broth
Additional chicken broth
2 tablespoons all-purpose flour
Garnishes: fresh rosemary
    sprigs, apple slices, nuts

• Remove giblets and neck; rinse turkey with cold water. Pat dry. Tie legs together with string; tuck wingtips under. Combine brown sugar and next 6 ingredients. Rub over turkey. Cover with plastic wrap; chill 8 hours.
• Remove plastic wrap. Place turkey on a rack in a roasting pan, breast side up. Arrange onion quarters around turkey. Pour 2 cans broth in bottom of pan.
• Bake, loosely covered with foil, at 325° for 1½ hours. Uncover and bake 1½ more hours or until meat thermometer inserted into meaty part of thigh registers 180°. (Cover with foil to prevent excessive browning, if necessary.) Remove onion; discard, reserving pan drippings. Let turkey stand 15 minutes before carving.
• Combine pan drippings and enough chicken broth to equal 2 cups in a saucepan over medium heat. Whisk in flour, and cook, whisking constantly, 5 minutes or until thickened. Serve with turkey. Garnish, if desired. Yield: 8 to 10 servings.

Cornbread Dressing

Prep: 30 min.   **Cook:** 1 hr., 19 min.   **Other:** 8 hrs.

1 cup butter or margarine, divided
3 cups white cornmeal
1 cup all-purpose flour
2 tablespoons sugar
2 teaspoons baking powder
1½ teaspoons salt
1 teaspoon baking soda
7 large eggs, divided
3 cups buttermilk
3 cups soft breadcrumbs

2 medium onions, diced (2 cups)
1 large bunch celery, diced (3 cups)
½ cup finely chopped fresh sage*
6 (10½-ounce) cans condensed chicken broth, undiluted
1 tablespoon pepper

• Place ½ cup butter in a 13- x 9-inch pan; heat in oven at 425° for 4 minutes.
• Combine cornmeal and next 5 ingredients; whisk in 3 eggs and buttermilk.
• Pour hot butter into batter, stirring until blended. Pour batter into pan.
• Bake at 425° for 30 minutes or until golden brown. Cool.
• Crumble cornbread into a large bowl; stir in breadcrumbs, and set aside.
• Melt remaining ½ cup butter in a large skillet over medium heat; add onions and celery, and sauté until tender. Stir in sage, and sauté 1 more minute.
• Stir vegetables, remaining 4 eggs, chicken broth, and pepper into cornbread mixture; pour evenly into 1 lightly greased 13- x 9-inch baking dish and 1 lightly greased 8-inch square baking dish. Cover and chill 8 hours.
• Bake, uncovered, at 375° for 35 to 40 minutes or until golden brown. Yield: 16 to 18 servings.

*Substitute 1 tablespoon dried rubbed sage for fresh sage, if desired.

Note: Freeze the dressing in the 8-inch square baking dish (before baking) up to 1 month. To serve, thaw overnight in refrigerator. Let stand at room temperature 30 minutes. Bake at 375° for 40 to 45 minutes or until golden.

Andouille Sausage, Apple, and Pecan Dressing: Brown ¾ pound diced andouille sausage in a skillet over medium heat; drain. Add sausage; 2 Granny Smith apples, chopped; and 2 cups chopped toasted pecans to dressing. Proceed as directed, baking 40 to 45 minutes or until done.

FREEZER FRIENDLY

Cooks Chat

"This is like my grandmother made. She did not make hers ahead of time, but doing so makes fixing a large meal so much easier."

"Very moist and delicious! I did not use condensed chicken broth in the 10½-ounce cans. I bought cans of regular chicken broth (fat-free) and used an equal amount. This recipe has replaced Grandma's!"

"This is the easiest, best-tasting recipe I have ever made! It truly is an old-fashioned type of dressing, and my family loved it. The fresh sage is so flavorful. I used biscuits for my breadcrumbs, and it turned out fine."

Cranberry Salsa

Prep: 6 min.   **Other:** 8 hrs.

3 cups fresh or frozen
   cranberries, thawed
½ medium-size red onion,
   chopped
2 jalapeño peppers, seeded and
   chopped

½ cup chopped fresh cilantro
½ cup honey
2 tablespoons fresh lime juice
1 tablespoon grated orange rind

• Process all ingredients in a food processor, pulsing 6 to 8 times or until coarsely chopped, stopping to scrape down sides. Cover and chill 8 hours. Yield: 2½ cups.

Squash Casserole

Prep: 15 min.   **Cook:** 45 min.

2½ pounds yellow squash or
   zucchini, sliced
½ cup butter or margarine
2 large eggs
¼ cup mayonnaise
1 (8-ounce) can sliced water
   chestnuts, drained
1 (4-ounce) jar diced pimiento,
   drained

½ cup chopped onion
¼ cup chopped green bell
   pepper
2 teaspoons sugar
1½ teaspoons salt
10 round buttery crackers,
   crushed (about ½ cup)
½ cup (2 ounces) shredded
   sharp Cheddar cheese

• Cook squash, covered, in a small amount of boiling water 8 to 10 minutes or until tender; drain well, pressing between paper towels.
• Combine squash and butter in a bowl; mash until butter melts. Stir in eggs and next 7 ingredients; spoon into a lightly greased shallow 2-quart baking dish. Sprinkle with crushed crackers.
• Bake at 325° for 30 minutes. Sprinkle with cheese; bake 5 more minutes or until cheese melts. Yield: 8 servings.

Brussels Sprouts with Apples

Prep: 25 min.   **Cook:** 42 min.

2¼ pounds fresh Brussels
   sprouts, halved
3 tablespoons fresh lemon juice
2 teaspoons salt, divided
¼ cup butter or margarine,
   divided
1 medium onion, diced
¼ cup apple juice
1 large Red Delicious apple,
   diced

1 garlic clove, minced
1 teaspoon sugar
1 (8-ounce) can sliced water
   chestnuts, drained
½ cup golden raisins
2 teaspoons grated lemon rind
½ teaspoon freshly ground
   pepper
⅛ teaspoon grated nutmeg

• Bring Brussels sprouts, lemon juice, 1½ teaspoons salt, and water
to cover to a boil in a saucepan. Cover, reduce heat, and simmer
5 to 10 minutes or until tender. Drain and keep warm.
• Melt 2 tablespoons butter in a large skillet over medium-high
heat; add onion, and sauté 15 to 20 minutes or until caramel-
colored. Add apple juice, and cook 2 minutes, stirring to loosen
browned particles.
• Add apple, garlic, and sugar; cook, stirring constantly, 5 to
6 minutes or until apple is tender. Add water chestnuts, next
4 ingredients, remaining ½ teaspoon salt, and remaining
2 tablespoons butter; cook, stirring constantly, 3 to 4 minutes.
Gently toss in Brussels sprouts. Yield: 6 to 8 servings.

Praline Coffee

Prep: 5 min.   **Cook:** 5 min.

3 cups hot brewed coffee
¾ cup half-and-half
¾ cup firmly packed light
   brown sugar

2 tablespoons butter or
   margarine
¾ cup praline liqueur
Sweetened whipped cream

• Cook first 4 ingredients in a large saucepan over medium heat,
stirring constantly, until thoroughly heated (do not boil). Stir in
liqueur; serve with sweetened whipped cream. Yield: 5¼ cups.

Stuffed Pumpkin with Cranberry-Raisin Bread Pudding

Prep: 35 min.   **Cook:** 1 hr.

1 (2½- to 3-pound) pumpkin*
2 tablespoons butter or margarine, melted and divided
2 tablespoons sugar, divided
2 large eggs
½ cup sugar
½ cup butter or margarine, melted

¾ cup half-and-half
¾ cup chopped pecans, toasted
1 (16-ounce) raisin bread loaf, cut into 1-inch cubes
½ cup fresh cranberries
Lemon-Vanilla Sauce

• Cut off top of pumpkin, reserving lid with stem. Scoop out pumpkin seeds and pulp, and reserve for another use. Brush inside of pumpkin shell with 1 tablespoon melted butter. Sprinkle with 1 tablespoon sugar. Top with lid.
• Bake at 350° for 35 minutes.
• Brush inside of baked pumpkin shell with 1 tablespoon butter; sprinkle with 1 tablespoon sugar.
• Stir together eggs and next 6 ingredients; spoon pudding mixture into a lightly greased 8-inch square pan.
• Bake pumpkin and bread pudding at 350° for 25 minutes. Let pumpkin cool; spoon bread pudding evenly into pumpkin shell. Serve with Lemon-Vanilla Sauce. Yield: 12 servings.

*For individual servings, substitute 12 (½-pound) pumpkins. Scoop out seeds and pulp; sprinkle each pumpkin shell with 1 teaspoon butter and 1 teaspoon sugar, and bake with the bread pudding. (Do not prebake as with the larger pumpkin.) Spoon bread pudding evenly into baked pumpkin shells.

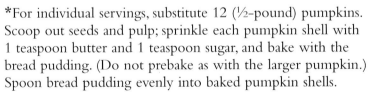

Lemon-Vanilla Sauce

Prep: 10 min.   **Cook:** 20 min.

1 vanilla bean, split
1 cup water
½ cup sugar
2 tablespoons cornstarch
⅛ teaspoon salt

1 tablespoon butter or margarine
2 tablespoons grated lemon rind
⅓ cup fresh lemon juice

• Cook vanilla bean, water, sugar, cornstarch, and salt in a saucepan over medium heat, stirring until smooth and thickened.
• Stir in butter and remaining ingredients, and cook until thoroughly heated. Remove vanilla bean. Yield: 1⅔ cups.

Casual Holiday Gathering

serves 6

Holiday Beef Tenderloin   *Skillet Creamed Corn*   *Marinated Asparagus*

Homemade Butter Rolls   *Mama's Pumpkin Pie*

Holiday Beef Tenderloin

Prep: 10 min.   **Cook:** 35 min.   **Other:** 8 hrs.

A hint of sweetness from the nutmeg balances the spice from the two peppers in this tenderloin that's great year-round, despite its title.

1 tablespoon salt
1½ teaspoons onion powder
1½ teaspoons garlic powder
1½ teaspoons black pepper
1 teaspoon ground red pepper
½ teaspoon ground cumin

½ teaspoon ground nutmeg
1 (5-pound) beef tenderloin, trimmed
¼ cup olive oil
Garnishes: fresh rosemary sprigs, fresh sage sprigs

• Combine first 7 ingredients.
• Rub tenderloin with oil; coat with spice mixture. Place in a roasting pan; cover and chill 8 hours.
• Bake at 500° for 15 minutes or until browned. Reduce temperature to 375° and bake 20 more minutes or until a meat thermometer registers 145° (medium rare) or 160° (medium). Let stand 10 minutes; slice. Garnish, if desired. Yield: 8 servings.

FOR THE HOLIDAYS
★ ★ ★ ★ ★

Cooks Chat

"Delicious and very tender. The seasoning was outstanding. Most importantly, it was extremely easy to prepare and serve. It was such a big hit at our family Christmas get-together last year, that everyone requested the same menu this year—only more of it."

Skillet Creamed Corn

Prep: 20 min.   **Cook:** 27 min.

6 bacon slices
½ Vidalia or other sweet onion, finely chopped
1 garlic clove, finely chopped
3 cups fresh corn kernels (about 6 ears)*
¼ cup all-purpose flour
1½ cups half-and-half
½ teaspoon salt
¼ teaspoon pepper
1 tablespoon butter or margarine
1 tablespoon chopped fresh basil*
Garnish: fresh basil sprigs

• Cook bacon in a large skillet until crisp; remove bacon, and drain on paper towels, reserving 2 tablespoons drippings in skillet. Crumble bacon, and set aside.
• Sauté onion and garlic in hot drippings 5 minutes or until tender. Stir in corn. Cook 5 to 7 minutes or until golden and remove from heat.
• Cook flour in a large clean skillet over medium heat, stirring occasionally, about 5 minutes or until golden. Gradually whisk in half-and-half until smooth. Add corn mixture, salt, and pepper; cook 5 minutes or until thickened. Remove from heat; stir in butter and basil. Sprinkle each serving with bacon. Garnish, if desired. Yield: 4 to 6 servings.

*Substitute 3 cups frozen corn and 1 teaspoon dried basil for fresh, if desired.

Marinated Asparagus

Prep: 15 min.   **Cook:** 3 min.   **Other:** 8 hrs.

2 pounds fresh asparagus
¾ cup olive oil
1 tablespoon sugar
½ cup white balsamic vinegar
4 garlic cloves, minced
1 teaspoon red pepper flakes

• Snap off tough ends of asparagus, and cook asparagus in boiling water to cover 3 minutes or until asparagus is crisp-tender; drain.
• Plunge asparagus into ice water to stop the cooking process; drain. Arrange asparagus in a 13- x 9-inch baking dish.
• Whisk together olive oil, sugar, balsamic vinegar, garlic, and red pepper flakes until well blended; pour over asparagus. Cover and chill 8 hours. Drain before serving. Yield: 6 to 8 servings.

Homemade Butter Rolls

Prep: 20 min. **Cook:** 10 min. **Other:** 10 hrs., 5 min.

2 (¼-ounce) envelopes active
    dry yeast
1 cup sugar, divided
2 cups warm water (100° to
    110°)

1 cup butter, melted
6 large eggs, lightly beaten
1½ teaspoons salt
8½ to 9½ cups all-purpose
    flour

• Stir together yeast, 2 tablespoons sugar, and 2 cups warm water in
a 4-cup glass measuring cup; let stand 5 minutes.
• Stir together yeast mixture, remaining sugar, and butter in a large
bowl; stir in egg and salt. Gradually stir in enough flour to make a
soft dough. Cover and chill 8 hours.
• Divide dough into 4 equal portions. Turn each portion out onto
a lightly floured surface, and roll each into a 12-inch circle. Cut
each circle into 12 wedges. Roll up each wedge, starting at wide
end; place on greased baking sheets. (Rolls may be frozen at this
point.) Cover and let rise in a warm place (85°), free from drafts, 2
hours or until doubled in bulk.
• Bake at 400° for 10 minutes or until golden. Yield: 4 dozen.

Note: If unbaked rolls are frozen, place frozen rolls on ungreased
baking sheets. Cover and let rise in a warm place (85°), free from
drafts, 2 hours or until doubled in bulk. Bake as directed.

Mama's Pumpkin Pie

Prep: 10 min. **Cook:** 1 hr., 5 min.

½ (15-ounce) package
    refrigerated piecrusts
1¾ cups canned pumpkin
1¾ cups sweetened condensed
    milk
2 large eggs, lightly beaten
⅔ cup firmly packed light
    brown sugar

2 tablespoons granulated sugar
1¼ teaspoons ground
    cinnamon
½ teaspoon salt
½ teaspoon ground ginger
½ teaspoon ground nutmeg
¼ teaspoon ground cloves

• Fit piecrust into a 9-inch pieplate according to package directions; fold edges under, and crimp.
• Combine pumpkin and remaining ingredients; beat at medium
speed with an electric mixer 2 minutes. Pour into piecrust.
• Bake at 425° for 15 minutes. Reduce heat to 350°; bake 50 minutes or until a knife inserted in center comes out clean. Cool on a
wire rack. Yield: 1 (9-inch) pie.

Christmas Cheer

serves 6

Baked Ham with Bourbon Glaze

Caramelized Onion-and-Gorgonzola Mashed Potatoes

Almond Broccoli in Sherry Sauce

Pineapple Wassail   Sweet Potato Crème Brûlée

Baked Ham with Bourbon Glaze

Prep: 10 min.   **Cook:** 1 hr., 30 min.

1 cup honey
½ cup molasses
½ cup bourbon*
¼ cup orange juice

2 tablespoons Dijon mustard
1 (6- to 8-pound) smoked fully
    cooked ham half
Garnish: fresh herb sprigs

• Microwave honey and molasses in a 1-quart glass microwave-safe dish at HIGH 1 minute; whisk to blend. Whisk in bourbon, juice, and mustard.
• Remove skin and excess fat from ham, and place ham in a roasting pan. Pour glaze over ham.
• Bake at 325° on lower oven rack for 1½ hours or until a meat thermometer inserted into thickest portion registers 140°, basting every 15 minutes with glaze.
• Remove from pan, reserving drippings. Cover ham, and chill, if desired. Chill reserved drippings.
• Remove and discard fat from drippings. Bring drippings to a boil in a small saucepan. Serve warm with ham. Garnish, if desired. Yield: 12 to 14 servings.

*Substitute ½ cup orange juice for bourbon, if desired.

Baked Ham with Bourbon Glaze

Caramelized Onion-and-Gorgonzola Mashed Potatoes

Prep: 30 min.   **Cook:** 30 min.

3 pounds Yukon gold potatoes, peeled and quartered
1¾ teaspoons salt, divided
2 tablespoons butter or margarine
1 tablespoon olive oil
2 medium onions, diced
4 garlic cloves, minced

2 teaspoons chopped fresh or ½ teaspoon dried rosemary
½ cup butter or margarine
¾ cup half-and-half
¾ cup crumbled Gorgonzola or blue cheese
¾ teaspoon pepper
Garnish: fresh rosemary sprigs

• Bring potato, 1 teaspoon salt, and water to cover to a boil in a Dutch oven; cook 20 to 25 minutes or until tender. Drain and keep warm.
• Melt 2 tablespoons butter with oil in a skillet over medium heat; add onion, and cook, stirring often, 12 to 17 minutes or until tender. Add garlic, and cook 3 minutes. Stir in rosemary; remove from heat.
• Mash potato with a potato masher; stir in ½ cup butter, half-and-half, and cheese until blended. Stir in onion mixture, remaining ¾ teaspoon salt, and pepper. Spoon enough mixture into a decorative ovenproof dish or 13- x 9-inch baking dish to fill bottom; pipe or dollop remaining mixture over top.
• Broil 3 inches from heat 5 minutes or until top is lightly browned. Garnish, if desired. Yield: 6 servings.

QUICK & EASY

Cooks Chat

"This was delightful! I've been looking for a new way to serve broccoli. This was a very different recipe with lots of flavor—but not too weird for my meat-and-potatoes husband. Mikey liked it!"

"I love broccoli but have never found a way of making it the way I like without using lots of cheese. Thank you."

Almond Broccoli in Sherry Sauce

Prep: 15 min.   **Cook:** 20 min.

1½ pounds fresh broccoli, trimmed and separated into florets
4 cups boiling water
1 chicken bouillon cube
¾ cup boiling water
¼ cup butter or margarine
¼ cup all-purpose flour

1 cup half-and-half
2 tablespoons sherry
2 tablespoons lemon juice
½ teaspoon salt
¼ teaspoon pepper
¾ cup (3 ounces) shredded Parmesan cheese
⅓ cup slivered almonds, toasted

• Cook florets in 4 cups boiling water in a Dutch oven over medium heat 4 to 5 minutes or until crisp-tender; drain. Place florets in a lightly greased 2-quart baking dish, and set aside.
• Dissolve bouillon cube in ¾ cup boiling water.
• Melt butter in a large saucepan over medium-high heat. Whisk in flour, and cook, whisking constantly, 1 minute. Gradually whisk in bouillon mixture and half-and-half; cook, stirring constantly, until mixture thickens and comes to a boil.
• Whisk in sherry and next 3 ingredients. Pour over broccoli; sprinkle with cheese and almonds.
• Bake at 375° for 20 minutes or until bubbly. Yield: 6 servings.

QUICK & EASY

Cooks Chat

"This is a good recipe for Christmas. We love it!"

Pineapple Wassail

Prep: 5 min.   **Cook:** 20 min.

4 cups unsweetened pineapple juice
1 (12-ounce) can apricot nectar
2 cups apple cider
1 cup orange juice

1 teaspoon whole cloves
3 (6-inch) cinnamon sticks, broken
Garnishes: orange wedges, whole cinnamon sticks

• Bring first 6 ingredients to a boil in a Dutch oven; reduce heat, and simmer 20 minutes. Pour through a wire-mesh strainer, discarding spices. Serve hot. Garnish, if desired. Yield: 2 quarts.

Sweet Potato Crème Brûlée

Prep: 20 min.   **Cook:** 1 hr., 7 min.   **Other:** 8 hrs., 5 min.

2 medium sweet potatoes,
   baked, skinned, and
   mashed
¼ cup firmly packed brown
   sugar
1 tablespoon fresh lemon juice
1 quart whipping cream

1 cup granulated sugar
8 large egg yolks
1 tablespoon vanilla extract
⅓ cup firmly packed brown
   sugar
Garnish: chopped toasted
   pecans

• Combine mashed sweet potatoes, ¼ cup brown sugar, and lemon juice; spoon potato mixture into a buttered 10-inch quiche dish to form a ¼-inch-thick layer.
• Stir together cream, 1 cup granulated sugar, egg yolks, and vanilla in medium saucepan. Cook over low heat, stirring constantly, about 5 minutes or until hot. Pour over sweet potato mixture in prepared dish. Place dish in a shallow baking pan. Add hot water to pan to a depth of 1 inch.
• Bake at 325° for 1 hour or until a knife inserted in center comes out almost clean. Remove from water. Cool on a wire rack. Cover and refrigerate at least 8 hours.
• Sprinkle custard with ⅓ cup brown sugar; place custard on a jellyroll pan. Broil 5½ inches from heat about 2 minutes or until sugar melts. Let stand 5 minutes to allow sugar to harden before serving. Garnish, if desired. Yield: 8 to 10 servings.

FOR THE HOLIDAYS
★ ★ ★ ★ ★

Cooks Chat

"This dish, though simple to make, is elegant and delicious. I made it for a Thanksgiving gathering, and every bite was devoured amidst oohing and aaahing! This recipe made me look like a gourmet chef! Thank you for a new Thanksgiving tradition."

"What a wonderfully smooth dessert to enjoy with your Thanksgiving feast! I think this will become a new family tradition! I wouldn't change a thing."

Lucky New Year's Celebration

serves 8

Collard 'n' Black-Eyed Pea Stew   Hot-Water Cornbread

Chocolate Martinis

SOUTHERN CLASSIC
★★★★★

Cooks Chat

"Since moving to the South, I've wanted to make a traditional New Year's Day meal. This recipe looked easy enough, even for me. I used prechopped ham and all fresh veggies. Then I doubled the recipe for leftovers. Excellent! Next year, I'll make more and invite some friends over. Don't forget the cornbread!"

"Easy, fast, and delicious! If you like collards, you will love this recipe. This will definitely become a New Year's tradition in my family!"

Collard 'n' Black-Eyed Pea Stew

Prep: 5 min.   **Cook:** 30 min.

2 cups chopped cooked ham
1 tablespoon vegetable oil
3 cups chicken broth
1 (16-ounce) package frozen chopped collard greens
1 (10-ounce) package frozen diced onion, red and green bell peppers, and celery*

1 teaspoon sugar
1 teaspoon seasoned pepper
1 (16-ounce) can black-eyed peas, drained

• Sauté ham in hot oil in a Dutch oven over medium-high heat 5 minutes or until lightly browned. Add broth and next 4 ingredients; bring to a boil. Cover, reduce heat to low, and simmer, stirring occasionally, 15 minutes. Stir in black-eyed peas, and cook 10 more minutes. Yield: 6 to 8 servings.

*For testing purposes only, we used McKenzie's Seasoning Blend for frozen diced onion, red and green bell peppers, and celery. Substitute 1 chopped onion, 1 chopped red bell pepper, 1 chopped green bell pepper, and 1 chopped celery rib, if desired.

Hot-Water Cornbread

Prep: 5 min.   **Cook:** 18 min.

Prepare this cornbread at the last minute so you can serve it piping hot.

Cooks Chat

"This is simply delicious—a true Southern favorite. It's good without sugar, too!"

2 cups white cornmeal
¼ teaspoon baking powder
1¼ teaspoons salt
1 teaspoon sugar
¼ cup half-and-half

1 tablespoon vegetable oil
¾ to 1¼ cups boiling water
Vegetable oil
Softened butter

• Combine cornmeal and next 3 ingredients in a bowl; stir in half-and-half and 1 tablespoon oil. Gradually add boiling water, stirring until batter is the consistency of grits.

• Pour oil to a depth of ½ inch into a large heavy skillet; place over medium-high heat. Scoop batter into a ¼-cup measure; drop into hot oil, and fry, in batches, 3 minutes on each side or until golden. Drain well on paper towels. Serve immediately with softened butter. Yield: 8 patties.

Note: Stone-ground (coarsely ground) cornmeal requires more liquid.

Country Ham Hot-Water Cornbread: Stir in 1 to 2 cups finely chopped country ham after adding boiling water.

Bacon-Cheddar Hot-Water Cornbread: Stir in 8 slices cooked and crumbled bacon, 1 cup (4 ounces) shredded sharp Cheddar cheese, and 4 minced green onions after adding boiling water.

Southwestern Hot-Water Cornbread: Stir in 1 seeded and minced jalapeño pepper; 1 cup (4 ounces) Mexican cheese blend; 1 cup frozen whole kernel corn, thawed; and ¼ cup minced fresh cilantro after adding boiling water.

Baked Hot-Water Cornbread: Omit skillet procedure. Pour ⅓ cup vegetable oil into a 15- x 10-inch jellyroll pan, spreading to edges. Drop batter as directed onto pan. Bake at 475° for 12 to 15 minutes. Turn cakes, and bake 5 more minutes or until golden brown.

Chocolate Martinis

Prep: 15 min.   **Other:** 1 hr., 5 min.

2 to 2½ cups vodka, chilled
1¼ cups chocolate liqueur
¼ cup raspberry liqueur

¼ cup half-and-half (optional)
Chocolate liqueur or syrup
Sweetened cocoa

• Stir together vodka, liqueurs, and, if desired, half-and-half in a large pitcher; chill at least 1 hour.
• Fill martini glasses with ice. Let stand 5 minutes; discard ice.
• Dip rims of chilled glasses in chocolate liqueur; dip in cocoa, coating rims.
• Pour vodka mixture into glasses. Serve immediately. Yield: 10 to 12 servings.

Note: For testing purposes only, we used Godiva Liqueur for chocolate liqueur, Chambord for raspberry liqueur, and Ghirardelli Sweet Ground Chocolate and Cocoa for sweetened cocoa.

Individual Chocolate Martini: Combine ¼ cup vodka, 2 tablespoons chocolate liqueur, 1½ teaspoons raspberry liqueur, 6 ice cubes, and, if desired, a dash of half-and-half in a martini shaker. Cover with lid, and shake until thoroughly chilled. Remove lid, and strain into a chilled martini glass. Serve immediately. Yield: 1 serving.

one-dish meals

★★★★★

Keep the kitchen clean and speed up weeknight meals with these top-rated wonders made in a single dish.

Chicken Cannelloni with Roasted Red Bell Pepper Sauce, page 96

Cooks Chat

"Wonderful! One of my family's favorite weeknight dinners."

"We call this 'Taco Salad' at our house. It's one of the few meals that we all love."

"This was just great! My family loved it. I left out the avocado. Next time, I'll put some sour cream on top. I will make this again and again."

Hamburger-Rice Skillet

Prep: 18 min.   Cook: 30 min.

1 pound ground chuck
1 small onion, chopped
1 small green bell pepper, chopped
1 (10-ounce) can mild diced tomatoes and green chiles
1½ cups water
1 cup uncooked long-grain rice
1 (1.25-ounce) envelope mild taco seasoning mix
½ teaspoon salt

2 cups chopped lettuce
3 green onions, chopped
1 tomato, chopped
1 avocado, sliced
1 (2¼-ounce) can sliced black olives, drained
1 cup (4 ounces) Mexican cheese blend
Tortilla chips
Salsa

• Cook first 3 ingredients in a large skillet over medium-high heat, stirring until beef crumbles and is no longer pink; drain.
• Stir in tomatoes and green chiles and next 4 ingredients. Cook, covered, over medium heat 15 minutes, stirring occasionally. Uncover and cook 15 more minutes; remove from heat.
• Sprinkle lettuce and next 5 ingredients over hamburger mixture. Stand tortilla chips around edge of skillet; serve with chips and salsa. Yield: 6 servings.

Cooks Chat

"This recipe was excellent! It had a wonderful flavor and was very easy to make. I made it for a group of about 20 people, and it got rave reviews. It is also great without the meat."

"This is an excellent basic recipe just as it is. You can also add mushrooms, decrease the garlic, and add Italian seasoning, or use ground chicken or turkey for those who don't eat red meat."

"This was really great! Thanks so much for the recipe. Simple, fun, and delicious!"

Ellie's Lasagna

Prep: 30 min.   Cook: 40 min.   Other: 10 min.

12 lasagna noodles
1 (15-ounce) container ricotta cheese
2 garlic cloves, pressed
1 pound ground beef

2 (26-ounce) jars spaghetti sauce
4 cups (16 ounces) shredded Italian three-cheese blend

• Cook noodles according to package directions. Drain; set aside.
• Stir together ricotta cheese and garlic; set aside.
• Cook beef in a large skillet, stirring until it crumbles and is no longer pink; drain. Stir in sauce.
• Layer one-third each of lasagna noodles, ricotta cheese mixture, shredded cheese, and beef mixture in a lightly greased 13- x 9-inch baking dish. Repeat layers twice.
• Bake at 375° for 35 to 40 minutes. Let stand 5 to 10 minutes before serving. Yield: 6 servings.

Note: For testing purposes only, we used Classico di Napoli Tomato & Basil Pasta Sauce.

Sicilian Spaghetti Sauce

Prep: 20 min.   **Cook:** 2 hrs., 40 min.

Italian sausage spices up traditional beefy spaghetti sauce in this Mediterranean classic. Freeze any leftovers to enjoy within 3 months.

½ pound mild Italian sausage
½ pound lean ground beef
1 large onion, chopped
2 garlic cloves, minced
4 (8-ounce) cans tomato
    sauce
1 (6-ounce) can Italian-style
    tomato paste
3 cups water
¼ cup sugar

1 to 1½ teaspoons salt
1 teaspoon dried parsley
1 teaspoon dried basil
¼ to ½ teaspoon ground red
    pepper
1 cup sliced fresh mushrooms
Hot cooked linguine
Shredded Parmesan cheese
Breadsticks (optional)

• Remove casings from sausage, and discard. Cook sausage and ground beef in a large skillet or Dutch oven over medium heat 6 minutes, stirring until meat crumbles. Add onion and garlic, and sauté 4 minutes or until beef and sausage are no longer pink. Drain and set aside. Wipe skillet clean.
• Combine tomato sauce and next 7 ingredients in skillet or Dutch oven; cook, stirring occasionally, 1 hour. Add sausage mixture and mushrooms. Cook, stirring occasionally, 1 hour and 30 minutes or until mixture thickens. Serve over linguine; sprinkle with cheese. Serve with breadsticks, if desired. Yield: 4 to 6 servings.

Cooks Chat

"This is the best spaghetti sauce I have ever made. The key is the lengthy cooking time, which allows the rich flavors to really develop. I used all ground beef, brown sugar, and oregano instead of parsley. It was even better the second day."

"I have cooked this meal for several guests in my home, and everyone has loved it. I would recommend this recipe to anyone who loves Italian food."

"This has become our favorite sauce—thick and hearty and delicious!"

Jack-o'-Lantern Cheeseburger Pie

Prep: 30 min.   **Cook:** 30 min.

1 pound ground beef
1 medium onion, chopped
2 garlic cloves, pressed
¾ teaspoon salt
½ teaspoon pepper
¼ cup ketchup
1 teaspoon Worcestershire sauce
1 (15-ounce) package
    refrigerated piecrusts

1 tablespoon prepared mustard
3 cups (12 ounces) shredded
    Monterey Jack cheese,
    divided
2 tablespoons water
1 large egg
Red and yellow liquid food
    coloring

• Cook first 5 ingredients in a large skillet over medium-high heat, stirring until beef crumbles and is no longer pink; drain. Stir in ketchup and Worcestershire sauce; cool.
• Unroll 1 piecrust, and place on a lightly greased baking sheet. Spread mustard evenly over crust. Stir together meat mixture and 2 cups cheese; spoon onto center of crust, leaving a 2-inch border.
• Unroll remaining piecrust, and cut out a jack-o'-lantern face, reserving pastry cutouts to use as a stem. Place crust over meat mixture; crimp edges of crust, and fold under. Place stem on top of jack-o'-lantern face.
• Whisk together 2 tablespoons water, egg, and 1 drop each of red and yellow food coloring; brush over crust.
• Bake at 425° for 20 minutes; remove from oven, and brush again with egg mixture. Fill eyes, nose, and mouth with remaining 1 cup cheese. Bake 5 to 10 more minutes or until golden brown. Yield: 6 to 8 servings.

Spaghetti-and-Spinach Casserole

Prep: 20 min.   **Cook:** 30 min.

To make ahead, bake as directed, cover, and freeze. Thaw overnight in the refrigerator. Bake, covered, at 350° for 30 minutes; uncover and bake 10 more minutes.

1½ pounds ground beef
2 garlic cloves, minced
½ teaspoon salt
½ teaspoon pepper
1 (26-ounce) jar spaghetti sauce
1 teaspoon Italian seasoning
1 (10-ounce) package frozen
  chopped spinach, thawed
  and drained

2 cups (8 ounces) shredded
  Monterey Jack cheese
1½ cups sour cream
1 large egg, lightly beaten
1 teaspoon garlic salt
8 ounces wide egg noodles,
  cooked
1½ cups (6 ounces) shredded
  Parmesan cheese

• Cook first 4 ingredients in a large nonstick skillet over medium heat, stirring until beef crumbles and is no longer pink. Drain and return to skillet. Stir in spaghetti sauce and Italian seasoning.
• Combine spinach and next 4 ingredients. Fold in noodles, and spoon mixture into a lightly greased 13- x 9-inch baking dish. Sprinkle with half of Parmesan cheese; top with beef mixture and remaining Parmesan cheese.
• Bake at 350° for 30 minutes or until bubbly and golden. Yield: 8 to 10 servings.

Cooks Chat

"This was wonderful. We served it over rice and added an extra can of beans, and our whole family loved it. Great to make for company!"

"This is delicious! Couldn't find red jalapeño jelly, so I used green jalapeño jelly. This freezes well."

Spicy-Sweet Ribs and Beans

Prep: 30 min.   **Cook:** 10 hrs., 20 min.

Slow cookers don't brown food, so here, we broil the ribs for extra flavor before adding them to the pot. Serve with cornbread and a simple green salad with creamy Italian or Ranch dressing.

2 (16-ounce) cans pinto beans, drained
4 pounds country-style pork ribs, trimmed
1 teaspoon garlic powder
½ teaspoon salt
½ teaspoon pepper
1 medium onion, chopped
1 (10.5-ounce) jar red jalapeño jelly
1 (18-ounce) bottle hickory-flavored barbecue sauce
1 teaspoon green hot sauce

• Place beans in a 5-quart electric slow cooker; set aside.
• Cut ribs apart; sprinkle with garlic powder, salt, and pepper. Place ribs on a broiling pan.
• Broil 5½ inches from heat 18 to 20 minutes or until browned, turning once. Add ribs to slow cooker, and sprinkle with onion.
• Combine jelly, barbecue sauce, and hot sauce in a saucepan; cook over low heat until jelly melts. Pour over ribs; stir gently.
• Cover and cook at HIGH 5 to 6 hours or at LOW 9 to 10 hours. Remove ribs. Drain bean mixture, reserving sauce. Skim fat from sauce. Arrange ribs over bean mixture; serve with sauce. Yield: 8 servings.

Note: For testing purposes only, we used Kraft Thick 'n Spicy Hickory Smoke Barbecue Sauce and Tabasco Green Pepper Sauce.

Ham-and-Greens Pot Pie with Cornbread Crust

Prep: 10 min.   **Cook:** 50 min.

4 cups chopped cooked ham
2 tablespoons vegetable oil
3 tablespoons all-purpose flour
3 cups chicken broth
1 (16-ounce) package frozen seasoning blend
1 (16-ounce) package frozen chopped collard greens
1 (16-ounce) can black-eyed peas, rinsed and drained
½ teaspoon dried crushed red pepper
Cornbread Crust Batter
Pimiento-Cheese Corn Sticks (optional)

• Sauté ham in hot oil in a Dutch oven over medium-high heat 5 minutes or until lightly browned. Add flour, and cook, stirring constantly, 1 minute. Gradually add chicken broth, and cook, stirring constantly, 3 minutes or until broth begins to thicken.
• Bring mixture to a boil, and add seasoning blend and collard greens; return to a boil, and cook, stirring often, 15 minutes. Stir in black-eyed peas and crushed red pepper; spoon hot mixture into a lightly greased 13- x 9-inch baking dish. Pour Cornbread Crust Batter evenly over hot filling mixture.
• Bake at 425° for 20 to 25 minutes or until cornbread is golden brown and set. Top with Pimiento-Cheese Corn Sticks, if desired. Yield: 8 to 10 servings.

Note: For testing purposes only, we used McKenzie's Seasoning Blend.

Cornbread Crust Batter

Prep: 5 min.

1½ cups white cornmeal mix
½ cup all-purpose flour
1 teaspoon sugar
2 large eggs, lightly beaten
1½ cups buttermilk

• Combine first 3 ingredients; make a well in the center of mixture. Add eggs and buttermilk to cornmeal mixture, stirring just until moistened. Yield: 1 (13- x 9-inch) crust.

Pimiento-Cheese Corn Sticks

Prep: 10 min.   **Cook:** 8 min.

Cornbread Crust Batter
1 cup (4 ounces) shredded
    Cheddar cheese

1 (7-ounce) jar diced pimiento,
    drained

• Prepare Cornbread Crust Batter, adding cheese and pimiento.
• Heat oven to 450°, and place cast-iron miniature corn stick pans in oven; heat 5 minutes or until hot. Remove pans from oven, and coat with cooking spray. Spoon batter into hot pans.
• Bake at 450° for 8 minutes or until golden brown. Remove from pans immediately. Yield: about 5 dozen.

Cheesy Bacon-and-Ham Casserole

Prep: 15 min.   **Cook:** 1 hr., 5 min.

½ pound bacon
½ pound chopped cooked ham
¾ cup quick-cooking grits
1 (16-ounce) loaf pasteurized prepared cheese product, cubed
¼ cup butter or margarine
6 large eggs, lightly beaten
½ cup milk
2 teaspoons baking powder
½ teaspoon freshly ground pepper

• Cook bacon in a large skillet until crisp; remove bacon, and drain on paper towels, reserving 1 tablespoon drippings in skillet. Crumble bacon, and set aside.
• Cook ham in reserved drippings in skillet over medium heat until browned.
• Cook grits according to package directions. Remove from heat; stir in cheese and butter until melted. Stir in bacon, ham, eggs, and remaining ingredients. Pour into a lightly greased 13- x 9-inch baking dish.
• Bake at 350° for 45 minutes or until set. Yield: 8 servings.

Note: Casserole may be prepared a day ahead; cover and chill. Remove from refrigerator the following day, and let stand at room temperature 30 minutes. Bake as directed.

Breakfast Casserole

Prep: 15 min.   **Cook:** 50 min.   **Other:** 8 hrs., 30 min.

1½ pounds ground pork sausage
3 to 4 bread slices, cubed
1½ cups (6 ounces) shredded Cheddar cheese
9 large eggs
3 cups milk
1½ teaspoons dry mustard
1 teaspoon salt
⅛ teaspoon pepper

• Cook sausage in a skillet, stirring until it crumbles and is no longer pink; drain well.
• Arrange bread cubes in bottom of a lightly greased 13- x 9-inch baking dish. Top with sausage and cheese.
• Whisk together eggs and next 4 ingredients; pour evenly over cheese. Cover and chill 8 hours.
• Let stand at room temperature 30 minutes. Bake at 350° for 45 minutes or until set. Yield: 8 to 10 servings.

Quiche Lorraine

Prep: 30 min.   **Cook:** 47 min.   **Other:** 10 min.

½ (15-ounce) package
   refrigerated piecrusts
8 bacon slices, cut into ½-inch
   pieces
4 green onions, chopped
2 cups (8 ounces) shredded
   Swiss cheese, divided

6 large eggs
1 cup whipping cream
½ teaspoon salt
⅛ teaspoon ground red pepper
⅛ teaspoon ground white
   pepper
⅛ teaspoon ground nutmeg

• Fit piecrust into a 9-inch pieplate according to package directions; fold edges under, and crimp.
• Bake at 400° for 7 minutes; remove from oven.
• Cook bacon pieces in a large skillet until crisp; drain on paper towels, and crumble. Sprinkle bacon, green onions, and 1 cup cheese into prepared crust.
• Whisk together eggs and next 4 ingredients; pour mixture into crust, and sprinkle with remaining 1 cup cheese and nutmeg.
• Bake at 350° for 35 to 40 minutes or until set. Let stand 10 minutes. Yield: 8 servings.

Spinach-and-Bacon Quiche

Prep: 20 min.   **Cook:** 45 min.

1 (10-ounce) package frozen
   chopped spinach, thawed
4 large eggs, lightly beaten
1½ cups half-and-half
1 (1.8-ounce) package leek
   soup mix
¼ teaspoon pepper
10 bacon slices, cooked and
   crumbled

½ cup (2 ounces) shredded
   sharp Cheddar cheese
½ cup (2 ounces) shredded
   mozzarella cheese
1 unbaked (9-inch) frozen
   deep-dish pastry shell*

• Drain spinach well, pressing between layers of paper towels.
• Whisk together eggs and next 3 ingredients. Stir in spinach, bacon, and cheeses. Pour mixture into frozen pastry shell; place on a baking sheet.
• Bake at 375° for 40 to 45 minutes. Yield: 8 servings.

*Substitute ½ (15-ounce) package refrigerated piecrusts for pastry shell, if desired. Prepare according to package directions.

Cooks Chat

*"I have made this recipe numerous
times, and everyone always loved
it. It's one that is good on a cold
night. This is ideal for a casual,
quick dinner for last-minute friends
who drop by."*

*"Excellent and easy! A hit with the
entire family, and that's amazing!"*

Sausage and Peppers with Parmesan Cheese Grits

Prep: 15 min.   **Cook:** 15 min.

1 (19-ounce) package sweet
   Italian sausage
3 red, yellow, or green bell
   peppers, cut into strips
1 large sweet onion, cut in half
   and thinly sliced
2 garlic cloves, minced
1 to 2 teaspoons Italian
   seasoning

1 teaspoon salt
½ teaspoon garlic powder
½ teaspoon pepper
Parmesan Cheese Grits
Garnish: shredded Parmesan
   cheese

• Remove sausage casings, and discard. Cook sausage and next
7 ingredients in a large skillet over medium-high heat, stirring
until sausage crumbles and is no longer pink and vegetables are
tender. Serve over Parmesan Cheese Grits. Garnish, if desired.
Yield: 4 servings.

Parmesan Cheese Grits

Prep: 3 min.   **Cook:** 5 min.

1 cup grits
4 cups water
¾ teaspoon salt
1 tablespoon butter or
   margarine

1 (5-ounce) package shredded
   Parmesan cheese

• Cook grits according to package directions, using 4 cups water.
Stir in salt, butter, and Parmesan cheese. Yield: 4 servings.

1-2-3 Jambalaya

Prep: 20 min.　**Cook:** 40 min.

1 large onion, diced
1 large green bell pepper, diced
1 pound smoked sausage, cut
　　into ¼-inch slices
1 tablespoon olive oil
4 cups chopped cooked chicken
3 cups uncooked long-grain
　　rice

2 (10½-ounce) cans French
　　onion soup, undiluted
1 (14-ounce) can chicken broth
1 (14-ounce) can beef broth
2 to 3 teaspoons Creole
　　seasoning
2 to 3 teaspoons hot sauce
Garnish: fresh cilantro sprigs

• Sauté onion, bell pepper, and sausage in hot oil in a Dutch oven 4 to 5 minutes or until sausage is browned. Stir in chicken and next 6 ingredients.
• Bake, covered, at 350° for 40 minutes, stirring after 30 minutes. Garnish, if desired. Yield: 8 to 10 servings.

Chicken-and-Sausage Jambalaya

Prep: 20 min.　**Cook:** 1 hr.　**Other:** 15 min.

We used a deli chicken to make this entrée easier. Be sure to remove all skin and bones.

1 (16-ounce) package Cajun-
　　style smoked sausage, cut
　　into ¼-inch slices
2 celery ribs, chopped
1 medium onion, chopped
1 medium-size green bell
　　pepper, chopped

4 cups chopped cooked chicken
1 (32-ounce) container chicken
　　broth
1¼ cups uncooked long-grain
　　rice
1 tablespoon Cajun seasoning
Garnish: chopped fresh parsley

• Cook smoked sausage in a Dutch oven over medium heat, stirring constantly, 3 minutes or until browned. Add celery, onion, and bell pepper, and sauté 6 to 8 minutes or until vegetables are tender.
• Stir in chicken and next 3 ingredients; bring to a boil. Cover, reduce heat, and simmer 45 minutes or until rice is done and liquid is absorbed. Remove from heat, and let stand 10 to 15 minutes before serving. Garnish, if desired. Yield: 6 to 8 servings.

Chicken Pot Pie

Prep: 10 min.   **Cook:** 40 min.   **Other:** 15 min.

This handy recipe makes four large casseroles—perfect for a crowd or for sharing with neighbors.

2 recipes Pot Pie Filling,
    prepared 1 at a time

4 (15-ounce) packages
    refrigerated piecrusts

• Divide filling evenly among 4 (15- x 12-inch) disposable aluminum roasting pans. Top each pan with 2 round piecrusts. Cut slits in piecrusts.
• Bake at 400° for 30 to 40 minutes or until golden. Let stand 15 minutes before serving. Yield: 100 servings (serving size: ⅔ cup).

Pot Pie Filling

Prep: 1 hr.   **Cook:** 15 min.

3 cups butter or margarine
2 large onions, chopped
6 celery ribs, chopped
3 cups all-purpose flour
2 (49-ounce) cans chicken
    broth
5 cups milk
16 cups chopped cooked
    chicken (about 8 roasted
    whole chickens)

3½ cups sliced carrots, cooked
    (about 1 pound)
3½ cups frozen green peas,
    thawed
1 to 2 tablespoons salt
1 tablespoon pepper
1½ teaspoons poultry
    seasoning
2 teaspoons hot sauce

• Melt butter in a 4- to 6-gallon stockpot over medium heat; add onions and celery, and sauté until tender.
• Add flour, stirring until blended; cook, stirring constantly, 2 minutes. Stir in broth and milk, stirring constantly. Bring to a boil, stirring constantly, and cook 2 minutes. Stir in chicken, sliced carrots, and remaining ingredients. Yield: 32 cups.

To prepare this recipe to serve 8: Use ⅔ cup butter; ⅔ cup chopped onion; ⅔ cup chopped celery; ⅔ cup all-purpose flour; 3½ cups chicken broth; 1⅓ cups milk; 4 cups chopped roasted chicken breast; 1 cup sliced carrots, cooked; ½ cup frozen green peas, thawed; ¾ teaspoon salt; ¼ teaspoon pepper; ¼ teaspoon poultry seasoning; and ¼ teaspoon hot sauce in place of the Pot Pie Filling ingredients above. Follow the Chicken Pot Pie method above using a 13- x 9-inch dish and 1 (15-ounce) package refrigerated piecrusts. Yield: 8 servings.

PARTY PLEASER

Cooks Chat

"I made this for a youth group fundraiser. It turned out so well that we made $1,000. People raved about these pies. This is an easy recipe to follow and my favorite so far. It is an appropriate recipe for special occasions. I didn't alter the ingredients, and I served it with green beans, stewed apples, and rolls."

Heavenly Chicken Lasagna

Prep: 30 min. **Cook:** 50 min. **Other:** 10 min.

1 tablespoon butter or margarine
½ large onion
1 (10¾-ounce) can reduced-fat cream of chicken soup, undiluted
1 (10-ounce) container refrigerated reduced-fat Alfredo sauce
1 (7-ounce) jar diced pimiento, undrained
1 (6-ounce) jar sliced mushrooms, drained
⅓ cup dry white wine
½ teaspoon dried basil
1 (10-ounce) package frozen chopped spinach, thawed
1 cup cottage cheese
1 cup ricotta cheese
½ cup grated Parmesan cheese
1 large egg, lightly beaten
9 lasagna noodles, cooked
2½ cups chopped cooked chicken
3 cups (12 ounces) shredded sharp Cheddar cheese, divided

• Melt butter in a skillet over medium-high heat. Add onion, and sauté 5 minutes or until tender. Stir in soup and next 5 ingredients. Reserve 1 cup sauce.
• Drain spinach well, pressing between layers of paper towels.
• Stir together spinach, cottage cheese, and next 3 ingredients.
• Place 3 lasagna noodles in a lightly greased 13- x 9-inch baking dish. Layer with half each of sauce, spinach mixture, and chicken. Sprinkle with 1 cup Cheddar cheese. Repeat procedure. Top with remaining 3 noodles and reserved 1 cup sauce. Cover and chill up to 1 day ahead.
• Bake at 350° for 45 minutes. Sprinkle with remaining 1 cup Cheddar cheese, and bake 5 more minutes or until cheese is melted. Let stand 10 minutes before serving. Yield: 8 to 10 servings.

Hearty Tex-Mex Squash-Chicken Casserole

Prep: 45 min. **Cook:** 35 min.

1 (10-ounce) package frozen chopped spinach, thawed
3 medium-size yellow squash, thinly sliced
1 large red bell pepper, cut into ½-inch pieces
1 yellow onion, thinly sliced
2 tablespoons peanut oil
3 cups shredded cooked chicken or turkey
12 (6-inch) corn tortillas, cut into 1-inch pieces

1 (10¾-ounce) can cream of celery soup, undiluted*
1 (8-ounce) container sour cream*
1 (8-ounce) jar picante sauce
1 (4.5-ounce) can chopped green chiles, undrained
1 (1.4-ounce) envelope fajita seasoning
2 cups (8 ounces) shredded sharp Cheddar cheese, divided*

• Drain chopped spinach well, pressing between paper towels to remove excess moisture.
• Sauté squash, bell pepper, and onion in hot oil in a large skillet over medium-high heat 6 minutes or until tender. Remove from heat. Stir in spinach, chicken, next 6 ingredients, and 1½ cups cheese. Spoon into a lightly greased 13- x 9-inch baking dish.
• Bake at 350° for 30 minutes. Sprinkle evenly with remaining ½ cup cheese, and bake 5 more minutes. Yield: 6 to 8 servings.

*Substitute reduced-sodium, reduced-fat cream of celery soup; light sour cream; and reduced-fat sharp Cheddar cheese, if desired.

SOUTHERN CLASSIC
★ ★ ★ ★ ★

Cooks Chat

"This is an awesome dish! I used leftover deli rotisserie chicken that we had for dinner the night before. I put the casserole together on the previous night and then baked it after I got home from work the next day—with great results! The dish had a wonderful taste without being too spicy. My 4-year-old son even asked for seconds!"

"This is one of the easiest and best-tasting casseroles I've had in a long time. Because of it, I actually got my husband to eat summer squash! There are just two of us, so whenever I fix this, I separate it into three small casseroles and freeze two; this works wonderfully. I also like to take this dish to potlucks."

Chicken with Polenta

Prep: 30 min.   **Cook:** 1 hr., 15 min.

To prepare this recipe ahead of time, grill the chicken, cut into strips, and chill. Make the polenta just before serving, and reheat the chicken in the microwave.

5 cups chicken broth, divided
1⅓ cups yellow cornmeal*
¾ cup half-and-half
1 cup grated Parmesan cheese
8 to 10 skinned and boned
   chicken breasts
1 teaspoon salt, divided
¼ teaspoon ground black
   pepper
2 red bell peppers, diced

1 large Vidalia onion, diced
1 tablespoon olive oil
3 cups fresh corn kernels (about
   4 ears)
¾ cup dry white wine
½ cup orange juice
⅛ to ¼ teaspoon ground red
   pepper
Garnish: chopped fresh chives

• Bring 4½ cups chicken broth to a boil in a 3-quart saucepan over medium heat. Gradually whisk in cornmeal. Reduce heat to low, and simmer, stirring often, 30 minutes. Remove from heat; stir in half-and-half and cheese.
• Sprinkle chicken with ½ teaspoon salt and black pepper.
• Grill chicken over medium-high heat (350° to 400°) 7 minutes on each side or until done. Cool to touch, and cut into thin strips; set aside.
• Sauté bell pepper and onion in hot oil in a large nonstick skillet over medium heat 7 minutes or until tender. Add corn; sauté 4 minutes. Stir in wine; simmer 5 minutes. Stir in juice, remaining ½ cup broth, remaining ½ teaspoon salt, and ground red pepper; simmer 10 minutes or until slightly thickened. Serve over polenta and chicken strips. Garnish, if desired. Yield: 10 servings.

*Substitute 1 cup regular grits for cornmeal, if desired. Bring 4 cups chicken broth to a boil, and stir in grits. Cover, reduce heat, and simmer 5 minutes. Remove from heat, and stir in half-and-half and cheese.

Chicken Cannelloni with Roasted Red Bell Pepper Sauce

Prep: 30 min. **Cook:** 30 min.

For quick weeknight solutions, prepare and stuff cannelloni shells. Wrap tightly with wax paper, and put in a zip-top freezer bag; freeze until ready to serve. Let thaw in the refrigerator. Unwrap and place in a baking dish; top with your favorite supermarket pasta sauce, and bake as directed.

1 (8-ounce) package cannelloni or manicotti shells
4 cups finely chopped cooked chicken
2 (8-ounce) containers chive-and-onion cream cheese
1 (10-ounce) package frozen chopped spinach, thawed and well drained
1 cup (8 ounces) shredded mozzarella cheese
½ cup Italian-seasoned breadcrumbs
1 teaspoon seasoned pepper
¾ teaspoon garlic salt
Roasted Red Bell Pepper Sauce
Garnish: chopped fresh basil or parsley

• Cook pasta according to package directions; drain.
• Stir together chicken and next 6 ingredients.
• Cut pasta shells lengthwise through 1 side. Spoon about ½ cup chicken mixture into each shell, gently pressing cut sides together. Place, cut sides down, in 2 lightly greased 11- x 7-inch baking dishes, and pour Roasted Red Bell Pepper Sauce evenly over shells.
• Bake, covered, at 350° for 25 to 30 minutes or until thoroughly heated. Garnish, if desired. Yield: 6 to 8 servings.

Roasted Red Bell Pepper Sauce

Prep: 5 min.

This sauce is also great over your favorite noodles.

2 (7-ounce) jars roasted red bell peppers, drained
1 (16-ounce) jar creamy Alfredo sauce
1 (3-ounce) package shredded Parmesan cheese

• Process all ingredients in a blender until smooth, stopping to scrape down sides. Yield: 3½ cups.

Note: For testing purposes only, we used Bertolli Creamy Alfredo Sauce.

"I thought this recipe sounded very interesting. My husband loved it, and I really liked it, but my kids wouldn't touch it. The Italian dressing had a rather strong taste, which my husband loved, but it was too much for the kids. I think it would be more kid-friendly without the dressing or possibly with Ranch instead. I'll certainly make it for my hubby again!"

Chicken-and-Wild Rice Casserole

Prep: 2 min.   **Cook:** 42 min.   **Other:** 10 min.

1 (6.2-ounce) package fast-cooking long-grain and wild rice mix
2 (10½-ounce) cans ready-to-serve low-sodium chicken broth
1 (8-ounce) package sliced fresh mushrooms
3 cups chopped cooked chicken
⅔ cup Italian dressing
1 (8-ounce) container sour cream

• Cook rice in a large saucepan according to package directions, using 2 cans chicken broth instead of water. Add mushrooms before the last 5 minutes.
• Stir in chicken, dressing, and sour cream; spoon into a lightly greased 2-quart baking dish.
• Bake at 325° for 30 minutes or until thoroughly heated. Let stand 10 minutes. Yield: 6 servings.

"My 13-year-old grandson made this dish tonight for his mom and dad. We did the prep work in the morning, and he had it on the table in about 30 minutes for dinner. It was wonderful. A fancy serve-to-anyone dish."

"I have tried this recipe several times, and it is now a family favorite. It's easy to make, and it comes out great every time. I prefer bow tie macaroni or noodles instead of rice."

"A family favorite!"

Strolling-Through-the-Holidays Stroganoff

Prep: 30 min.   **Cook:** 28 min.

2 pounds unpeeled, large fresh shrimp
½ cup butter or margarine, divided
2 cups chopped cooked chicken
½ pound smoked Polish sausage, cut into ½-inch slices
1 (8-ounce) package sliced fresh mushrooms
½ small onion, diced
1 garlic clove, minced
¼ cup all-purpose flour
1 cup chicken broth
½ cup milk
½ cup white wine
1 teaspoon ketchup
½ teaspoon Worcestershire sauce
1 (8-ounce) container sour cream
1 tablespoon chopped fresh dillweed
Hot cooked rice

• Peel shrimp, and devein, if desired.
• Melt ¼ cup butter in a Dutch oven over medium-high heat. Add shrimp; cook 3 to 5 minutes or just until shrimp turn pink. Remove shrimp, and set aside. Add chicken and sausage to pan; cook 5 minutes or until thoroughly heated. Remove from pan; keep warm.

- Melt remaining ¼ cup butter in Dutch oven over medium-high heat. Add mushrooms; sauté 5 minutes. Add onion and garlic; sauté 5 minutes or until tender. Whisk in flour; cook, whisking constantly, 1 minute. Add broth, milk, and wine; cook, whisking constantly, 5 minutes or until thickened. Stir in ketchup, Worcestershire sauce, and shrimp.
- Remove from heat, and stir in sour cream and dillweed. Stir in chicken mixture; serve over rice. Yield: 6 to 8 servings.

Fabulous Tuna-Noodle Casserole

Prep: 10 min.   **Cook:** 40 min.

¼ cup butter or margarine
1 small red or green bell pepper, chopped
1 small onion, chopped
1 cup sliced fresh mushrooms
¼ cup all-purpose flour
2½ cups milk
2 cups (8 ounces) shredded Cheddar cheese
2 (9-ounce) cans solid white tuna in spring water, drained and flaked
1 (12-ounce) package egg noodles, cooked
2 teaspoons dried parsley flakes
½ teaspoon salt
½ teaspoon pepper
½ cup fine, dry breadcrumbs
2 tablespoons butter or margarine, melted

- Melt ¼ cup butter in a large skillet over medium heat; add bell pepper, onion, and mushrooms, and sauté 5 minutes or until tender.
- Whisk together flour and milk until smooth; stir into vegetable mixture, and cook, stirring constantly, 5 minutes or until thickened. Remove from heat; add cheese, stirring until melted.
- Stir in tuna and next 4 ingredients; spoon into a lightly greased 13- x 9-inch baking dish.
- Bake, covered, at 350° for 25 minutes. Stir together breadcrumbs and 2 tablespoons melted butter; sprinkle over casserole, and bake 5 more minutes. Yield: 6 to 8 servings.

KIDS LOVE IT

Cooks Chat

"Having made the same tuna-noodle casserole—the one with cream of mushroom soup—for the last 30 years, I was delighted to find this recipe. It was absolutely delicious and so easy to make! I loved the fresh bell pepper and mushrooms, and the sauce pulled it all together. The casserole didn't dry out in the oven, and the consistency was perfect."

"Best tuna casserole I've tried! This one is smooth and rich. Use only solid tuna—it makes a big difference. My family and our guests all liked this casserole. When guests rave about it, you know you have a hit."

Spicy Catfish with Vegetables and Basil Cream

Prep: 25 min.   **Cook:** 25 min.

This recipe shows the versatility and creativity of sautéing.

3 tablespoons butter, divided
1 (16-ounce) package frozen whole kernel corn, thawed
1 medium onion, chopped
1 medium-size green bell pepper, chopped
1 medium-size red bell pepper, chopped
¾ teaspoon salt
¾ teaspoon pepper
½ cup all-purpose flour
¼ cup yellow cornmeal
1 tablespoon Creole seasoning
4 (6- to 8-ounce) catfish fillets
⅓ cup buttermilk
1 tablespoon vegetable oil
½ cup whipping cream
2 tablespoons chopped fresh basil
Garnish: fresh basil sprigs

• Melt 2 tablespoons butter in a large skillet over medium-high heat. Add corn, onion, and peppers; sauté 6 to 8 minutes or until tender. Stir in salt and pepper. Spoon onto serving dish; keep warm.
• Combine flour, cornmeal, and Creole seasoning in a large shallow dish. Dip fillets in buttermilk, and dredge in flour mixture.
• Melt remaining 1 tablespoon butter with oil in skillet over medium-high heat. Cook fillets, in batches, 2 to 3 minutes on each side or until golden. Remove and arrange over vegetables.
• Add cream to skillet, stirring to loosen particles from bottom of skillet. Add chopped basil, and cook, stirring often, 1 to 2 minutes or until thickened. Serve sauce with fillets and vegetables. Garnish, if desired. Yield: 4 servings.

Shrimp Enchiladas

Prep: 20 min.   **Cook:** 30 min.

6 cups water
1½ pounds unpeeled, medium-
    size fresh shrimp*
1 (10¾-ounce) can cream of
    shrimp soup, undiluted
1 (10¾-ounce) can cream of
    onion soup, undiluted
1 cup picante sauce
1 (8-ounce) package cream
    cheese, softened*

½ cup sour cream
2 cups (8 ounces) shredded
    Monterey Jack cheese,
    divided*
9 green onions, chopped
1 (4.5-ounce) can chopped
    green chiles
10 (6-inch) flour tortillas*
Garnish: chopped fresh cilantro

• Bring 6 cups water to a boil; add shrimp, and cook 3 to 5 minutes or just until shrimp turn pink. Drain; rinse with cold water.
• Peel shrimp, and devein, if desired. Coarsely chop shrimp, and set aside.
• Combine soups and picante sauce in a saucepan over medium-high heat, stirring often until thoroughly heated. Spoon 1 cup mixture into bottom of a lightly greased 13- x 9-inch baking dish; reserve remaining mixture, and keep warm.
• Beat cream cheese and sour cream at medium speed with an electric mixer until smooth; stir in shrimp, 1 cup Monterey Jack, green onions, and chiles.
• Heat tortillas according to package directions. Spoon 3 to 4 tablespoons shrimp mixture down center of each tortilla. Roll up tortillas, and place, seam side down, in baking dish.
• Pour remaining soup mixture over enchiladas; top with remaining 1 cup Monterey Jack cheese.
• Bake at 350° for 30 minutes. Garnish, if desired. Yield: 4 to 6 servings.

*Substitute 2 cups chopped cooked chicken for shrimp, if desired. Substitute reduced-fat cream cheese, Monterey Jack cheese, and flour tortillas, if desired.

KITCHEN COMFORT
★ ★ ★ ★ ★

Cooks Chat

"I cherish the recipes I read in Southern Living, *especially since I live overseas! This recipe is wonderful and receives rave reviews from friends and family. Since so many people are allergic to shellfish, I usually make it with cream of mushroom soup and then make some enchiladas with shrimp and some with chicken so that everyone has a choice."*

"A great change from more traditional types of enchiladas. I served mine with pinto beans, guacamole, and a great Mexican rice. I had many requests for the recipe. Very easy to assemble."

"Just prepared this for the first time for a luncheon, and it received raves. It was easy and tasted great. Hint: Cream of onion soup isn't available in my area, so I substituted a second can of cream of shrimp soup."

Sautéed Shrimp and Pasta

Prep: 15 min.   **Cook:** 6 min.

8 ounces uncooked linguine
2 pounds unpeeled, medium-size fresh shrimp
1 small onion, chopped
2 garlic cloves, minced
1 tablespoon hot sesame oil
6 plum tomatoes, peeled and chopped
1 teaspoon dried oregano

½ teaspoon salt
½ teaspoon dried basil
½ teaspoon freshly ground pepper
¼ cup chopped fresh parsley
¼ cup kalamata olives, sliced
¼ cup lemon juice
2 ounces crumbled feta cheese

• Cook linguine according to package directions. Drain; keep warm.
• Peel shrimp, and devein, if desired.
• Sauté onion and garlic in oil in a large skillet until tender. Stir in tomato and next 4 ingredients; cook, stirring constantly, 3 minutes.
• Add shrimp, and cook, stirring occasionally, 3 minutes or until shrimp turn pink. Stir in parsley, olives, and lemon juice; cook just until thoroughly heated. Serve over linguine; sprinkle with cheese. Yield: 4 servings.

Cheesy Shrimp-and-Grits Casserole

Prep: 15 min.   **Cook:** 1 hr., 15 min.

4 cups chicken broth
½ teaspoon salt
1 cup regular grits
1 cup (4 ounces) shredded sharp Cheddar cheese, divided
1 cup (4 ounces) shredded Monterey Jack cheese with peppers
2 tablespoons butter or margarine

6 green onions, chopped
1 green bell pepper, chopped
1 garlic clove, minced
1 pound small fresh shrimp, peeled and cooked
1 (10-ounce) can diced tomatoes and green chiles, drained
¼ teaspoon salt
¼ teaspoon pepper

• Bring 4 cups chicken broth and ½ teaspoon salt to a boil in a large saucepan; stir in grits. Cover, reduce heat, and simmer 20 minutes.
• Stir together grits, ¾ cup Cheddar cheese, and Monterey Jack cheese.

- Melt butter in a large skillet over medium heat; add green onions, bell pepper, and garlic, and sauté 5 minutes or until tender.
- Stir together green onion mixture, grits mixture, shrimp, and next 3 ingredients. Pour into a lightly greased 2-quart baking dish. Sprinkle top with remaining ¼ cup shredded Cheddar cheese.
- Bake at 350° for 30 to 45 minutes. Yield: 10 to 12 servings.

Shrimp with Roasted Red Pepper Cream

Prep: 15 min. **Cook:** 8 min.

1 (7-ounce) package vermicelli
1 (12-ounce) jar roasted red bell peppers, drained
1 (8-ounce) package ⅓-less-fat cream cheese, softened
½ cup low-sodium fat-free chicken broth
3 garlic cloves, chopped
½ teaspoon ground red pepper
2 pounds cooked, peeled large shrimp
¼ cup chopped fresh basil
Garnish: fresh basil sprig

- Prepare pasta according to package directions, omitting salt and oil. Keep pasta warm.
- Process red bell peppers and next 4 ingredients in a blender or food processor until smooth, scraping down sides. Pour mixture into a large skillet.
- Cook over medium heat 5 minutes, stirring often, until thoroughly heated. Add shrimp, and cook, stirring occasionally, 2 to 3 minutes or until thoroughly heated. Remove from heat. Serve over hot cooked pasta. Sprinkle with basil. Garnish, if desired. Yield: 6 servings.

Note: For testing purposes only, we used Alessi Sweet Pimento Fire Roasted Italian Style Peppers.

QUICK & EASY
★ ★ ★ ★ ★

Cooks Chat

"This recipe is fast and simple, and it tastes great."

"I found this dish to be very easy and quick. It was also delicious! This recipe will become one that I make over and over."

"I've tried this with fresh roasted red bell peppers (roasted in the oven), and it was wonderful. I recommend it so very much."

Crawfish Étouffée

Prep: 25 min.   **Cook:** 35 min.

Seafood markets sell frozen, peeled crawfish tails harvested in Louisiana or China. You can substitute peeled shrimp, but the color won't be as intense.

½ cup butter or margarine
1 large onion, chopped
¼ cup finely chopped celery
¼ cup chopped green bell pepper
2 garlic cloves, minced
1 pound peeled crawfish tails
1 teaspoon salt
½ teaspoon ground black pepper
½ teaspoon onion powder

¼ teaspoon ground white pepper
½ teaspoon hot sauce
1½ tablespoons all-purpose flour
¾ cup water
½ cup finely chopped green onions
¼ cup finely chopped fresh parsley
Hot cooked rice

• Melt butter in a large skillet over medium heat. Add onion and next 3 ingredients; sauté, stirring constantly, 5 minutes.
• Stir in crawfish and next 5 ingredients; cook 5 minutes. Stir in flour; cook, stirring constantly, 2 minutes.
• Stir in water gradually; cook over low heat 20 minutes, stirring mixture occasionally.
• Stir in green onions and parsley; cook 3 minutes. Serve over rice. Yield: 4 to 6 servings.

Crabmeat-Parmesan Quiche

Prep: 15 min.   **Cook:** 52 min.   **Other:** 15 min.

Decked with lump crabmeat, guests will gobble up this dish for brunch, lunch, or dinner.

½ (15-ounce) package
    refrigerated piecrusts
3 to 4 green onions, chopped
2 teaspoons olive oil
2 (6-ounce) cans lump crabmeat,
    rinsed and drained
1 teaspoon grated lemon rind
½ teaspoon Old Bay seasoning

⅛ teaspoon ground red pepper
1 cup half-and-half
3 large eggs
¼ teaspoon salt
¼ teaspoon black pepper
1 (5-ounce) package shredded
    Parmesan cheese

• Unroll piecrust, and place on a lightly floured surface. Roll to ⅛-inch thickness. Carefully place piecrust in a 9-inch pieplate; fold edges under, and crimp.
• Bake on lowest oven rack at 400° for 8 minutes. Cool.
• Sauté chopped green onions in hot oil in a large skillet over medium-high heat 2 minutes. Stir in crabmeat and next 3 ingredients; sauté 2 minutes.
• Whisk together half-and-half and next 3 ingredients in a large bowl. Stir in cheese and crabmeat mixture; pour into prepared crust.
• Bake on lowest oven rack at 400° for 35 to 40 minutes or until set. Let stand 15 minutes. Yield: 6 servings.

Cooks Chat

"This recipe was very easy to make and was so delicious! Even my 2- and 6-year-old kids ate it! I will definitely recommend it and cook it again and again."

"I made this for my husband (a truck driver!), and he absolutely loved it. He's requested it several times since and has eaten the entire thing in 2 days by himself! It was quick and easy to prepare, and it reheated nicely."

"This quiche is so easy and yummy! I used fresh jumbo lump crabmeat; it was a huge hit at brunch!"

Shellfish Crêpes in Wine-Cheese Sauce

Prep: 30 min.   **Cook:** 20 min.   **Other:** 3 hrs., 30 min.

½ cup butter or margarine, divided
2 cups chopped cooked shrimp (about 1 pound)
1 cup (8 ounces) fresh crabmeat
2 green onions, minced
¼ cup dry vermouth*
⅛ teaspoon salt
¼ teaspoon pepper
½ tablespoon butter or margarine, melted
Wine-Cheese Sauce
Crêpes
2 cups (8 ounces) shredded Swiss cheese
Garnish: sliced green onions

• Melt ¼ cup butter in a large skillet over medium-high heat. Add shrimp, crabmeat, and green onions, and sauté for 1 minute. Stir in vermouth, salt, and pepper. Bring mixture to a boil, and cook 7 minutes or until most of liquid is absorbed. Remove mixture from heat, and set aside.
• Drizzle ½ tablespoon melted butter into a 13- x 9-inch baking dish.
• Stir 2 cups Wine-Cheese Sauce into shrimp mixture. Spoon about 3 tablespoons shrimp mixture down center of each Crêpe.
• Roll up, and place, seam side down, in prepared dish. Spoon remaining 2 cups Wine-Cheese Sauce over Crêpes. Sprinkle with Swiss cheese, and dot with remaining ¼ cup butter. Cover and chill 3 hours. Let stand at room temperature 30 minutes.
• Bake at 450° for 20 minutes or until thoroughly heated. Garnish, if desired. Yield: 12 servings.

Wine-Cheese Sauce

Prep: 10 min.   **Cook:** 10 min.

¼ cup cornstarch
¼ cup milk
⅓ cup dry vermouth*
3 cups whipping cream
¼ teaspoon salt
¼ teaspoon pepper
2 cups (8 ounces) shredded Swiss cheese

• Whisk together cornstarch and milk in a small bowl.
• Bring vermouth to a boil in a large skillet, and cook until vermouth is reduced to 1 tablespoon. Remove from heat, and whisk in cornstarch mixture. Add whipping cream, salt, and pepper; cook over medium-high heat, whisking constantly, 2 minutes or until mixture comes to a boil. Boil 1 minute or until mixture is thickened, and add Swiss cheese. Reduce heat, and simmer, whisking constantly, 1 minute or until sauce is smooth. Yield: 4 cups.

*Substitute clam juice for vermouth, if desired.

Crêpes

Prep: 8 min.　**Cook:** 36 min.　**Other:** 1 hr.

4 large eggs
2 cups all-purpose flour
1 cup cold water
1 cup cold milk

¼ cup butter or margarine,
　melted
½ teaspoon salt

• Process all ingredients in a blender or food processor until
smooth, stopping to scrape down sides. Cover and chill 1 hour.
• Place a lightly greased 8-inch nonstick skillet over medium heat
until skillet is hot.
• Pour 3 tablespoons batter into skillet; quickly tilt in all directions
so batter covers bottom of skillet.
• Cook 1 minute or until crêpe can be shaken loose from skillet.
Turn crêpe, and cook about 30 seconds. Repeat procedure with
remaining batter. Stack crêpes between sheets of wax paper. Yield:
2 dozen.

Note: To make ahead, prepare crêpes as directed, and freeze up to
1 month. Casserole may be prepared 1 day ahead; cover and chill.
Let stand at room temperature 30 minutes before baking; proceed
as directed.

Cooks Chat

"This is a terrific dish for the whole family. It has a surprisingly deep and somewhat smoky flavor for a light dish. My finicky children even loved it. I substituted regular mushrooms for portobello and used only half the onion."

"This recipe was great. We buy a lot of kale over the summer, and I am always looking for different ways to use it. This made a very nice light summer dish."

"Quick and easy! My kids asked for seconds, and they are picky eaters!"

Pasta with Beans and Greens

Prep: 20 min.   **Cook:** 21 min.

Besides being a delicious and colorful main dish,
this recipe boasts generous amounts of protein, fiber, complex
carbohydrates, iron, and calcium.

8 ounces uncooked bow tie
   pasta
1 large onion, chopped
1 (6-ounce) package portobello
   mushroom caps, halved
   and sliced*
2 teaspoons olive oil
4 cups chopped fresh kale or
   spinach (about 6 ounces)
1 cup reduced-sodium chicken
   broth

2 garlic cloves, minced
½ teaspoon salt
½ teaspoon pepper
1 (15-ounce) can great
   Northern beans, rinsed and
   drained
¼ cup shredded Parmesan
   cheese

• Cook pasta according to package directions, omitting salt and fat; drain. Place pasta in a large bowl; set aside.
• Sauté onion and mushrooms in hot oil in a large skillet over medium heat 5 minutes. Add kale and next 4 ingredients; cook, stirring often, 15 minutes or until kale is tender. Add beans, and cook 1 minute.
• Add bean mixture to pasta; toss gently. Sprinkle with cheese. Yield: 6 servings.

*Substitute 1 (8-ounce) package sliced fresh mushrooms for portobello mushroom caps, if desired.

Bean Ragoût with Cilantro-Cornmeal Dumplings

Prep: 25 min.   **Cook:** 55 min.

2 large onions, chopped
5 garlic cloves, minced
2 tablespoons vegetable oil
1 poblano chile pepper, seeded and chopped
2 large red bell peppers, chopped
3 tablespoons chili powder
2 teaspoons ground cumin
1 teaspoon dried oregano
1¼ teaspoons salt, divided
1 (28-ounce) can whole tomatoes, undrained and chopped
2 small zucchini, chopped

1 (15-ounce) can pinto beans, undrained
1 (15-ounce) can black beans, undrained
½ teaspoon freshly ground pepper
½ cup all-purpose flour
½ cup cornmeal
1 teaspoon baking powder
2 tablespoons shortening
¼ cup (1 ounce) shredded Cheddar cheese
2 tablespoons minced fresh cilantro
½ cup milk

• Sauté onion and garlic in hot oil in a large Dutch oven until tender. Add poblano pepper and bell pepper, and sauté 2 to 3 minutes. Stir in chili powder, cumin, and oregano; cook, stirring constantly, 1 to 2 minutes.

• Add ¾ teaspoon salt, tomatoes, and next 4 ingredients; bring mixture to a boil. Reduce heat, and simmer 15 to 20 minutes or until zucchini is tender.

• Combine flour, cornmeal, baking powder, and remaining ½ teaspoon salt in a medium bowl. Cut in shortening with a pastry blender until mixture is crumbly. Stir in cheese and cilantro. Add milk, stirring just until ingredients are moistened.

• Drop dough by heaping tablespoonfuls into simmering ragoût. Cook 5 minutes. Cover and cook 10 to 15 more minutes or until dumplings are done. Yield: 6 to 8 servings.

PARTY PLEASER
★★★★★

Cooks Chat

"This recipe is excellent as written! The only substitutions I made were to use leftover pinto beans for the canned pinto beans and to substitute dried cilantro for fresh. The red bell peppers and poblano chile are integral parts of this recipe."

Bean-and-Cheese Chimichangas

Prep: 10 min.   **Cook:** 20 min.

Chimichangas may be frozen in zip-top freezer bags
up to 3 months.

1 (16-ounce) can refried beans
1 cup (4 ounces) shredded
    Monterey Jack cheese
⅓ cup medium salsa
1 tablespoon taco seasoning mix
½ (5-ounce) package yellow
    rice mix, cooked (optional)

5 (10-inch) flour tortillas
2 cups vegetable oil
Shredded lettuce
Toppings: salsa, guacamole,
    sour cream

• Stir together first 4 ingredients. Stir in rice, if desired. Place ⅓ cup mixture just below center of each tortilla. Fold opposite sides of tortillas over filling, forming rectangles; secure with picks.
• Pour oil into a large skillet; heat to 325°. Fry in batches 4 to 5 minutes on each side or until lightly browned. Drain on paper towels. Remove picks; arrange on lettuce. Serve with toppings, if desired. Yield: 2 to 4 servings.

Note: To serve 4 to 6, double all ingredients, and process as directed. To bake, place on a baking sheet, and coat both sides with cooking spray. Bake at 425° for 8 minutes; turn chimichangas, and bake 5 more minutes. Remove picks.

Super Special Spinach Pie

Prep: 10 min.   **Cook:** 25 min.   **Other:** 10 min.

2 (6-ounce) packages fresh baby
    spinach
¼ cup butter
3 tablespoons all-purpose flour
¼ teaspoon salt
¼ teaspoon pepper

¼ teaspoon garlic powder
4 large eggs, lightly beaten
¾ cup whipping cream
½ cup (2 ounces) shredded
    Parmesan cheese

• Rinse spinach well; drain.
• Melt butter in a large skillet over medium heat. Add spinach, and cook just until wilted.
• Combine flour, salt, pepper, and garlic powder in a large bowl. Add spinach, eggs, whipping cream, and Parmesan cheese, stirring well. Pour mixture into a lightly greased 9-inch pieplate.
• Bake at 350° for 25 minutes or until pie is set. Let stand 10 minutes. Cut pie into wedges. Yield: 8 servings.

healthy & light

★★★★★

There's no need to resist culinary indulgence with this mouth-watering array of lightened recipes.

Blueberry-Cinnamon Muffins, page 114

Creamy Vegetable Dip

Prep: 10 min.

1 (8-ounce) package fat-free cream cheese, softened
2 tablespoons fat-free milk
2 tablespoons freshly grated Parmesan cheese
4 teaspoons Ranch-style dressing mix

¼ cup chopped red bell pepper
1 green onion, chopped (about 2 tablespoons)
Assorted fresh vegetables

• Beat cream cheese and milk at medium speed with an electric mixer until creamy; add cheese and dressing mix, beating until blended. Stir in bell pepper and green onions. Cover and chill until ready to serve. Serve with assorted fresh vegetables. Yield: 1½ cups (serving size: ¼ cup).

Per serving (¼ cup): Calories 62 (17% from fat); Fat 1.2g (sat 0.7g, mono 0.1g, poly 0g); Protein 6.3g; Carb 4.3g; Fiber 0.2g; Chol 5mg; Iron 0mg; Sodium 406mg; Calc 104mg

Baked Cheese Grits

Prep: 15 min.   **Cook:** 40 min.

2⅔ cups water
⅔ cup quick-cooking grits
2 tablespoons light margarine
2 large eggs, lightly beaten
½ (8-ounce) loaf light pasteurized prepared cheese product, cut into ½-inch pieces

¼ teaspoon salt
¼ teaspoon ground red pepper
Vegetable cooking spray

• Bring 2⅔ cups water to a boil; add grits, and cook, stirring often, 5 minutes or until thickened. Remove from heat. Add margarine and next 4 ingredients, stirring until blended. Spoon mixture into a 2-quart baking dish coated with cooking spray.
• Bake at 350° for 40 minutes or until lightly browned. Yield: 3½ cups (serving size: ½ cup).

Note: Casserole may be chilled up to 8 hours. Let stand at room temperature 30 minutes; bake as directed.

Per serving (½ cup): Calories 131 (36% from fat); Fat 5g (sat 1.9g, mono 1.3g, poly 1g); Protein 6.3g; Carb 14g; Fiber 0.3g; Chol 67mg; Iron 0.3mg; Sodium 389mg; Calc 101mg

Confetti Twice-Baked Potatoes

Prep: 15 min.   **Cook:** 1 hr., 10 min.   **Other:** 10 min.

4 medium baking potatoes
½ cup fat-free sour cream
¼ cup fat-free milk
2 tablespoons butter or
    margarine
¼ cup chopped fresh basil
¼ cup chopped fresh parsley
2 green onions, chopped

2 garlic cloves, minced
Butter-flavored vegetable
    cooking spray
2 plum tomatoes, chopped
½ cup (2 ounces) shredded
    reduced-fat sharp Cheddar
    cheese

Cooks Chat

"Easy, fast (except for the baking time), and light. And they taste great, too! After I scooped out the potato, I sprayed inside the shells and returned them to the oven for 5 to 10 minutes to crisp them up a bit. I highly recommend this recipe to potato lovers!"

• Bake potatoes at 375° for 1 hour or until tender; cool 10 minutes. Reduce oven temperature to 350°.
• Cut potatoes in half lengthwise; carefully scoop out pulp into a large bowl, leaving shells intact. Stir together pulp, sour cream, milk, and butter; stir in basil and next 3 ingredients.
• Coat insides of potato shells with cooking spray. Spoon potato mixture evenly into shells; sprinkle evenly with tomato and cheese.
• Bake potatoes at 350° for 10 minutes or until thoroughly heated and cheese is melted. Yield: 8 servings (serving size: 1 potato half).

Note: To make ahead, place unbaked stuffed potato halves, covered, in the refrigerator. Bring potato halves to room temperature before baking at 350°.

Per serving (1 potato half): Calories 129 (26% from fat); Fat 3.7g (sat 2.3g, mono 1g, poly 0.2g); Protein 4.6g; Carb 20g; Fiber 1.9g; Chol 11mg; Iron 1.2mg; Sodium 96mg; Calc 80mg

Cooks Chat

"I brought these to a family Sunday breakfast, and they were devoured! The cinnamon added a different touch, which was great. I used whole buttermilk and 2 eggs instead of egg substitute. My extended family loved these!"

"I took these to the beach for my extended family, and they were a hit. I made the batter into a loaf of bread for traveling purposes, which worked well. I also used eggs and whole buttermilk."

Blueberry-Cinnamon Muffins

Prep: 25 min.   **Cook:** 20 min.   **Other:** 5 min.

To prevent the berries from bleeding, toss them in flour, and then gently fold them into the batter.

¼ cup uncooked regular oats
2 tablespoons brown sugar
1 teaspoon ground cinnamon, divided
¼ cup butter, softened
1 cup granulated sugar
½ cup egg substitute
1 teaspoon vanilla extract

2 cups all-purpose flour
1 teaspoon baking soda
½ teaspoon baking powder
½ teaspoon salt
1¼ cups fat-free buttermilk
1 cup fresh blueberries
Vegetable cooking spray

• Stir together oats, brown sugar, and ½ teaspoon cinnamon; set aside.
• Beat butter and granulated sugar at medium speed with an electric mixer until fluffy. Add egg substitute, beating until blended. Stir in vanilla.
• Combine all-purpose flour, baking soda, baking powder, salt, and remaining ½ teaspoon cinnamon; add to butter mixture alternately with buttermilk, ending with flour mixture.

- Gently stir in blueberries. Spoon batter evenly into muffin pans coated with cooking spray, filling two-thirds full. Sprinkle evenly with oat mixture.
- Bake at 350° for 15 to 20 minutes or until tops are golden. Cool muffins in pans 5 minutes; remove from pans, and cool on wire racks. Yield: 15 muffins.

Per muffin: Calories 174 (21% from fat); Fat 4g (sat 2g, mono 1.1g, poly 0.4g); Protein 3.7g; Carb 31g; Fiber 0.9g; Chol 9mg; Iron 1.1mg; Sodium 249mg; Calc 39mg

Fruit-and-Bran Muffins

Prep: 15 min.   **Cook:** 20 min.   **Other:** 5 min.

These muffins serve up a good dose of fiber.

1 cup fat-free milk
2 cups O-shaped sweetened oat-and-wheat bran cereal
1 large Granny Smith apple, peeled and diced
1¼ cups uncooked oat bran hot cereal
⅓ cup golden raisins
¼ cup firmly packed dark brown sugar
¼ cup egg substitute
1 tablespoon baking powder
½ teaspoon ground cinnamon
¼ teaspoon ground nutmeg
3 tablespoons applesauce
Vegetable cooking spray

- Bring milk to a boil in a large saucepan; remove from heat, and stir in O-shaped cereal. Let stand 5 minutes or until cereal is softened.
- Stir in apple and next 8 ingredients until blended.
- Place paper baking cups in muffin pans, and lightly coat with cooking spray. Spoon batter evenly into cups.
- Bake at 375° for 18 to 20 minutes or until a wooden pick inserted in center comes out clean. Yield: 1 dozen.

Note: For testing purposes only, we used Cracklin' Oat Bran Cereal for sweetened cereal and Hodgson Mill Oat Bran Hot Cereal for uncooked cereal.

Per muffin: Calories 150 (17% from fat); Fat 2.9g (sat 0.6g, mono 1.1g, poly 0.4g); Protein 5.2g; Carb 27.3g; Fiber 4.1g; Chol 0.5mg; Iron 1.9mg; Sodium 158mg; Calc 118mg

KITCHEN COMFORT
★ ★ ★ ★ ★

Cooks Chat

"Delicious! The fruit makes the muffins so moist and gives them just the right amount of sweetness. I will make these regularly."

Italian-Style Beef-and-Pepperoni Soup

Prep: 25 min.   **Cook:** 45 min.

1 pound extra-lean ground beef
1 cup sliced turkey pepperoni
    (3 ounces)
Vegetable cooking spray
1 cup sliced fresh mushrooms
1 green bell pepper, seeded and
    chopped
1 bunch green onions, chopped
2 garlic cloves, minced
1 teaspoon olive oil
2 tablespoons tomato paste
1 (28-ounce) can crushed
    tomatoes

4 cups low-sodium fat-free
    chicken broth
1 tablespoon chopped fresh or
    1 teaspoon dried basil
1 tablespoon chopped fresh or
    1 teaspoon dried oregano
1 teaspoon freshly ground
    pepper
Garnishes: sliced fresh basil,
    shredded Parmesan cheese
Parmesan Toast Points (optional)

• Cook ground beef and pepperoni in a Dutch oven coated with cooking spray over medium-high heat 8 minutes or until beef crumbles and is no longer pink. Rinse and drain beef mixture.
• Sauté mushrooms and next 3 ingredients in hot oil in Dutch oven 5 minutes. Stir in beef mixture, tomato paste, and next 5 ingredients. Bring to a boil; reduce heat, and simmer 30 minutes. If desired, garnish and serve with Parmesan Toast Points. Yield: 10 cups.

Per serving (1 cup, not including Parmesan Toast Points): Calories 147 (43% from fat);
Fat 7g (sat 2.7g, mono 2.7g, poly 0.3g); Protein 13g; Carb 6.1g; Fiber 0.5g; Chol 40mg;
Iron 1.7mg; Sodium 289mg; Calc 35mg

Parmesan Toast Points

Prep: 5 min.   **Cook:** 5 min.

1 small sourdough loaf

Parmesan cheese, shredded

• Cut 1 small sourdough loaf into thin wedges. Arrange wedges on a baking sheet. Sprinkle evenly with shredded Parmesan cheese. Bake at 400° for 5 minutes.

Cooks Chat

"Great soup for cold winter nights. My four children loved the soup with a little mozzarella cheese on top and crusty bread on the side. Great as leftovers."

"I served this recently at a party. Everyone wanted the recipe! Very easy and delicious on a cold day."

Creamy Tomato-Stuffed Chicken

Prep: 20 min.   **Cook:** 45 min.   **Other:** 10 min.

1 pound skinned and boned chicken breasts (4 breast halves)
½ teaspoon salt, divided
½ teaspoon pepper, divided
½ (8-ounce) package ⅓-less-fat cream cheese
3 garlic cloves, minced and divided
¼ cup chopped dried tomatoes (not in oil)
½ cup chopped fresh basil, divided
¼ cup (1 ounce) shredded Parmesan cheese
Vegetable cooking spray
6 plum tomatoes, chopped
2 teaspoons olive oil
2 teaspoons red wine vinegar

• Place chicken between 2 sheets of heavy-duty plastic wrap, and flatten to ¼-inch thickness using a meat mallet or rolling pin. Sprinkle evenly with ¼ teaspoon salt and ¼ teaspoon pepper.
• Stir together cream cheese, two-thirds of minced garlic, and dried tomatoes. Spread cream cheese mixture evenly over 1 side of each chicken breast, leaving a ¼-inch border. Sprinkle ¼ cup basil and Parmesan cheese evenly over breasts; roll up, jellyroll fashion, and secure with wooden picks, if necessary. Arrange in an 8-inch square baking dish coated with cooking spray.
• Bake at 350° for 30 to 45 minutes or until chicken is done. Remove from oven, and let stand 10 minutes.
• Stir together plum tomatoes, olive oil, vinegar, remaining ¼ teaspoon salt, remaining ¼ teaspoon pepper, remaining one-third minced garlic, and remaining ¼ cup basil.
• Cut chicken into slices. Serve with tomato mixture. Yield: 4 servings.

Note: Fresh tomato mixture may also be served with toasted or grilled French bread slices.

Per serving: Calories 262 (34% from fat); Fat 9.9g (sat 4.7g, mono 2.5g, poly 0.7g); Protein 32.3g; Carb 9.5g; Fiber 1.8g; Chol 83mg; Iron 1.8mg; Sodium 662mg; Calc 133mg

White Spaghetti and Meatballs

Prep: 30 min.   **Cook:** 45 min.   **Other:** 20 min.

1½ pounds skinned and boned chicken breasts, cut into chunks
1 large garlic clove
1 large egg
10 saltine crackers, finely crushed
1 teaspoon Italian seasoning
Vegetable cooking spray
1 (8-ounce) package sliced fresh mushrooms
⅛ teaspoon ground nutmeg
1 teaspoon olive oil
1 large garlic clove, minced
2 tablespoons all-purpose flour
½ cup dry white wine
3 cups low-sodium fat-free chicken broth
1 (8-ounce) package ⅓-less-fat cream cheese
¼ teaspoon ground red pepper
¼ cup chopped fresh Italian parsley
1 (8-ounce) package spaghetti

• Process chicken and garlic clove in a food processor until ground.
• Stir together chicken mixture, egg, and next 2 ingredients in a large bowl. Cover and chill 20 minutes.
• Shape mixture into 1-inch balls. Place a rack coated with cooking spray in an aluminum foil-lined broiling pan. Arrange meatballs on rack; lightly spray meatballs with cooking spray.
• Bake at 375° for 13 minutes or until meatballs are golden and thoroughly cooked.
• Sauté mushrooms and nutmeg in hot oil in a Dutch oven over medium-high heat 8 to 10 minutes or until mushrooms are tender. Add minced garlic; sauté 1 minute. Sprinkle with flour; cook, stirring constantly, 1 minute. Add wine, stirring to loosen browned particles from bottom of pan. Whisk in broth. Bring to a boil; reduce heat, and simmer, stirring occasionally, 15 minutes. Add cream cheese, whisking until smooth and sauce is thickened.
• Add meatballs, red pepper, and parsley to sauce; simmer 10 minutes. Meanwhile, cook pasta according to package directions, omitting salt and oil; drain. Serve sauce with meatballs over pasta. Yield: 6 servings.

Per serving: Calories 431 (24% from fat); Fat 11.2g (sat 5.2g, mono 3.5g, poly 1.1g); Protein 40g; Carb 39g; Fiber 1.7g; Chol 122mg; Iron 3.8mg; Sodium 629mg; Calc 78mg

Easy Mexican Lasagna

Prep: 15 min.   **Cook:** 1 hr.

This simple and delicious one-dish supper calls for almost no preparation (especially if you buy precooked cut-up chicken).

3 cups chopped cooked chicken breast
1 (15-ounce) can black beans, rinsed and drained
⅔ cup canned diced tomatoes and green chiles
1 teaspoon garlic powder
1 teaspoon ground cumin
½ teaspoon pepper
1 (10¾-ounce) can fat-free cream of chicken soup
1 (10¾-ounce) can fat-free cream of mushroom soup

1 (10-ounce) can enchilada sauce
Vegetable cooking spray
9 (6-inch) corn tortillas
1 cup (4 ounces) shredded reduced-fat Cheddar cheese
1 cup (4 ounces) shredded Monterey Jack cheese
Toppings: shredded lettuce, nonfat sour cream, mild chunky salsa

• Cook first 6 ingredients in a saucepan over medium heat 10 minutes or until thoroughly heated.
• Stir together chicken and mushroom soups and enchilada sauce in a saucepan; cook, stirring often, 10 minutes or until thoroughly heated.
• Spoon one-third of sauce into a 13- x 9-inch baking dish coated with cooking spray; top with 3 tortillas. Spoon half of chicken mixture and one-third of sauce over tortillas; sprinkle with half of Cheddar cheese. Top with 3 tortillas; repeat layers once with remaining chicken, sauce, Cheddar cheese, and tortillas, ending with tortillas. Sprinkle with Monterey Jack cheese.
• Bake at 350° for 30 to 40 minutes or until lasagna is bubbly. Serve with desired toppings. Yield: 8 servings.

*To lower sodium, substitute reduced-sodium soups, canned tomato products, and cheeses.

Per serving: Calories 303 (39% from fat); Fat 13.6g (sat 7.0g, mono 2.7g, poly 0.8g); Protein 25g; Carb 24g; Fiber 3.7g; Chol 65mg; Iron 1.2mg; Sodium 896mg; Calc 250mg

KIDS LOVE IT
★★★★★

Cooks Chat

"This is an easy, fantastic dish that pleases any crowd (even in-laws)!"

"There were no leftovers after serving this to my family of five. Mexican rice would be a great side dish to serve with this. The recipe calls for 3 tortillas per layer, but I added extra. This is so tasty that it is hard to believe it's a light entrée!"

"You can also use this as a dip. Leave out the tortillas, and just bake the other ingredients in the oven. Serve with warm tortillas."

Fried Pork Chops with Cream Gravy

Prep: 5 min.   **Cook:** 25 min.

1 cup all-purpose flour
1 teaspoon Cajun seasoning
¼ teaspoon garlic powder
¼ teaspoon pepper
8 (4-ounce) boneless center-cut
   pork chops

1 cup nonfat buttermilk
Vegetable cooking spray
3 tablespoons vegetable oil
1 cup fat-free milk
¼ teaspoon salt
Garnish: coarsely ground pepper

• Reserve 2 tablespoons flour, and set aside. Place remaining flour in a shallow dish.
• Combine Cajun seasoning, garlic powder, and ¼ teaspoon pepper. Rub pork chops evenly on both sides with seasoning mixture.
• Dip pork in buttermilk; dredge in flour. Lightly coat both sides of pork with cooking spray.
• Cook pork, in batches, in hot oil in a large heavy skillet over medium-high heat 5 minutes on each side or until golden brown. Drain on paper towels.
• Add reserved 2 tablespoons flour to pan drippings in skillet; stir in milk and salt, and cook, stirring constantly, until thickened and bubbly. Serve immediately with pork. Garnish, if desired. Yield: 8 servings.

Per serving: Calories 267 (42% from fat); Fat 12.3g (sat 3.7g, mono 4.9g, poly 2.6g); Protein 26.2g; Carb 11.2g; Fiber 0.3g; Chol 69mg; Iron 1.5mg; Sodium 250mg; Calc 63mg

Layered Potato Salad

Prep: 15 min.   **Cook:** 30 min.   **Other:** 1 hr.

4 pounds red potatoes,
   unpeeled
1 (8-ounce) container fat-free
   sour cream
¾ cup light mayonnaise
2 tablespoons Creole mustard
½ teaspoon pepper

¼ teaspoon salt
1 bunch green onions, chopped
   (about 1 cup)
¾ cup chopped Italian parsley
3 reduced-fat, reduced-sodium
   bacon slices, cooked and
   crumbled

• Bring potatoes and water to cover to a boil in a large Dutch oven over medium-high heat. Boil 25 minutes or until tender. Drain and let cool.
• Cut potatoes into thin slices.

- Stir together sour cream and next 4 ingredients.
- Layer one-third each of potatoes, sour cream mixture, green onions, and parsley in a large glass bowl. Repeat layers twice, ending with parsley. Cover and chill 1 hour. Sprinkle with bacon just before serving. Yield: 12 servings.

Note: Salad may be prepared a day in advance and chilled.

Per serving: Calories 192 (27% from fat); Fat 5.8g (sat 1g, mono 0g, poly .01g); Protein 4.8g; Carb 30g; Fiber 3.4g; Chol 8mg; Iron 1.5mg; Sodium 270mg; Calc 51mg

Creamy Hash Brown Casserole

Prep: 10 min.　**Cook:** 1 hr.　**Other:** 10 min.

1 (32-ounce) package frozen
　hash brown potatoes
1 (10¾-ounce) can fat-free
　cream of chicken soup
1 (8-ounce) container light
　sour cream
1 small onion, chopped
1 (5-ounce) can low-fat
　evaporated milk
¼ cup light butter or
　margarine, melted

½ teaspoon salt
¼ teaspoon pepper
1 teaspoon dried rosemary
　(optional)
Vegetable cooking spray
1 cup (4 ounces) shredded
　reduced-fat Cheddar
　cheese

- Stir together first 8 ingredients and, if desired, rosemary in a large bowl.
- Spoon mixture into an 11- x 7-inch baking dish coated with cooking spray. Sprinkle cheese evenly over top.
- Bake at 350° for 1 hour or until bubbly and golden. Remove from oven, and let stand 10 minutes. Yield: 6 servings.

Per serving: Calories 308 (37% from fat); Fat 13g (sat 7.4g, mono 0.4g, poly 0.5g); Protein 13g; Carb 37g; Fiber 2.6g; Chol 44mg; Iron 1.7mg; Sodium 811mg; Calc 230mg

SOUTHERN CLASSIC
★ ★ ★ ★ ★

Cooks Chat

"This is the best hash brown casserole I have ever made. I will make this again and again."

Spicy Beans with Coconut Milk

Prep: 20 min.   **Cook:** 37 min.

We enjoy the spicy, tangy taste of this dish, but feel free to adjust the curry paste and lime juice to your liking. This recipe is an excellent source of fiber—you need at least 25 grams per day.

1 sweet onion, chopped
Vegetable cooking spray
2 garlic cloves, minced
1 to 2 tablespoons red curry paste
2 (15-ounce) cans kidney beans, rinsed and drained
1 (14½-ounce) can diced tomatoes, undrained
1 (14-ounce) can light coconut milk

1 teaspoon grated lime rind
2 to 3 tablespoons fresh lime juice
2 tablespoons sugar
1 to 1½ teaspoons salt
4 cups hot cooked basmati or long-grain rice
Toppings: 2 green onions, chopped; 2 tablespoons chopped fresh cilantro (optional)

• Sauté chopped onion in a Dutch oven coated with cooking spray over medium-high heat 5 minutes; add garlic, and sauté 1 minute. Add red curry paste; sauté 1 minute. Stir in kidney beans, diced tomatoes, coconut milk, and next 4 ingredients. Bring to a boil; reduce heat, and simmer 30 minutes. Serve over basmati rice, and sprinkle with toppings, if desired. Yield: 6 servings.

Note: Red curry paste may be found in the Asian section of large supermarkets or in Asian markets.

Per serving: Calories 335 (11% from fat); Fat 4.2g (sat 2.2g, mono 0.2g, poly 0.1g); Protein 11g; Carb 64g; Fiber 11g; Chol 0mg; Iron 2.3mg; Sodium 495mg; Calc 40mg

appetizers & beverages

★★★★★

Please every guest at your next gathering with these scrumptious appetizers and refreshing beverages.

Tomato Tart, page 137

Nutty Stuffed Celery

Prep: 15 min.

3 ounces ⅓-less-fat cream cheese, softened
1 tablespoon half-and-half
½ teaspoon onion powder
½ teaspoon seasoned salt

¼ teaspoon curry powder
4 celery stalks, cut into 4-inch pieces
¼ cup coarsely chopped honey-roasted peanuts

• Stir together first 5 ingredients. Cover and chill mixture until ready to serve.
• Spread mixture on celery pieces, and sprinkle with peanuts. Yield: 4 servings.

Deviled Eggs

Prep: 10 min.

5 hard-cooked eggs, peeled
1½ tablespoons Dijon mustard
1½ tablespoons mayonnaise

5 pimiento-stuffed olives, halved
1 teaspoon Cajun seasoning

• Cut eggs in half lengthwise; carefully remove yolks.
• Mash yolks, and stir in mustard and mayonnaise; blend well.
• Spoon yolk mixture evenly into egg whites. Place an olive half in the center of each; sprinkle with Cajun seasoning. Yield: 10 eggs.

Pumpkin Cheese Ball

Prep: 30 min.   **Other:** 4 hrs.

2 (8-ounce) blocks extra-sharp
  Cheddar cheese, shredded
1 (8-ounce) package cream
  cheese, softened
1 (8-ounce) container chive-
  and-onion cream cheese

2 teaspoons paprika
½ teaspoon ground red pepper
1 broccoli stalk
Red and green apple wedges

• Combine Cheddar cheese and next 4 ingredients in a bowl until blended. Cover and chill 4 hours or until mixture is firm enough to be shaped.
• Shape mixture into a ball to resemble a pumpkin. Smooth entire outer surface with a frosting spatula or table knife. Make vertical grooves in ball, if desired, using fingertips.
• Cut florets from broccoli stalk, and reserve for another use. Cut stalk to resemble a pumpkin stem, and press into top of cheese ball. Serve cheese ball with apple wedges. Yield: 16 appetizer servings.

Note: To make ahead, wrap cheese ball in plastic wrap without stalk; store in refrigerator up to 2 days. Attach stalk before serving.

Pesto Goat Cheese

Prep: 25 min.   **Other:** 2 hrs.

2 (3-ounce) logs goat cheese,
  softened
1 (8-ounce) package cream
  cheese, softened
1 (7-ounce) jar basil pesto,
  drained

1 tablespoon fresh lemon juice
1 tablespoon chopped fresh
  parsley
1 (¾-ounce) package fresh
  thyme sprigs
Assorted crackers

• Stir together first 5 ingredients until well blended. Remove ¼ cup mixture, and wrap in plastic wrap; chill. Press remaining cheese mixture into a 6-cup or 1.5-liter plastic wrap-lined bowl. Cover and chill 2 hours.
• Remove plastic wrap from chilled ¼ cup cheese mixture. Shape heaping teaspoonfuls of cheese mixture into egg shapes. Chill until ready to serve.
• Unmold cheese mixture; remove plastic wrap, and place on a serving platter. Press a 2-inch indention into center of cheese mold. Press thyme sprigs around top edge and sides of mold to resemble a nest. Arrange eggs in center of nest. Serve with crackers. Yield: about 3 cups.

Southwestern Cheese Appetizer

Prep: 30 min.   **Other:** 8 hrs.

½ cup olive oil
½ cup white wine vinegar
¼ cup fresh lime juice
½ (7-ounce) jar roasted red bell peppers, drained and diced
3 green onions, minced
3 tablespoons chopped fresh parsley
3 tablespoons chopped fresh cilantro
1 teaspoon sugar
½ teaspoon salt
½ teaspoon freshly ground pepper
1 (8-ounce) block sharp Cheddar cheese, chilled
1 (8-ounce) block Monterey Jack cheese with peppers, chilled
1 (8-ounce) package cream cheese, chilled

• Whisk together first 3 ingredients until mixture is blended; stir in diced red bell peppers and next 6 ingredients. Set marinade aside.
• Cut block of Cheddar cheese in half lengthwise. Cut halves crosswise into ¼-inch-thick slices. Repeat procedure with Monterey Jack cheese and cream cheese.
• Arrange cheese slices alternately in a shallow baking dish, standing slices on edge. Pour marinade over cheeses. Cover and chill at least 8 hours. Transfer cheese to a serving plate, and spoon any remaining marinade over top. Serve with assorted crackers. Yield: 16 appetizer servings.

Warmed Cranberry Brie

Prep: 10 min.   **Cook:** 5 min.

1 (15-ounce) round Brie
1 (16-ounce) can whole-berry cranberry sauce
¼ cup firmly packed brown sugar
2 tablespoons spiced rum*
½ teaspoon ground nutmeg
¼ cup chopped pecans, toasted

• Trim rind from top of Brie, leaving a ⅓-inch border on top. Place Brie on a baking sheet.
• Stir together cranberry sauce and next 3 ingredients; spread mixture evenly over top of Brie. Sprinkle evenly with pecans.
• Bake Brie at 500° for 5 minutes. Serve with assorted crackers and apple and pear slices. Yield: 8 appetizer servings.

*Substitute 2 tablespoons orange juice for spiced rum, if desired.

Layered Crabmeat Spread

Prep: 20 min.   **Other:** 20 min.

For a lighter version, use ⅓-less-fat cream cheese, light mayonnaise, and 2% reduced-fat Monterey Jack cheese.

1 (8-ounce) package cream
 cheese, softened
2 tablespoons lemon juice
1 tablespoon mayonnaise
½ teaspoon seasoned salt
½ teaspoon lemon pepper
¼ teaspoon Worcestershire
 sauce
¾ cup cocktail sauce

1 (16-ounce) container lump
 crabmeat, drained
2 cups (8 ounces) shredded
 Monterey Jack cheese
3 green onions, chopped
½ green bell pepper, chopped
½ cup sliced ripe olives
Assorted crackers and fresh
 vegetables

• Beat cream cheese at medium speed with an electric mixer until smooth; add lemon juice and next 4 ingredients, beating until blended. Spoon mixture into a 9-inch serving dish. Cover and chill at least 20 minutes.

• Spread cocktail sauce evenly over cream cheese mixture. Top with crabmeat; sprinkle with cheese, green onions, bell pepper, and ripe olives. Serve spread with crackers and fresh vegetables. Yield: 12 to 15 appetizer servings.

Cooks Chat

"This recipe turned out great. I carried it to a party, and everyone raved about how good it was and how much time I must have spent making it. The colors were great. I used green, yellow, and red bell peppers to make it colorful."

Goat Cheese Spread

Prep: 30 min.   **Other:** 8 hrs.

To garnish, cut 1 dried tomato into slivers. Gently press tomato slivers and fresh oregano sprigs in a decorative pattern over the top of the cheese after it is inverted.

2 (8-ounce) packages cream
   cheese, softened
8 ounces goat cheese
2 garlic cloves, minced
4 teaspoons chopped fresh or
   1¼ teaspoons dried
   oregano
⅛ teaspoon freshly ground
   pepper

¼ cup basil pesto
½ cup dried tomatoes in oil,
   drained and chopped
Garnishes: dried tomato slivers,
   fresh oregano sprigs
French bread slices or crackers

• Process first 5 ingredients in a food processor until smooth. Spread one-third of cheese mixture in bottom of a plastic wrap-lined 8- x 4-inch loafpan. Top with pesto; spread one-third cheese mixture over pesto. Sprinkle with dried tomatoes, and top with remaining cheese mixture. Cover and chill 8 hours.
• Invert spread onto a serving plate, discarding plastic wrap. Garnish, if desired. Serve with French bread slices or crackers. Yield: 12 to 16 appetizer servings.

Baked Vidalia Onion Dip

Prep: 15 min. **Cook:** 25 min. **Other:** 10 min.

2 tablespoons butter or
 margarine
3 large Vidalia onions, coarsely
 chopped
2 cups (8 ounces) shredded
 Swiss cheese
2 cups mayonnaise

1 (8-ounce) can sliced water
 chestnuts, drained and
 chopped
¼ cup dry white wine
1 garlic clove, minced
½ teaspoon hot sauce

• Melt butter in a large skillet over medium-high heat; add onion, and sauté 10 minutes or until tender.
• Stir together shredded Swiss cheese and next 5 ingredients; stir in onion, blending well. Spoon mixture into a lightly greased 2-quart baking dish.
• Bake at 375° for 25 minutes, and let stand 10 minutes. Serve with tortilla chips or crackers. Yield: 6 cups.

To lighten: Substitute vegetable cooking spray for butter; substitute reduced-fat Swiss cheese and light mayonnaise.

Pumpkin Pie Dip

Prep: 5 min. **Other:** 8 hrs.

1 (8-ounce) package cream
 cheese, softened
2 cups powdered sugar
1 (15-ounce) can pumpkin

1 teaspoon ground cinnamon
½ teaspoon ground ginger
Garnishes: ground cinnamon,
 cinnamon sticks

• Beat cream cheese and sugar at medium speed with an electric mixer until smooth. Add pumpkin, 1 teaspoon cinnamon, and ginger, beating well. Cover and chill 8 hours. Garnish, if desired. Serve with gingersnaps and apple or pear slices. Yield: 3 cups.

Corn-and-Field Pea Dip

Prep: 10 min.   **Other:** 8 hrs.

2 (15.8-ounce) cans field peas with snaps, rinsed and drained

2 (11-ounce) cans white shoepeg corn, drained

2 (10-ounce) cans diced tomatoes and green chiles

1 (14½-ounce) can diced tomatoes

5 green onions, diced

1 (16-ounce) bottle zesty Italian dressing

2 garlic cloves, minced

1 tablespoon finely chopped fresh parsley

• Stir together all ingredients. Cover and chill 8 hours. Drain before serving. Serve with corn chips. Yield: 8 cups.

Chunky Black Bean Salsa

Prep: 15 min.

3 tomatoes, seeded and chopped

1 (15-ounce) can black beans, rinsed and drained

1 jalapeño pepper, seeded and diced

½ small sweet onion, chopped

¼ cup chopped fresh cilantro

½ teaspoon grated lime rind

3 tablespoons fresh lime juice

½ teaspoon salt

½ teaspoon pepper

Baked tortilla chips

• Combine first 9 ingredients in a bowl. Cover and chill until ready to serve. Serve with baked tortilla chips. Yield: 6 cups.

Goblin Dip with Bone Crackers

Prep: 10 min.   **Cook:** 15 min.

1 (16-ounce) can chili without beans
1 (16-ounce) can refried beans
1 (8-ounce) package cream cheese
1 (8-ounce) jar chunky pico de gallo
1 (4.5-ounce) can chopped green chiles, undrained

½ teaspoon ground cumin
Toppings: shredded Cheddar or Monterey Jack cheese with peppers, chopped black olives, sliced green onions
Bone Crackers

• Cook first 6 ingredients in a heavy saucepan over low heat, stirring often, 15 minutes or until cream cheese is melted. Sprinkle with desired toppings; serve warm with Bone Crackers. Yield: 6 cups.

Bone Crackers

Prep: 20 min.   **Cook:** 30 min. per batch

2 (13.5-ounce) packages 9-inch flour tortillas
½ cup butter or margarine, melted

¼ teaspoon garlic salt

• Cut tortillas with a 3½-inch bone-shaped cutter, and place on baking sheets. Stir together butter and garlic salt; brush mixture on tortillas.
• Bake at 250° for 30 minutes or until crisp. Yield: 60 crackers.

Note: Flour tortillas may be cut into bone shapes using kitchen shears.

Cooks Chat

"I made this for a Halloween party at an elementary school. It was a hit with the kids as well as the adults! It takes a bit of work to make the bone crackers, but the effort is well worth it. I've made this numerous times and have never had any left over. Fun and tasty!"

Fruit Salsa with Cinnamon Crisps

Prep: 35 min.   **Cook:** 8 min. per batch

1 pint fresh strawberries, chopped
1 large banana, chopped
1 Red Delicious apple, chopped
1 kiwifruit, peeled and chopped
¼ cup fresh lemon juice
¼ cup sugar
¼ teaspoon ground nutmeg
1¼ teaspoons ground cinnamon, divided
4 (7½-inch) flour tortillas
Vegetable cooking spray
2 tablespoons sugar

• Combine first 4 ingredients. Stir together lemon juice, ¼ cup sugar, nutmeg, and ½ teaspoon cinnamon; toss with fruit. Chill.
• Cut each tortilla into eighths. Arrange pieces on baking sheets. Lightly coat with cooking spray. Combine remaining ¾ teaspoon cinnamon and 2 tablespoons sugar. Sprinkle over tortilla chips.
• Bake at 350° for 6 to 8 minutes or until lightly browned. Serve with fruit salsa. Yield: 4 servings.

Spinach Crostini

Prep: 25 min.   **Cook:** 18 min.

1 (10-ounce) package frozen chopped spinach, thawed and drained
2 plum tomatoes, diced
1 small onion, diced
1 garlic clove, minced
½ cup crumbled feta cheese
¼ cup mayonnaise
¼ cup sour cream
¼ teaspoon pepper
1 (16-ounce) French bread loaf, cut into ½-inch slices

• Combine first 8 ingredients; spread on 1 side of each bread slice. Place on a baking sheet.
• Bake at 350° for 18 minutes or until golden. Yield: 8 appetizer servings.

Blue Cheese Crisps

Prep: 8 min.   **Cook:** 10 min. per batch

½ cup butter or margarine,
   softened
1 (4-ounce) package crumbled
   blue cheese, softened
½ cup finely chopped pecans
   or walnuts
1 French baguette, sliced
Garnish: fresh parsley

• Stir together softened butter and blue cheese until blended; stir in chopped nuts. Set mixture aside.
• Place baguette slices in a single layer on baking sheets.
• Bake at 350° for 3 to 5 minutes. Turn slices, and spread evenly with blue cheese mixture. Bake 5 more minutes. Garnish, if desired. Serve crisps immediately. Yield: 32 servings.

Roasted Pepper-Tomato Bruschetta

Prep: 15 min.

Seeding the tomatoes will enhance the appearance of these appetizers.

1 (7-ounce) jar roasted red bell
   peppers, drained and
   chopped
6 ripe tomatoes, seeded and
   diced
3 tablespoons shredded
   Parmesan cheese
2 tablespoons chopped fresh
   basil
1 garlic clove, minced
½ teaspoon coarse-grained sea
   salt or kosher salt
¼ teaspoon freshly ground
   pepper
24 French bread slices, toasted

• Combine first 7 ingredients; spoon 1 heaping tablespoon over each toasted bread slice. Yield: 2 dozen.

Tomato Tart

Tomato Tart

Prep: 45 min. **Cook:** 1 hr., 24 min. **Other:** 10 min.

½ (15-ounce) package
    refrigerated piecrusts
1 garlic bulb
½ teaspoon olive oil
1½ cups shredded fontina
    cheese, divided

4 large tomatoes
½ teaspoon salt
¼ teaspoon pepper

• Press refrigerated piecrust on bottom and up sides of a square 9-inch tart pan. Bake at 450° for 9 minutes or until piecrust is lightly browned; set aside.
• Cut off pointed end of garlic bulb; place garlic on a piece of aluminum foil, and drizzle with olive oil. Fold foil to seal.
• Bake garlic at 425° for 30 minutes; cool. Squeeze pulp from garlic cloves into bottom of baked piecrust.
• Sprinkle ½ cup fontina cheese over garlic.
• Slice tomatoes, and sprinkle evenly with salt and pepper. Place on folded paper towels, and let stand 10 minutes. Arrange tomato slices over shredded cheese. Sprinkle with remaining 1 cup cheese.
• Bake at 350° for 45 minutes or until tart is lightly browned. Yield: 4 to 6 servings.

Southwestern Chicken Salad Spirals

Prep: 15 min. **Other:** 2 hrs.

1 (7-ounce) jar roasted red bell
    peppers
2 cups chopped cooked chicken
1 (8-ounce) package cream
    cheese, softened
1 (0.4-ounce) envelope Ranch-
    style buttermilk dressing
    mix
¼ cup chopped ripe olives

½ small onion, diced
1 (4.5-ounce) can chopped
    green chiles, drained
2 tablespoons chopped fresh
    cilantro
½ teaspoon pepper
¼ cup pine nuts (optional)
8 (6-inch) flour tortillas
Garnish: fresh cilantro

• Drain roasted peppers well, pressing between layers of paper towels; chop.
• Stir together roasted peppers, chicken, and next 7 ingredients. Cover and chill at least 2 hours.
• Stir pine nuts, if desired, into chicken mixture. Spoon evenly over tortillas, and roll up. Cut each roll into 5 slices, securing with wooden picks, if necessary. Garnish, if desired. Yield: 40 appetizers.

Southwestern Rollups

Prep: 25 min.   **Cook:** 7 min.   **Other:** 30 min.

For neater slices, avoid overfilling the tortillas, and roll tightly. Before serving, cut each tortilla on the diagonal.

1 (10-ounce) package frozen chopped spinach, thawed
1 (1-ounce) envelope fajita seasoning mix
½ cup chicken broth or water
3 (6-ounce) packages refrigerated Southwestern-flavored chicken breast strips, chopped
1 (15-ounce) can black beans, rinsed and drained

1 (11-ounce) can yellow corn with red and green bell peppers, drained
2 cups (8 ounces) shredded Monterey Jack cheese with peppers
6 (10-inch) flour tortillas
Salsa

• Combine spinach and fajita seasoning in a large nonstick skillet; add broth. Cook over medium heat, stirring often, 5 minutes. Stir in chicken and next 3 ingredients; simmer until cheese melts.
• Spread 1 cup chicken mixture on 1 side of each tortilla, leaving a ½-inch border around edges.
• Roll up tortillas tightly; wrap in plastic wrap. Chill 30 minutes.
• Unwrap rollups, and cut into slices. Serve with salsa. Yield: 8 to 10 appetizer servings.

Note: For testing purposes only, we used refrigerated Louis Rich Carving Board Southwestern Chicken Breast Strips.

Shanghai Spring Rolls with Sweet Chili Sauce

Prep: 30 min.   **Cook:** 6 min. per batch

½ pound unpeeled fresh
    shrimp
2 large eggs, lightly beaten
½ pound ground pork
1 (8-ounce) can sliced water
    chestnuts, drained and
    minced
1 (8-ounce) can bamboo
    shoots, drained and minced
3 garlic cloves, minced
2 green onions, diced

2 tablespoons minced fresh
    ginger
1 tablespoon soy sauce
⅛ teaspoon salt
⅛ teaspoon pepper
1 (12-ounce) package spring
    roll wrappers
Vegetable oil
Sweet Chili Sauce
Lettuce leaves (optional)

• Peel shrimp, and devein, if desired; finely chop.
• Stir together shrimp, 1 egg, pork, and next 8 ingredients. Spoon
1 tablespoon mixture in center of each spring roll wrapper. Fold
top corner of each wrapper over filling, tucking tip of corner
under filling, and fold left and right corners over filling. Lightly
brush remaining corner with remaining egg; tightly roll filled end
toward remaining corner, and gently press to seal.
• Pour vegetable oil to a depth of 2 inches into a medium saucepan,
and heat to 350°. Fry spring rolls, a few at a time, 6 minutes or
until golden. Drain on paper towels. Serve spring rolls with Sweet
Chili Sauce and over lettuce leaves, if desired. Yield: 15 spring rolls.

Sweet Chili Sauce

Prep: 5 min.

1 (7-ounce) bottle hot chili
    sauce with garlic
½ cup water
½ cup rice wine vinegar

¼ cup sugar
¼ cup lemon juice
2 tablespoons chili paste

• Stir together all ingredients until blended. Chill until ready to
serve. Yield: 2 cups.

Cooks Chat

*"Yummy! I made these, and my hus-
band and all of our neighbors loved
them. They were begging for more! I
added more filling (2 heaping tablespoons), which made them bigger. I
served them with duck sauce from a
jar. A real winner! I am making a
huge platter of them to take over to
a friend's for the Super Bowl.
Thanks for the recipe."*

*"Very, very good! There wasn't one
left at the end of the party. You can
fry them and keep them warm in the
oven for a little while before the
guests arrive."*

"The chili sauce is divine."

Chicken-and-Brie Quesadillas with Chipotle Salsa

Prep: 15 min.   **Cook:** 10 min.   **Other:** 1 hr.

2 cups chopped plum tomato
1 small onion, chopped
3 garlic cloves, minced
3 tablespoons fresh lime juice
2 teaspoons minced canned
 chipotle chiles in adobo
 sauce
½ teaspoon salt
5 green onions, minced and
 divided

½ cup chopped fresh cilantro,
 divided
1 cup finely chopped cooked
 chicken
1 (4.5-ounce) can diced green
 chiles, drained
8 (7-inch) flour tortillas
8 ounces Brie, trimmed and
 diced

• Stir together first 6 ingredients, ¼ cup green onions, and ¼ cup cilantro. Let stand 1 hour.
• Stir together remaining green onions, remaining ¼ cup cilantro, chicken, and diced green chiles.
• Arrange 4 tortillas on a large lightly greased baking sheet. Top evenly with cheese, chicken mixture, and remaining tortillas, pressing down slightly.
• Bake at 425° for 8 to 10 minutes or until cheese melts. Cut into wedges, and serve immediately with salsa. Yield: 12 appetizer servings.

Note: Freeze remaining chipotle chiles in adobo sauce, if desired.

Quick Quesadillas

Prep: 10 min.   **Cook:** 18 min.

For easier flipping, place 1 tortilla in the skillet, top one side with half the amount of filling, and fold in half. Cook as directed, and cut into 3 triangles.

6 (6-inch) flour tortillas
6 tablespoons shredded
 Monterey Jack cheese
6 tablespoons shredded
 Cheddar cheese
1 (4.5-ounce) can chopped
 green chiles, undrained

3 medium plum tomatoes,
 chopped
Sour cream
Salsa

• Place 1 flour tortilla in a small lightly greased nonstick skillet. Sprinkle with 2 tablespoons each of shredded cheeses. Spread with 1 tablespoon chiles; sprinkle with 3 tablespoons chopped tomato. Top with 1 tortilla, and coat with cooking spray.
• Cook quesadilla over low heat 2 to 3 minutes on each side or until golden. Remove from skillet; keep warm.
• Repeat procedure with remaining tortillas, cheeses, chiles, and tomato. Cut each quesadilla into 6 triangles. Serve with sour cream and salsa. Yield: 6 appetizer servings.

Southwestern Pull-Apart Ring

Prep: 15 min.   **Cook:** 30 min.   **Other:** 10 min.

1 (12-ounce) package ground hot or mild pork sausage
1 red bell pepper, diced
1 green bell pepper, diced
1 (1-ounce) package fajita seasoning mix

2 (12-ounce) cans refrigerated biscuits
1½ cups (6 ounces) shredded Mexican four-cheese blend

• Cook sausage in a skillet over medium heat, stirring until it crumbles and is no longer pink. Stir in peppers, and cook 3 to 5 minutes or until tender. Sprinkle with seasoning mix, and cook 1 to 2 more minutes; drain well, pressing with paper towels.
• Separate refrigerated biscuits, and cut into quarters; place in a large mixing bowl. Fold in sausage mixture, tossing to coat.
• Layer biscuit mixture and cheese in a lightly greased 10-inch tube pan.
• Bake at 400° for 15 minutes or until golden brown. Let stand in pan 5 to 10 minutes. Invert onto a serving plate, and serve immediately. Yield: 12 to 16 appetizer servings.

Veggie Southwestern Pull-Apart Ring: Sauté 1 red bell pepper, diced, and 1 green bell pepper, diced, in 1 teaspoon olive oil 3 to 5 minutes or until tender. Separate 2 (12-ounce) cans refrigerated biscuits; cut into quarters. Place in a large mixing bowl. Fold in peppers, 2 tablespoons melted butter, and fajita seasoning, tossing to coat. Layer biscuits and ¾ cup (3 ounces) shredded Mexican four-cheese blend in a lightly greased 10-inch tube pan. Bake, cool, and invert as directed. Brush with melted butter.

KIDS LOVE IT

Cooks Chat

"Easy to prepare—make sure to drain the sausage. We have served it at two Christmas parties, and it was a big hit. Every last bite was eaten."

"The recipe was easy to prepare. It needs more cooking time when using the larger-sized cans of biscuit dough. I made it for a Christmas party, and everyone seemed to enjoy it."

Cooks Chat

"I have made these a number of times, and there were never any leftovers. I think they taste better without freezing."

"Yummm. Big hit—everyone was very impressed. Easy to make."

Spinach Quiches

Prep: 15 min.   **Cook:** 45 min.

1 (15-ounce) package
 refrigerated piecrusts
2 tablespoons butter or
 margarine
1 small onion, chopped
2 green onions, chopped
¼ cup chopped fresh parsley
1 (10-ounce) package frozen
 chopped spinach, thawed
 and well drained

1 tablespoon Worcestershire
 sauce
1 teaspoon salt
½ teaspoon pepper
3 large eggs
¼ cup milk
1 cup (4 ounces) shredded
 Swiss cheese

• Roll each piecrust into a 12-inch square; cut each square into 24 pieces. Shape into balls, and press into lightly greased miniature muffin pans.
• Melt butter in a large skillet over medium heat. Add onions and parsley; sauté until onions are tender. Add spinach; cook 2 minutes. Stir in Worcestershire sauce, salt, and pepper. Remove from heat.
• Whisk together eggs and milk until blended; stir in cheese. Add egg mixture to spinach mixture; spoon evenly into prepared pans.
• Bake at 350° for 30 to 35 minutes. Remove immediately from pans, and cool on wire racks. Freeze quiches up to 2 months. Yield: 4 dozen.

Note: Thaw frozen quiches in refrigerator; bake at 300° for 10 minutes or until thoroughly heated.

Wiener Worms

Prep: 5 min. **Cook:** 3 min.

8 bun-length hot dogs
8 buns (optional)

Mustard and ketchup

• Cut bun-length hot dogs lengthwise into quarters. Place on grill rack crosswise, and grill, uncovered, over medium-high heat 2 to 3 minutes or until they begin to curl. Serve alone or in buns with mustard and ketchup. In addition to red, offer colored ketchups, such as green and purple. Yield: 8 servings.

Shrimp-Stuffed Mushrooms

Prep: 35 min. **Cook:** 20 min.

Purchase steamed shrimp at the supermarket. Stuff the mushrooms ahead, but bake just before serving.

12 large fresh mushrooms
  (1 pound)
Butter-flavored cooking spray
½ cup chopped cooked shrimp
⅓ cup Italian-seasoned
  breadcrumbs

¼ cup low-sodium fat-free
  chicken broth
¼ teaspoon salt
⅛ teaspoon ground red pepper
1 tablespoon grated Parmesan
  cheese (optional)

• Remove stems from mushrooms; chop stems.
• Spray mushroom caps with butter-flavored cooking spray.
• Stir together chopped mushrooms, shrimp, and next 4 ingredients. Spoon evenly into mushroom caps; sprinkle evenly with cheese, if desired. Place on a lightly greased rack in a broiler pan.
• Bake at 375° for 20 minutes. Yield: 12 appetizers.

Artichoke-Stuffed Mushrooms

Prep: 25 min.   **Cook:** 22 min.

1½ pounds large fresh mushrooms
¼ cup chopped onion
2 garlic cloves, chopped
1 tablespoon olive oil
¼ cup dry white wine
¼ cup soft breadcrumbs
1 (14-ounce) can artichoke hearts, drained and chopped

3 green onions, chopped
½ cup grated Parmesan cheese
½ cup mayonnaise
¼ teaspoon salt
¼ teaspoon pepper

• Rinse and pat mushrooms dry. Remove stems, and chop; reserve mushroom caps.
• Sauté mushroom stems, onion, and garlic in hot oil in a large skillet over medium heat 5 minutes or until onion is tender.
• Add wine, and cook 2 minutes or until liquid evaporates. Stir in breadcrumbs. Remove from heat, and let cool.
• Combine onion mixture, artichoke, and next 5 ingredients. Spoon 1 teaspoonful into each mushroom cap. Place on a lightly greased rack in a roasting pan.
• Bake at 350° for 12 to 15 minutes or until golden. Yield: 25 to 30 appetizer servings.

Grilled Zucchini-Wrapped Shrimp

Prep: 45 min.   **Cook:** 6 min.   **Other:** 15 min.

Add a thin slice of pickled jalapeño to each appetizer for extra heat.

1 pound unpeeled, large fresh
 shrimp
½ cup fresh lime juice
8 tablespoons vegetable oil,
 divided

2 garlic cloves, pressed
¾ teaspoon salt
½ teaspoon ground red pepper
2 large zucchini
Fresh cilantro sprigs (optional)

- Peel shrimp; devein, if desired.
- Combine lime juice, 3 tablespoons vegetable oil, and next
3 ingredients in a zip-top freezer bag, gently squeezing to blend;
add shrimp. Seal and chill mixture 15 minutes.
- Remove shrimp from marinade, reserving marinade.
- Bring reserved marinade to a boil in a small saucepan; remove
from heat.
- Cut zucchini lengthwise into thin slices with a vegetable peeler.
Wrap each shrimp with a zucchini slice, and secure with a wooden
pick. Brush rolls with remaining 5 tablespoons vegetable oil.
- Grill rolls, without grill lid, over medium-high heat (350° to
400°) about 4 minutes.
- Brush with reserved marinade; turn and brush again. Grill
2 more minutes or just until shrimp turn pink. Serve hot or at
room temperature on a cilantro-lined platter, if desired. Yield:
6 appetizer servings.

Cooks Chat

"When you taste the shrimp and smell the aroma of the freshly grilled zucchini, you'll know that this is a great way to cook shrimp. It was really delicious. My fiancée loved it."

"This recipe was very easy. Instead of using the shrimp as appetizers, I used skewers and made kebabs out of them for an entrée. I also cut up raw lobster tail meat and did the same thing. A big hit!"

Crab-and-Scallop Cakes

Prep: 30 min.   **Cook:** 8 min. per batch   **Other:** 2 hrs.

The day before, mix and shape the cakes, and make the sauces. Sauté the cakes 1 hour before the party; cover and keep warm in a 200° oven.

1 pound bay scallops, drained
⅓ cup whipping cream
1 large egg
1 teaspoon Old Bay seasoning
½ teaspoon salt
¼ teaspoon pepper
6 green onions, thinly sliced
3 medium tomatoes, peeled, seeded, and diced

2 pounds fresh lump crabmeat, drained
2 tablespoons butter or margarine
Red Pepper Sauce
Yellow Pepper Sauce
Garnishes: parsley sprigs, lemon wedges

• Process scallops in a food processor until chopped. Add cream and next 4 ingredients; process until combined, stopping to scrape down sides.
• Combine scallop mixture, onions, and tomato; gently fold in crabmeat. Cover and chill at least 2 hours.
• Shape mixture into 8 patties (about ⅓ cup each).
• Melt butter in a large skillet over medium-high heat; add cakes, and cook, in batches, 3 to 4 minutes on each side or until golden. Serve with Red Pepper Sauce and Yellow Pepper Sauce. Garnish, if desired. Yield: 8 servings.

Red Pepper Sauce

Prep: 10 min.   **Cook:** 30 min.

2 large red bell peppers, coarsely chopped

1 cup whipping cream
¼ teaspoon salt

• Combine all ingredients in a saucepan over medium heat; cover and simmer 30 minutes.
• Process mixture in a blender or food processor until smooth. Pour puree through a wire-mesh strainer into a bowl. Serve warm. Yield: 1 cup.

Yellow Pepper Sauce

Prep: 10 min.   **Cook:** 30 min.

2 large yellow bell peppers,
   coarsely chopped

1 cup whipping cream
¼ teaspoon salt

• Combine all ingredients in a saucepan over medium heat; cover and simmer 30 minutes.
• Process mixture in a blender or food processor until smooth. Pour puree through a wire-mesh strainer into a bowl. Serve warm. Yield: 1 cup.

Spicy Crab-and-Ginger Salsa with Sesame Wontons

Prep: 25 min.   **Cook:** 1 min. per batch

3 tablespoons rice wine vinegar
2 tablespoons vegetable oil
1 tablespoon lime juice
1 to 2 teaspoons Asian
   garlic-chili sauce or paste*
1 teaspoon sesame oil
½ teaspoon salt
12 ounces lump crabmeat,
   drained and coarsely
   chopped

1 cucumber, peeled, seeded, and
   diced
2 green onions, sliced
2 tablespoons chopped pickled
   ginger
Peanut oil
24 wontons
2 tablespoons sesame seeds,
   toasted

• Whisk together rice wine vinegar and next 5 ingredients. Stir in crabmeat and next 3 ingredients. Cover and chill until ready to serve.
• Pour peanut oil to a depth of ½ inch into a large skillet. Fry wontons, in batches, in hot oil over medium-high heat 30 seconds on each side or until golden. Drain on paper towels; sprinkle with sesame seeds. Serve wontons with salsa. Yield: 8 appetizer servings.

Note: Garlic-chili sauce or paste may be found in the Asian section of the supermarket or in gourmet stores.

*For testing purposes only, we used A Taste of Thai Garlic Chili Pepper Sauce.

PARTY PLEASER

Cooks Chat

"This is a fabulous recipe! It is the best fusion recipe I have ever tried! The sweetness of the crab blends so well with the pungent flavor of the ginger, and the sesame creates a perfect balance. A must-try recipe!"

*"I tried this recipe, and it was
fantastic—almost like eating in a
tropical resort! Well worth the effort
on cold winter days, as it's very
refreshing."*

Citrus-Marinated Shrimp with Louis Sauce

Prep: 35 min.   **Cook:** 5 min.   **Other:** 25 min.

2 lemons, halved
2 limes, halved
½ orange, halved
1 tablespoon dried crushed red
   pepper
4 pounds unpeeled, large fresh
   shrimp
2 cups fresh orange juice
2 cups grapefruit juice
2 cups pineapple juice
½ cup fresh lemon juice

½ cup fresh lime juice
1 lemon, sliced
1 orange, sliced
1 lime, sliced
1 grapefruit, sliced
1 teaspoon dried crushed red
   pepper
Lettuce leaves
Louis Sauce
Garnish: citrus fruit slices

• Combine lemon halves, next 3 ingredients, and salted water to
cover in a Dutch oven. Bring to a boil; add shrimp, and cook 2 to
3 minutes or just until shrimp turn pink. Plunge shrimp into ice
water to stop the cooking process; drain.
• Peel shrimp, leaving tails on. Devein, if desired.
• Combine orange juice and next 9 ingredients in a large shallow
dish or zip-top freezer bag. Add shrimp, cover or seal, and chill
25 minutes. Drain off liquid. Serve shrimp over lettuce leaves with
Louis Sauce. Garnish, if desired. Yield: 10 to 12 appetizer servings.

Louis Sauce

Prep: 10 min.

This sauce can be prepared a day ahead.

1 (12-ounce) bottle chili sauce
2 cups mayonnaise
2 tablespoons grated onion
2 tablespoons grated lemon
   rind
3 tablespoons lemon juice
1 tablespoon prepared
   horseradish

1½ teaspoons Greek seasoning
1½ teaspoons Worcestershire
   sauce
½ teaspoon hot sauce
¼ teaspoon ground red pepper
Garnish: lemon zest

• Stir together first 10 ingredients. Cover and chill until ready to
serve. Garnish, if desired. Yield: 3 cups.

Cottontail Punch

Prep: 5 min.

6 cups peach-flavored white
    grape juice
1 (12-ounce) can frozen
    lemonade concentrate

1 (1-liter) bottle club soda
Lemonade Ice Cubes

• Stir together first 3 ingredients in a large container; add
Lemonade Ice Cubes. Yield: 12 cups.

Lemonade Ice Cubes

Prep: 10 min.   **Other:** 8 hrs.

1 (6-ounce) can frozen
    lemonade concentrate

Red and green liquid food
    coloring

• Prepare lemonade according to package directions. Divide into
2 equal portions. Stir 2 drops red food coloring into 1 portion;
pour into an ice cube tray, and freeze 8 hours. Repeat procedure
with green food coloring and remaining lemonade. Yield: 2 trays.

Cooks Chat

*"Light, delicious, and lovely for
showers. I didn't use the colored ice
cubes. I froze some fresh lemon
slices and extra punch (without the
soda) into an ice ring using a Bundt
pan. Serve this in a punch bowl."*

Brew-Ha-Ha Punch

Prep: 5 min.

2 cups sugar
2 quarts water
2 (0.13-ounce) envelopes
    unsweetened lemon-lime
    drink mix

1 (46-ounce) can pineapple
    juice
1 quart ginger ale

• Stir together sugar and 2 quarts water until sugar is dissolved. Stir
in remaining ingredients. Chill. Yield: 4 quarts.

Note: For a scary presentation, place punch bowl into a larger
bowl, and add dry ice to larger bowl.

Cooks Chat

*"I fixed this years ago when my
children were little. It was always a
big hit. Don't forget the dry ice."*

*"This is a wonderful alternative to
regular pop. For a fun presentation,
I froze gummy spiders and worms in
ice cubes and added the cubes to
the punch."*

Minted Tea Punch

Prep: 20 min.   **Other:** 2 hrs.

4 cups boiling water
4 family-size decaffeinated tea
  bags
½ cup loosely packed fresh
  mint leaves
¾ cup sugar

1 (6-ounce) can frozen
  lemonade concentrate,
  thawed and undiluted
4 cups cold water
Garnishes: lemon slices, fresh
  mint sprigs

• Pour 4 cups boiling water over tea bags and mint leaves. Cover and steep 3 minutes; remove and discard tea bags and mint. Stir in sugar until dissolved. Stir in lemonade concentrate and 4 cups cold water; chill at least 2 hours. Serve punch over ice. Garnish, if desired. Yield: 9 cups.

Strawberry Slush

Prep: 10 min.   **Other:** 8 hrs., 15 min.

2 (10-ounce) cans frozen
  strawberry daiquiri mix
  concentrate, thawed and
  divided

1 cup water, divided
Ice cubes
3 cups lemon-lime soft drink,
  chilled

• Combine 1 can daiquiri mix, ½ cup water, and enough ice cubes to reach 4-cup level in a blender container; process until smooth. Pour into a 3-quart container; set aside.
• Repeat procedure with remaining 1 can daiquiri mix, remaining ½ cup water, and enough ice cubes to reach 4-cup level in blender container; process until smooth. Add to first batch in 3-quart container; cover and freeze 8 hours or until firm.
• Remove from freezer; let stand 15 minutes or until slush can be broken up. Add lemon-lime soft drink, stirring until smooth. Yield: about 11 cups.

Note: To make ahead, place each blended batch of strawberry daiquiri mixture into a large zip-top freezer bag; seal and freeze. When ready to use, proceed with recipe as directed, using 1½ cups lemon-lime soft drink per batch.

Raspberry Lemonade

Prep: 10 min.

1 (14-ounce) package frozen
    raspberries, thawed
1 (16-ounce) jar maraschino
    cherries without stems
1¼ cups sugar

¾ cup fresh lemon juice
    (about 5 lemons)
¼ cup fresh lime juice
    (about 1 large lime)
3 cups water

• Process first 5 ingredients in a blender until smooth, stopping to
scrape down sides. Pour fruit mixture through a wire-mesh strainer
into a pitcher, discarding solids. Stir in 3 cups water. Serve over ice.
Yield: about 6 cups.

Blackberry Lemonade: Substitute 1 (14-ounce) package frozen
blackberries, thawed, for frozen raspberries. Proceed as directed.
Yield: about 6 cups.

Cherry-Berry Lemonade: Substitute 1 (16-ounce) package
frozen mixed berries, thawed, for frozen raspberries. Proceed as
directed, using 2 cups water. Yield: about 5 cups.

Cherry-Berry Lemonade Pops: Pour Cherry-Berry
Lemonade evenly into 14 (4-ounce) plastic pop molds. Insert
plastic pop sticks, and freeze 4 hours or until firm. Yield: about
14 pops.

Fresh-Squeezed Lemonade

Prep: 20 min.

1½ cups sugar
½ cup boiling water
1 tablespoon grated lemon rind

1½ cups fresh lemon juice
    (8 large lemons)
5 cups water

• Stir together sugar and ½ cup boiling water until sugar dissolves.
Stir in lemon rind, lemon juice, and 5 cups water. Chill. Serve over
ice. Yield: 8 cups.

Strawberry-Lemonade Slush

Prep: 20 min.   **Other:** 30 min.

Fresh lemon juice offers a tart tang to this beverage.

2 (16-ounce) containers fresh
   strawberries, sliced
1½ cups sugar
2 cups water, divided

1½ cups fresh lemon juice
   (about 6 to 9 medium
   lemons), divided
4 cups ice cubes, divided

• Stir together sliced strawberries and sugar; let stand 30 minutes.
• Process half of strawberry mixture, 1 cup water, ¾ cup lemon juice, and 2 cups ice in a blender until smooth. Repeat procedure with remaining ingredients, and serve immediately. Yield: about 8 cups.

Ginger Beer

Prep: 10 min.   **Other:** 4 hrs.

This pungent refresher also tastes great hot. Just heat it in the microwave by the mugful.

1 quart water
1 cup sugar
⅓ cup grated fresh ginger

1½ teaspoons grated lime rind
2 tablespoons fresh lime juice

• Combine all ingredients, stirring until sugar dissolves. Cover and chill 4 hours.
• Pour ginger mixture through a wire-mesh strainer into a large pitcher, discarding solids. Serve over crushed ice. Yield: 5 cups.

Apricot-Apple Cider Sipper

Prep: 10 min.   **Cook:** 15 min.

1 gallon apple cider
1 (11.5-ounce) can apricot
   nectar
2 cups sugar
2 cups orange juice

¾ cup lemon juice
4 (3-inch) cinnamon sticks
2 teaspoons ground allspice
1 teaspoon ground cloves
½ teaspoon ground nutmeg

• Bring all ingredients to a boil in a Dutch oven; reduce heat, and simmer 10 minutes. Remove cinnamon sticks. Serve hot. Yield: 21 cups.

Apple Cider Sipper: Omit nectar. Yield: 19 cups.

Cooks Chat

"This is a wonderful recipe. When I made it the first time, however, it was too sweet, so the next time I made it, I used 1½ cups of sugar. It was great. It really depends on your taste."

"I served this at a bridal luncheon and received numerous requests for the recipe. The dessert wine was rather pricey, but the result was well worth it."

"Delicious! My friends and I used this punch for a baby shower, and the guests raved about it. It was so refreshing and delicate. We omitted the dessert wine because we thought it might be too sweet. It was wonderful. Mimosas have now been replaced!"

Champagne Punch

Prep: 15 min.   **Other:** 8 hrs.

2 cups cranberry juice cocktail
1 (12-ounce) can frozen orange
    juice concentrate, thawed
1 cup lemon juice
1 cup sugar

1 (375-milliliter) bottle
    Sauterne or dessert wine*
2 (750-milliliter) bottles
    champagne, chilled
Ice Ring

• Combine first 4 ingredients, stirring well; chill at least 8 hours.
• Pour juice mixture into a chilled punch bowl. Gently stir in Sauterne and champagne just before serving. Float Ice Ring, fruit side up, in punch. Yield: 20 servings.

*Substitute either (375 ml) Bonny Doon Muscat Vin de Glacière or (375 ml) Quady Electra for Sauterne, if desired.

Ice Ring

Prep: 10 min.   **Other:** 10 hrs.

1½ to 2 cups orange juice
½ cup cranberry juice
6 to 8 seedless red grape
    clusters

10 to 12 orange slices, seeded
8 to 10 whole strawberries
Fresh mint sprigs

• Combine juices. Line bottom of 6-cup ring mold with grape clusters and half of orange slices, using grapes to stand orange slices vertically. Pour a thin layer of juices into mold, and freeze until firm, about 2 hours. Arrange remaining orange slices, strawberries, and mint sprigs around grapes. Pour remaining juices around fruit almost to top of mold. Freeze 8 hours.
• Unmold by dipping bottom half of mold in several inches of warm water 5 to 10 seconds to loosen, repeating as necessary to release ring (do not immerse entire mold in water). Invert ring onto plate. Yield: 1 ice ring.

Easy Ice Ring: Combine juices. Fill bottom of 6-cup ring mold with 2 cups crushed ice. Lay grape clusters over ice. Arrange orange slices, strawberries, and fresh mint sprigs around grapes. Pour juices around fruit almost to top of mold. Freeze 8 hours or until firm.

Hurricane Punch

Prep: 10 min.

½ (64-ounce) bottle red fruit
    punch
½ (12-ounce) can frozen
    limeade juice concentrate,
    thawed

1 (6-ounce) can frozen orange
    juice concentrate, thawed
1⅔ cups light rum
1⅔ cups dark rum

• Stir together all ingredients. Serve over ice. Yield: 8¼ cups.

Berry-Colada Punch

Prep: 5 min.

1 (16-ounce) package frozen
    sliced strawberries, thawed
1 (16-ounce) can cream of
    coconut

3 cups pineapple juice, chilled
3 cups club soda, chilled
2 cups rum (optional)

• Process strawberries and cream of coconut in a blender until smooth; pour into a pitcher or large bowl. Stir in pineapple juice, club soda, and, if desired, rum. Serve over crushed ice. Yield: 2½ quarts.

Cherry Cordial Hot Chocolate

Prep: 10 min.   **Cook:** 10 min.

5½ cups milk
1½ cups half-and-half
1½ cups chocolate syrup
½ cup maraschino cherry juice, divided

1¾ cups whipping cream
1 tablespoon powdered sugar
Maraschino cherries with stems (optional)

• Heat first 3 ingredients and 7 tablespoons cherry juice in a Dutch oven over medium-low heat, stirring often.
• Beat whipping cream at medium speed with an electric mixer until foamy; gradually add powdered sugar and reserved cherry juice, beating until soft peaks form. Serve with hot chocolate; top each serving with a cherry, if desired. Yield: 8½ cups.

Brandy Cream

Prep: 5 min.

2 pints vanilla ice cream, softened
½ cup brandy

⅓ cup crème de cacao
¼ cup hazelnut liqueur
¼ teaspoon ground nutmeg

• Process first 4 ingredients in a blender until smooth. Sprinkle each serving with nutmeg, and serve immediately. Yield: 5 cups.

Eggnog

Prep: 10 min.   **Cook:** 20 min.   **Other:** 8 hrs.

6 large eggs, lightly beaten
¾ cup sugar
2 cups milk
1 cup brandy
¼ cup rum

1 tablespoon vanilla extract
2 cups whipping cream
Garnishes: whipped cream,
   grated fresh nutmeg

• Stir together egg and sugar in a large saucepan; gradually stir in milk. Cook over medium heat, stirring constantly, 18 to 20 minutes or until mixture thickens and coats a metal spoon. Remove from heat; stir in brandy, rum, and vanilla. Cover and chill 8 hours.
• Beat whipping cream at high speed with an electric mixer until soft peaks form; fold into chilled egg mixture. Garnish, if desired. Yield: 8 cups.

Cooks Chat

"I have never liked eggnog until this. My boss gave me the recipe to try, and it was awesome. It tasted almost like a dessert."

"After trying this recipe, I have decided eggnog is no longer just for the holidays!"

Eggnog-Coffee Punch

Prep: 10 min.

1 quart coffee ice cream
1 quart vanilla ice cream
1 quart eggnog
2 cups hot brewed coffee
½ cup coffee liqueur or strong
    brewed coffee
½ cup bourbon (optional)
Frozen whipped topping,
    thawed
Nutmeg

• Scoop ice cream into a punch bowl. Add eggnog, coffee, liqueur, and, if desired, bourbon, stirring until ice cream melts slightly. Serve in glass mugs. Dollop punch with whipped topping; sprinkle with nutmeg. Serve immediately. Yield: 10 to 12 servings.

Note: For testing purposes only, we used Kahlúa coffee liqueur.

Cooks Chat

"I made this recipe exactly as stated and thought it was just wonderful. How perfect for a sweltering summer day!"

Classic Mint Julep

Prep: 10 min.

3 fresh mint leaves
1 tablespoon Mint Simple
 Syrup
Crushed ice
1½ to 2 tablespoons
 (1 ounce) bourbon

1 (4-inch) cocktail straw or
 coffee stirrer
1 fresh mint sprig
Powdered sugar (optional)

• Place mint leaves and Mint Simple Syrup in a chilled julep cup. Gently press leaves against cup with back of spoon to release flavors. Pack cup tightly with crushed ice; pour bourbon over ice. Insert straw; place mint sprig directly next to straw, and serve immediately. Sprinkle with powdered sugar, if desired. Yield: 1 (8-ounce) julep.

Note: For testing purposes only, we used Woodford Reserve Distiller's Select Bourbon.

Mint Simple Syrup

Prep: 5 min.   **Cook:** 10 min.   **Other:** 24 hrs.

1 cup granulated sugar
1 cup water

10 to 12 fresh mint sprigs

• Bring sugar and water to a boil in a medium saucepan. Boil, stirring often, 5 minutes or until sugar dissolves. Remove from heat; add mint, and let cool completely. Pour into a glass jar; cover and chill 24 hours. Remove and discard mint. Yield: 2 cups.

breads

★★★★★

Friends and family will find warmth and comfort in these aromatic breads fresh from the oven.

Spoon Rolls, page 174

Sweet Beer Bread

Prep: 5 min.   **Cook:** 55 min.

3 cups self-rising flour
½ cup sugar
1 (12-ounce) bottle beer*

¼ cup butter or margarine,
  melted

• Stir together first 3 ingredients; pour into a lightly greased 9- x 5-inch loafpan.
• Bake at 350° for 45 minutes. Pour melted butter over top. Bake 10 more minutes. Yield: 1 loaf.

*Substitute nonalcoholic or light beer for regular beer, if desired.

Cheddar-Chive Beer Bread: Add ¾ cup shredded sharp Cheddar cheese and 2 tablespoons chopped fresh chives to dry ingredients. Garnish with chive sprigs, if desired. Proceed as directed.

Banana-Nut Bread

Prep: 10 min.   **Cook:** 1 hr.   **Other:** 10 min.

Use very ripe bananas for the best flavor in this recipe.

1 cup sugar
½ cup shortening
2 large eggs
3 small bananas, mashed
1 teaspoon vanilla extract

2 cups all-purpose flour
1 teaspoon baking powder
½ teaspoon baking soda
1 teaspoon salt
½ cup chopped walnuts, toasted

• Beat sugar and shortening at medium speed with an electric mixer until creamy. Add eggs, banana, and vanilla, beating well.
• Combine flour and next 3 ingredients; add to banana mixture, beating until combined. Stir in chopped walnuts.
• Pour into a greased and floured 8-inch loafpan.
• Bake at 350° for 1 hour or until a wooden pick inserted in center comes out clean. Cool on a wire rack 10 minutes; remove loaf from pan, and cool completely on wire rack. Yield: 1 loaf.

Cheddar-Chive Beer Bread

Pumpkin-Pecan Bread

Prep: 12 min.   **Cook:** 1 hr., 15 min.   **Other:** 10 min.

3 cups sugar
1 cup vegetable oil
4 large eggs
1 (15-ounce) can pumpkin
3½ cups all-purpose flour
2 teaspoons baking soda
2 teaspoons salt
1 teaspoon ground cinnamon
1 teaspoon ground allspice
1 teaspoon ground nutmeg
½ teaspoon ground cloves
⅔ cup water
1 to 1½ cups chopped pecans, toasted

• Beat first 11 ingredients at low speed with an electric mixer 3 minutes or until blended. Add ⅔ cup water, beating until blended. Stir in pecans. Pour batter into 2 greased and floured 9- x 5-inch loafpans.
• Bake at 350° for 1 hour and 15 minutes or until a wooden pick inserted in center comes out clean. Cool in pans on a wire rack 10 minutes; remove from pans, and cool completely on wire rack. Yield: 2 loaves.

Note: Bread may be frozen up to 3 months.

Blueberry-Orange Bread

Prep: 20 min.   **Cook:** 1 hr.   **Other:** 15 min.

1 cup wheat bran cereal, crushed
¾ cup water
1 tablespoon grated orange rind
¼ cup fresh orange juice
½ teaspoon vanilla extract
2 cups all-purpose flour
1 cup sugar
1½ teaspoons baking powder
½ teaspoon baking soda
½ teaspoon salt
1 large egg
2 tablespoons vegetable oil
1 cup frozen blueberries, thawed

• Stir together first 5 ingredients in a large bowl; let stand 10 minutes or until cereal softens.
• Stir in flour and next 6 ingredients just until dry ingredients are moistened. Gently fold in blueberries. Pour batter into a greased 9- x 5-inch loafpan.
• Bake at 350° for 1 hour or until a long wooden pick inserted in center comes out clean. Cool on a wire rack 10 to 15 minutes; remove from pan, and cool completely on wire rack. Yield: 1 loaf.

Old Southern Biscuits

Prep: 10 min.　**Cook:** 14 min.

¼ cup shortening
2 cups self-rising flour

1 cup buttermilk
Melted butter (optional)

• Cut shortening into flour with a pastry blender or fork until crumbly. Add buttermilk, stirring the mixture just until moistened.
• Pat dough to ½-inch thickness; cut with a 2-inch round cutter. Place on a lightly greased baking sheet.
• Bake at 425° for 14 minutes or until golden. Brush hot biscuits with melted butter, if desired. Yield: 1 dozen.

Cooks Chat

"This recipe is the same as one taught to me by an Alabama native. Being a Yankee, I had never made biscuits from scratch until I made these. They are wonderful! Yes, I know—I've led a deprived life. Bring on the sausage gravy!"

Drop Scones

Prep: 8 min.　**Cook:** 14 min.

½ cup milk
1½ teaspoons white vinegar
½ cup butter or margarine,
　　softened
½ cup sugar

2 cups all-purpose flour
1 teaspoon baking soda
2 teaspoons cream of tartar
¼ teaspoon salt
Sugar

• Stir together milk and vinegar; set aside.
• Stir together butter and ½ cup sugar in a large bowl.
• Combine flour and next 3 ingredients; stir into butter mixture alternately with milk mixture, beginning and ending with flour mixture, until dry ingredients are moistened. Drop by rounded 2 tablespoonfuls onto an ungreased baking sheet; sprinkle with additional sugar.
• Bake at 450° for 12 to 14 minutes or until golden. Yield: 10 scones.

Cooks Chat

"My child's school used this recipe to help kids make a scone mix that they could take home. The scones were delicious and very easy to make. We added cinnamon, which made them even better!"

Classic Cream Scones

Prep: 10 min.   **Cook:** 15 min.

Be careful not to overwork scone dough. A light touch will produce tender results.

2 cups all-purpose flour
2 teaspoons baking powder
⅛ teaspoon salt
¼ cup sugar
⅓ cup butter or margarine, cubed

½ cup whipping cream
1 large egg
1½ teaspoons vanilla extract
1 egg white
1 teaspoon water
Sugar

• Combine first 4 ingredients. Cut in butter with a pastry blender until mixture is crumbly.
• Whisk together cream, egg, and vanilla; add to flour mixture, stirring just until dry ingredients are moistened.
• Turn dough out onto a lightly floured surface. Pat dough to ½-inch thickness; cut with a 2½-inch round cutter, and place on a baking sheet.
• Whisk together egg white and 1 teaspoon water; brush mixture over tops of scones. Sprinkle scones with additional sugar.
• Bake at 425° for 13 to 15 minutes or until lightly browned. Yield: 1 dozen.

Pecan-Pie Muffins

Prep: 5 min.   **Cook:** 25 min.

1 cup chopped pecans
1 cup firmly packed brown
   sugar
½ cup all-purpose flour

2 large eggs
½ cup butter or margarine,
   melted

• Combine first 3 ingredients in a large bowl; make a well in center of mixture.
• Beat eggs until foamy. Stir together eggs and butter; add to dry ingredients, stirring just until moistened.
• Place foil baking cups in muffin pans, and coat with cooking spray; spoon batter into cups, filling two-thirds full.
• Bake at 350° for 20 to 25 minutes or until done. Remove from pans immediately, and cool on wire racks. Yield: 9 muffins.

Date Muffins

Prep: 10 min.   **Cook:** 30 min.   **Other:** 1 hr.

1 cup finely chopped dates
1 cup boiling water
1 tablespoon shortening
1 large egg, lightly beaten
1 teaspoon vanilla extract

1½ cups all-purpose flour
1 cup sugar
1 teaspoon baking powder
½ teaspoon salt
1 cup chopped pecans

• Combine first 3 ingredients, and let stand 1 hour. Stir in egg and vanilla.
• Combine flour and next 4 ingredients in a bowl; make a well in center of mixture. Add date mixture, stirring just until moistened. Spoon into greased muffin pans, filling three-fourths full.
• Bake at 350° for 25 to 30 minutes. Yield: 1 dozen.

Ham-and-Cheddar Muffins

Prep: 15 min.   **Cook:** 23 min.   **Other:** 3 min.

3 tablespoons butter or
   margarine
1 medium-size sweet onion,
   finely chopped
1½ cups all-purpose baking
   mix
2 cups (8 ounces) shredded
   Cheddar cheese, divided

½ cup milk
1 large egg
1 cup finely chopped cooked
   ham
Poppy seeds (optional)

• Melt butter in a skillet over medium-high heat; add onion, and sauté 3 to 5 minutes or until tender.
• Combine baking mix and 1 cup cheese in a large bowl; make a well in center of mixture.
• Stir together milk and egg, blending well; add to cheese mixture, stirring until moistened. Stir in onion and ham. Spoon into lightly greased muffin pans, filling two-thirds full. Sprinkle with remaining 1 cup cheese. Sprinkle with poppy seeds, if desired.
• Bake at 425° for 18 minutes or until golden. Let stand 2 to 3 minutes before removing from pans. Yield: 1 dozen (3-inch) muffins.

Note: Substitute mini muffin pans for regular pans, if desired. Bake at 425° for 14 minutes or until golden. Yield: 2½ dozen mini muffins.

Reduced-Fat Ham-and-Cheddar Muffins: Substitute low-fat baking mix, fat-free or low-fat shredded Cheddar cheese, and fat-free milk. Reduce butter to 1 tablespoon; proceed with recipe as directed.

Ham-and-Swiss Muffins: Substitute shredded Swiss cheese for Cheddar; whisk in 2 tablespoons Dijon mustard with milk and egg. Proceed with recipe as directed.

Sausage-and-Cheese Muffins: Substitute 1 cup hot or mild ground pork sausage, cooked and crumbled, for chopped ham. Proceed with recipe as directed.

Chicken-and-Green Chile Muffins: Substitute 1 cup finely chopped cooked chicken for ham and 2 cups shredded Mexican four-cheese blend for Cheddar; add 1 (4.5-ounce) can chopped green chiles. Proceed with recipe as directed.

Barbecue Muffins

Prep: 15 min.   **Cook:** 20 min.   **Other:** 5 min.

1 (12-ounce) can refrigerated
    buttermilk biscuits
½ pound lean ground beef
¼ cup ketchup
1½ tablespoons brown sugar

1½ teaspoons apple cider
    vinegar
¼ teaspoon chili powder
½ cup (2 ounces) shredded
    Cheddar cheese

• Separate biscuits; pat or roll into 5-inch circles on a lightly floured
surface, and press into lightly greased muffin pans.
• Brown ground beef in a large skillet, stirring until it crumbles;
drain. Stir in ketchup and next 3 ingredients; spoon beef mixture
into muffin cups.
• Bake at 375° for 15 minutes; sprinkle with cheese, and bake
5 more minutes or until cheese melts. Cool in pan on a wire
rack 5 minutes. Yield: 10 muffins.

Note: Baked muffins may be frozen in an airtight container up to
1 week.

Cheesy Witches' Brooms

Prep: 15 min.   **Cook:** 12 min.

2 (11.5-ounce) packages
    cornbread twists or
    breadsticks

½ cup shredded Parmesan
    cheese

• Separate cornbread twists, and place on a baking sheet. Flatten
1 end of dough; cut dough into small strips to resemble a broom.
• Sprinkle cut end with cheese.
• Bake brooms at 375° for 10 to 12 minutes or until lightly
browned. Yield: 16 servings.

Cinnamon Toast Rollups

Prep: 10 min.   **Cook:** 12 min.

¼ cup firmly packed light
   brown sugar
½ cup granulated sugar
½ teaspoon ground cinnamon

1 (8-ounce) can refrigerated
   crescent rolls
¼ cup butter or margarine,
   melted

• Stir together first 3 ingredients.
• Unroll crescent rolls; brush with melted butter, and sprinkle evenly with sugar mixture.
• Separate dough into triangles. Roll up each triangle, starting with shortest side; place on a lightly greased baking sheet.
• Bake at 350° for 10 to 12 minutes or until golden brown; remove to a wire rack to cool. To carry in a lunchbox, wrap in aluminum foil sandwich wrapper sheets. Yield: 8 rollups.

Pecan Crescent Twists

Prep: 15 min.   **Cook:** 12 min.

2 (8-ounce) cans refrigerated
   crescent rolls
3 tablespoons butter or
   margarine, melted and
   divided
½ cup chopped pecans

¼ cup powdered sugar
1 teaspoon ground cinnamon
⅛ teaspoon ground nutmeg
½ cup powdered sugar
2½ teaspoons maple syrup or
   milk

• Unroll crescent rolls, and separate each can into 2 rectangles, pressing perforations to seal. Brush evenly with 2 tablespoons melted butter.
• Stir together chopped pecans and next 3 ingredients; sprinkle 3 tablespoons pecan mixture onto each rectangle, pressing in gently.
• Roll up, starting at 1 long side, and twist. Cut 6 shallow ½-inch-long diagonal slits in each roll.
• Shape rolls into rings, pressing ends together; place on a lightly greased baking sheet. Brush rings evenly with remaining 1 tablespoon butter.
• Bake at 375° for 12 minutes or until rings are golden.
• Stir together ½ cup powdered sugar and maple syrup until glaze is smooth; drizzle over warm rings. Cut rings in half, and serve. Yield: 8 servings.

Brunch Popover Pancake

Prep: 10 min.   **Cook:** 25 min.

Complete with fruit and a "pancake," this recipe needs little else served with it. If you want a heavier meal, consider serving it with scrambled eggs and bacon or thinly sliced ham.

4 large eggs, lightly beaten
1 cup milk
1 cup all-purpose flour
¼ teaspoon salt
⅓ cup butter or margarine, melted
3 tablespoons orange marmalade
3 tablespoons butter or margarine

1 tablespoon lemon juice
1 (16-ounce) package frozen sliced peaches, thawed and drained
1 cup frozen blueberries, thawed

• Place a well-greased 12-inch cast-iron skillet in a 425° oven for 5 minutes.
• Combine first 5 ingredients, stirring with a wire whisk until blended.
• Remove skillet from oven. Pour batter into hot skillet.
• Bake at 425° for 20 to 25 minutes. (Pancake resembles a giant popover and will fall quickly after removing from oven.)
• Meanwhile, combine marmalade, 3 tablespoons butter, and lemon juice in a saucepan; bring to a boil. Add peaches, and cook over medium heat, stirring constantly, 2 to 3 minutes. Spoon on top of baked pancake. Sprinkle with blueberries. Yield: 4 servings.

Cooks Chat

"When in season, use fresh peaches and blueberries. Also, I suggest using seedless raspberry jam in place of the marmalade. I use the pancake recipe all the time, varying a fresh fruit topping, depending upon what is readily available. It rates 'A+' with all my friends! Bon appétit!"

Apple Pancakes

Prep: 10 min.   **Cook:** 16 min.

2 cups all-purpose flour
¼ cup sugar
1 teaspoon baking soda
¼ teaspoon salt
2 cups buttermilk

2 large eggs
2 tablespoons butter, melted
1 large Granny Smith apple, peeled and chopped

• Combine first 4 ingredients in a large bowl; make a well in center of mixture.
• Stir together buttermilk, eggs, and butter. Add to dry ingredients, stirring just until moistened. Fold in apple.
• Pour ¼ cup batter for each pancake onto a hot lightly greased griddle. Cook until tops are covered with bubbles and edges look cooked; turn and cook other side. Yield: 16 (4-inch) pancakes.

Cooks Chat

"Fluffy and delicious! The whole family loved them! I will definitely serve them to guests."

Chocolate Chip Mandelbread

Chocolate Chip Mandelbread

Prep: 10 min. **Cook:** 35 min.

2 cups sugar, divided
3 large eggs
1 cup vegetable oil
3¾ cups all-purpose flour
2 teaspoons baking powder
½ teaspoon salt

1 teaspoon vanilla extract
1 (6-ounce) package semisweet
   chocolate mini-morsels
1½ teaspoons ground
   cinnamon

• Beat 1½ cups sugar and eggs at medium speed with an electric mixer until blended. Add oil and next 4 ingredients; beat until blended. Stir in mini-morsels.
• Divide dough in half; shape each portion into a 10- x 3-inch log on lightly greased baking sheets. (Dough will be sticky. Shape dough with floured hands, if necessary.)
• Bake at 350° for 25 to 30 minutes or until lightly browned. Cool slightly; cut diagonally into ¾-inch-thick slices.
• Combine remaining ½ cup sugar and cinnamon; sprinkle over slices. Bake 5 more minutes; cool completely on wire racks. Yield: 36 servings.

Orange-Pecan Biscotti

Prep: 10 min. **Cook:** 55 min. **Other:** 35 min.

4 large eggs
1 cup sugar
1½ tablespoons grated orange
   rind
2 tablespoons vegetable oil

1 teaspoon vanilla extract
1 teaspoon almond extract
3⅓ cups all-purpose flour
2 teaspoons baking powder
1 cup chopped pecans

• Beat eggs and sugar at high speed with an electric mixer for 5 minutes or until foamy. Add orange rind, oil, and extracts, beating until blended.
• Combine flour and baking powder; add to sugar mixture, beating well. Fold in pecans. Cover and freeze 30 minutes or until firm.
• Divide dough in half; shape each portion into an 8- x 5-inch log on a lightly greased baking sheet.
• Bake at 325° for 25 minutes or until firm. Cool on baking sheet 5 minutes. Remove to wire racks to cool.
• Cut each log diagonally into ½-inch-thick slices with a serrated knife, using a gentle sawing motion. Place on greased baking sheets.
• Bake at 325° for 15 minutes. Turn cookies over; bake 15 more minutes. Remove cookies to wire racks to cool. Yield: 2 dozen.

Cocoa-Almond Biscotti

Prep: 30 min.   **Cook:** 44 min.   **Other:** 5 min.

½ cup butter or margarine,
    softened
1 cup sugar
2 large eggs
1½ tablespoons coffee liqueur*
2¼ cups all-purpose flour

1½ teaspoons baking powder
¼ teaspoon salt
1½ tablespoons cocoa
1 (6-ounce) can whole almonds
    (1 cup)

• Combine butter and sugar in a large bowl; beat at medium speed with an electric mixer until light and fluffy. Add eggs, beating well. Mix in liqueur.
• Combine flour and next 3 ingredients; add to butter mixture, beating well. Stir in almonds.
• Divide dough in half; shape each portion into a 9- x 2-inch log on a greased baking sheet.
• Bake at 350° for 30 minutes or until firm. Cool on baking sheet 5 minutes. Remove to wire racks to cool completely.
• Cut each log diagonally into ½-inch-thick slices with a serrated knife, using a gentle sawing motion. Place on ungreased baking sheets.
• Bake at 350° for 5 to 7 minutes. Turn cookies over; bake 5 to 7 more minutes. Remove to wire racks to cool. Yield: 2½ dozen.

*Substitute 1½ tablespoons chocolate syrup for liqueur, if desired.

Spoon Rolls

Prep: 10 min.   **Cook:** 20 min.   **Other:** 5 min.

1 (¼-ounce) envelope active
    dry yeast
2 cups warm water (100° to
    110°)
4 cups self-rising flour

¼ cup sugar
¾ cup butter or margarine,
    melted
1 large egg, lightly beaten

• Combine yeast and 2 cups warm water in a large bowl; let mixture stand 5 minutes.
• Stir in flour and remaining ingredients until blended. Spoon into well-greased cast-iron muffin pans, filling two-thirds full, or into well-greased cast-iron drop biscuit pans, filling half full.
• Bake at 400° for 20 minutes or until rolls are golden brown. Yield: 14 rolls.

Note: Unused batter may be stored in an airtight container in the refrigerator for up to 1 week.

Spoon Rolls

Oatmeal Dinner Rolls

Prep: 15 min.   **Cook:** 15 min.   **Other:** 1 hr., 35 min.

These dinnertime delights yield a lightly sweet flavor from brown sugar.

2 cups water
1 cup quick-cooking oats
3 tablespoons butter or
    margarine
2 (¼-ounce) envelopes active
    dry yeast
½ cup warm water (100° to
    110°)

1 tablespoon granulated sugar
4 cups all-purpose flour
1½ teaspoons salt
⅓ cup firmly packed brown
    sugar

• Bring 2 cups water to a boil in a medium saucepan; stir in oats and butter. Boil, stirring constantly, 1 minute. Remove from heat; let cool to 110°.

• Stir together yeast, ½ cup warm water, and 1 tablespoon granulated sugar in a 2-cup measuring cup; let stand 5 minutes.

• Beat oat mixture, yeast mixture, flour, salt, and brown sugar at medium speed with an electric mixer until smooth.

• Turn dough out onto a lightly floured surface; knead until smooth and elastic (about 5 minutes). Place in a well-greased bowl, turning to grease top.

• Cover and let rise in a warm place (85°), free from drafts, 1 hour or until doubled in bulk.

• Punch dough down, and divide in half; shape each portion into 16 (1½-inch) balls. Place evenly into 2 lightly greased 9- x 1¾-inch round cakepans.

• Cover and let rise in a warm place, free from drafts, 30 minutes or until doubled in bulk.

• Bake at 375° for 15 minutes or until golden brown. Yield: 32 rolls.

Two-Seed Bread Knots

Prep: 30 min.   **Cook:** 17 min.   **Other:** 25 min.

These savory bread knots offer a showy presentation with sprinklings of sesame and poppy seeds.

1 (¼-ounce) envelope
   rapid-rise yeast
1 cup warm water (100° to
   110°)
3½ cups bread flour
2 tablespoons sugar

1½ teaspoons salt
3 tablespoons olive oil
1 egg yolk
1 tablespoon water
1 tablespoon sesame seeds
1 teaspoon poppy seeds

• Preheat oven to 200°. Combine yeast and 1 cup warm water in a 1-cup liquid measuring cup; let mixture stand 5 minutes.
• Combine flour, sugar, and salt in a heavy-duty mixing bowl. Add yeast mixture and oil. Beat at low speed with an electric mixer 1 minute; beat at medium speed 5 minutes.
• Divide dough into 20 equal portions. Shape each portion into a 7-inch rope, and shape into a knot.
• Combine egg yolk and 1 tablespoon water; brush over rolls. Sprinkle with seeds; place on parchment paper-lined baking sheets.
• Turn oven off, cover rolls loosely with plastic wrap; place in oven, and let rise 15 to 20 minutes or until doubled in bulk. Remove from oven, and preheat oven to 400°. Discard plastic wrap.
• Bake at 400° for 15 to 17 minutes or until golden. Yield: 20 rolls.

KITCHEN COMFORT
★ ★ ★ ★ ★

Cooks Chat

"Excellent recipe that only requires the dough to rise for 20 minutes. This makes a great recipe for any night of the week. I made honey butter to accompany these."

Anillos

Prep: 20 min. **Cook:** 15 min. **Other:** 25 min.

These airy jelly-filled breads are probably the closest thing we know to baked doughnuts.

1 (¼-ounce) envelope active
   dry yeast
1 cup warm water (100° to
   110°)
½ cup granulated sugar, divided
5 cups bread flour

2 large eggs
6 tablespoons shortening
¼ teaspoon salt
¾ cup strawberry preserves
1 cup powdered sugar
⅓ cup water

• Stir together yeast, 1 cup warm water, and 2 tablespoons sugar in a 2-cup liquid measuring cup; let stand 5 minutes.
• Stir together remaining 6 tablespoons sugar, flour, and next 3 ingredients in bowl of a heavy-duty electric stand mixer. Add yeast mixture, and beat at medium speed with mixer, using dough hook attachment, 6 minutes.
• Divide dough into 12 equal portions; shape into balls, and place on 2 lightly greased baking sheets (6 balls per baking sheet). Flatten to 4-inch-wide circles with hand; press thumb in center of each circle to make an indentation (about the size of a quarter). Spoon 1 tablespoon preserves in each indentation.
• Cover and let stand in a warm place (85°), free from drafts, 20 minutes (dough will not double in bulk).
• Bake at 375° for 13 to 15 minutes or until golden brown. Cool on baking sheets on wire racks. Stir together powdered sugar and ⅓ cup water; drizzle evenly over breads. Yield: 1 dozen.

main dishes

★★★★★

Sit down to home-cooked bliss with this bounty of entrées ranging from meat to chicken to seafood.

Peppery Chicken Fried Chicken, page 208

Grilled Flank Steak

Prep: 10 min.   **Cook:** 14 min.   **Other:** 8 hrs., 5 min.

2 tablespoons dry red wine
1 tablespoon red wine vinegar
1 tablespoon prepared
   horseradish
1 tablespoon ketchup

1 teaspoon dried thyme leaves
1 teaspoon minced garlic
½ teaspoon pepper
2 pounds flank steak

• Combine first 7 ingredients in a shallow dish or zip-top freezer bag; add steak. Cover or seal, and chill 8 hours, turning occasionally.
• Remove steak from marinade, discarding marinade.
• Grill, covered with grill lid, over high heat (400° to 500°) about 7 minutes on each side or to desired degree of doneness. Let stand 5 minutes. Cut steak diagonally across the grain into thin slices. Yield: 6 servings.

Cilantro-Garlic Sirloin with Zesty Corn Salsa

Prep: 15 min.   **Cook:** 24 min.   **Other:** 2 hrs., 10 min.

1 cup (1 bunch) fresh cilantro,
   packed
2 garlic cloves
3 tablespoons fresh lime juice
1 tablespoon grated lime rind
½ teaspoon salt
½ teaspoon ground cumin

¼ to ½ teaspoon ground red
   pepper
2 pounds top sirloin steak
   (1¼ inches thick)
Zesty Corn Salsa
Garnish: fresh cilantro sprig

• Process first 7 ingredients in a food processor or blender until blended, and rub cilantro mixture over sirloin steak. Chill 2 hours.
• Grill, covered with grill lid, over medium-high heat (350° to 400°) 10 to 12 minutes on each side or to desired degree of doneness. Let stand 10 minutes.
• Cut steak diagonally across the grain into thin slices. Serve with Zesty Corn Salsa. Garnish, if desired. Yield: 8 servings.

Zesty Corn Salsa

Prep: 15 min.　**Cook:** 20 min.

6 ears fresh corn, husks
  removed
¼ cup fresh lime juice
2 teaspoons olive oil

½ teaspoon grated lime rind
1 small jalapeño pepper, minced
¼ teaspoon salt
¼ teaspoon ground cumin

• Grill corn, covered with grill lid, over medium-high heat
(350° to 400°) 10 minutes on each side or until browned on all
sides. Remove from grill; cool.
• Cut corn from cob into a bowl; stir in juice and remaining
ingredients. Yield: 2 cups (about 8 servings).

Cooks Chat

"My daughter, Katie, made this for my 50th birthday dinner. What a wonderful gift! The tenderloin was fabulously flavored, and the recipe proved to be cook-friendly. Thanks to Katie and Southern Living *for making my 50th memorable!"*

"This was one of the best beef tenderloin recipes that I have tried. It was absolutely delicious."

"This is a great recipe—everyone really loves it."

Beef Tenderloin in Wine Sauce

Prep: 20 min.   **Cook:** 35 min.   **Other:** 10 min.

1 (3-pound) beef tenderloin
½ teaspoon salt
½ teaspoon pepper
½ cup butter or margarine
1 onion, thinly sliced
1 garlic clove, minced
1 (8-ounce) package sliced fresh mushrooms
½ cup dry red wine
1 teaspoon Italian seasoning
1 teaspoon hot sauce
1½ teaspoons Worcestershire sauce
1 cup beef broth
1 teaspoon all-purpose flour

• Sprinkle beef evenly with salt and pepper. Place in an aluminum foil-lined roasting pan.
• Bake at 450° for 15 minutes.
• Meanwhile, melt butter in a medium saucepan over medium heat. Add onion, garlic, and mushrooms. Cook, stirring often, 7 minutes. Stir in wine and next 3 ingredients. Whisk together beef broth and all-purpose flour, and stir into wine mixture. Reduce heat, and simmer, stirring occasionally, 10 minutes or until onion is tender.
• Remove beef from oven, and top with sauce. Bake beef 18 more minutes or until a meat thermometer registers 145° (medium rare) or 160° (medium), basting once. Transfer beef to a serving platter, reserving sauce in pan. Let beef stand 10 minutes before slicing. Serve with sauce. Yield: 6 to 8 servings.

Garlic-and-Rosemary Beef Tenderloin

Prep: 10 min.   **Cook:** 35 min.   **Other:** 8 hrs., 40 min.

½ cup soy sauce
½ cup olive oil
¼ cup balsamic or red wine
    vinegar
8 garlic cloves, minced

4 teaspoons dried rosemary
1 (5-pound) beef tenderloin,
    trimmed
1 tablespoon pepper

• Combine first 5 ingredients in a large shallow dish or zip-top freezer bag; add beef. Cover or seal, and chill at least 8 hours, turning occasionally.
• Remove beef from marinade, discarding marinade. Place in a roasting pan; sprinkle evenly with pepper, and let stand 30 minutes.
• Bake at 500° for 15 minutes or until lightly browned. Reduce temperature to 375°; bake 20 more minutes or until a meat thermometer registers 145° (medium rare) or 160° (medium). Let tenderloin stand 10 minutes before slicing. Yield: 8 to 10 servings.

Fillet of Beef with Red Pepper Butter

Prep: 10 min.   **Cook:** 13 min.   **Other:** 1 hr.

⅓ cup butter, softened
¼ cup finely chopped red bell
    pepper
¾ teaspoon seasoned salt

¼ to ½ teaspoon ground red
    pepper
2 (2½-inch-thick) beef
    tenderloin fillets

• Combine first 4 ingredients, stirring well. Shape into 4 (2-inch) rounds on a wax paper-lined baking sheet; cover and refrigerate 1 hour or until firm.
• Place beef tenderloin fillets on a rack in a broiler pan.
• Broil 6 inches from heat 6 minutes. Turn fillets over, and top each with a butter round.
• Broil 6 to 7 minutes or until a meat thermometer registers 145° (medium rare) or 160° (medium), or to desired degree of doneness. Turn fillets over, and transfer to a serving platter; top with remaining butter rounds. Yield: 2 servings.

Steaks with Caramel-Brandy Sauce

Prep: 5 min.   **Cook:** 10 min.

This recipe cooks the steaks to medium-rare doneness. Lower the temperature and increase cook time for more well-done steaks.

4 (6-ounce) beef tenderloin
  fillets
1 teaspoon salt
1 teaspoon pepper
3 tablespoons butter, divided

3 tablespoons brandy
1 tablespoon light brown sugar
¼ cup whipping cream
Garnish: fresh chives

• Sprinkle steaks evenly with salt and pepper.
• Melt 1 tablespoon butter in a medium skillet over medium-high heat. Add steaks, and cook 3 minutes on each side or to desired degree of doneness. Remove steaks from skillet, and keep warm.
• Add brandy to skillet, stirring to loosen particles from bottom of skillet. Add remaining 2 tablespoons butter and sugar; cook, stirring constantly, until sugar dissolves and browns.
• Remove skillet from heat; whisk in cream until blended. Return to heat, and bring to a boil; cook, stirring constantly, 1 minute or until thickened. Serve immediately over steaks. Garnish, if desired. Yield: 4 servings.

Rosemary Rib Roast

Prep: 10 min.   **Cook:** 1 hr., 35 min.   **Other:** 50 min.

Prime rib is often on sale around the holidays, so it's a fairly economical choice. Have the butcher remove the chine bone and then tie it back on—this will give you the flavor from the bone but allow you to easily remove it for carving.

6 garlic cloves, pressed
2 teaspoons salt
2 teaspoons pepper
1 teaspoon crushed rosemary
2 tablespoons olive oil

1 (7-pound) 4-rib prime rib
   roast, chine bone removed
1 cup sour cream
2 tablespoons lemon juice
2 tablespoons horseradish

• Combine first 5 ingredients in a small bowl; rub over roast. Let stand at room temperature 30 minutes.
• Bake roast at 450° for 45 minutes on lower rack of oven. Reduce temperature to 350°; bake roast 45 to 50 additional minutes or until a meat thermometer registers 145° (medium rare) or 160° (medium). Let roast stand 20 minutes.
• Combine sour cream, lemon juice, and horseradish; serve with roast. Yield: 8 servings.

Italian Pot Roast

Prep: 35 min. **Cook:** 3 hrs., 30 min.

To make ahead, chill baked roast overnight. Cut into thin
slices, and place in a 13- x 9-inch baking dish. Top with gravy.
Bake at 350° for 30 minutes or until thoroughly heated.
Serve with roasted potatoes.

1 (4½-pound) rib-eye roast,
    trimmed*
2 tablespoons vegetable oil
1 (15-ounce) can tomato sauce
½ cup red wine
2 large tomatoes, chopped
1 medium onion, minced
4 garlic cloves, minced
1 tablespoon salt
1 tablespoon pepper
2 teaspoons chopped fresh or
    1 teaspoon dried basil

2 teaspoons chopped fresh or
    1 teaspoon dried oregano
1 (16-ounce) package red
    potatoes, cut into wedges
½ teaspoon salt
¼ teaspoon pepper
3 tablespoons all-purpose flour
1 cup beef broth or water
Garnish: chopped fresh parsley

• Cook roast in hot oil in a large Dutch oven over medium-high
heat 5 to 6 minutes or until browned on all sides.
• Combine tomato sauce and next 8 ingredients; pour sauce
mixture over roast in Dutch oven.
• Bake, covered, at 325° for 3 hours or until roast is tender.
Remove roast from Dutch oven, and keep warm; reserve drippings
in Dutch oven.
• Place potato wedges in a lightly greased 15- x 10-inch jellyroll
pan. Bake at 450° for 30 minutes. Sprinkle with ½ teaspoon salt
and ¼ teaspoon pepper.
• Skim fat from drippings in Dutch oven. Whisk together flour and
beef broth until smooth; add to drippings. Cook mixture, stirring
constantly, over low heat 8 minutes or until thickened.
• Cut roast into thin slices. Arrange roast and potatoes on a serving
platter. Garnish, if desired. Serve with tomato gravy. Yield: 6 to
8 servings.

*Substitute 1 (4½-pound) boneless beef rump roast, trimmed,
for rib-eye roast, if desired. Bake, covered, at 325° for 2 hours and
20 minutes or until tender.

MAKE AHEAD

Cooks Chat

*"I served this at a party for eight,
and everyone thought it was delicious. I used a 5½-pound rib roast,
and it was the perfect amount. This
dish can be kept warm while your
guests are enjoying appetizers—a
nice plus."*

Smoky Barbecue Brisket

Prep: 10 min.   **Cook:** 6 hrs.   **Other:** 8 hrs.

This is even better if it stays in your refrigerator a day after cooking to absorb the flavors. Slice and reheat in the oven or microwave.

1 (4- to 6-pound) beef brisket, trimmed
1 (5-ounce) bottle liquid smoke
1 onion, chopped
2 teaspoons garlic salt
1 to 2 teaspoons salt
⅓ cup Worcestershire sauce
1 (12- to 18-ounce) bottle barbecue sauce

• Place brisket in a large shallow dish or extra-large zip-top freezer bag; pour liquid smoke over brisket. Sprinkle evenly with onion, garlic salt, and salt. Cover or seal, and chill 8 hours, turning occasionally.
• Remove brisket, and place on a large piece of heavy-duty aluminum foil, discarding liquid smoke mixture. Pour Worcestershire sauce evenly over brisket, and fold foil to seal; place wrapped brisket in a roasting pan.
• Bake at 275° for 5 hours. Unfold foil; pour barbecue sauce evenly over brisket. Bake 1 more hour, uncovered. Yield: 8 servings.

Baby Loin Back Ribs

Prep: 20 min.   **Cook:** 2 hrs., 30 min.   **Other:** 3 hrs.

2 slabs baby loin back ribs (about 4 pounds)
3 tablespoons Dry Spices
1 cup Basting Sauce
1 cup Sweet Sauce

• Place ribs in a large shallow pan. Rub Dry Spices evenly over ribs. Cover and chill 3 hours.
• Prepare a hot fire by piling charcoal or lava rocks on 1 side of grill, leaving other side empty. (For gas grill, light only 1 side.) Place food rack on grill. Arrange ribs over unlit side.
• Grill ribs, covered with grill lid, over medium heat (300° to 350°) for 2 to 2½ hours, basting every 30 minutes with Basting Sauce and turning occasionally. Brush ribs with Sweet Sauce the last 30 minutes. Yield: 3 to 4 servings.

Note: Use remaining Dry Spices as a rub on pork or chicken.

Dry Spices

Prep: 5 min.

3 tablespoons paprika
2 teaspoons seasoned salt
2 teaspoons garlic powder
2 teaspoons ground black
    pepper

1 teaspoon dry mustard
1 teaspoon ground oregano
1 teaspoon ground red pepper
½ teaspoon chili powder

• Combine all ingredients in a small bowl. Yield: 6½ tablespoons.

Basting Sauce

Prep: 5 min.　**Other:** 8 hrs.

¼ cup firmly packed brown
    sugar
1½ tablespoons Dry Spices
2 cups red wine vinegar

2 cups water
¼ cup Worcestershire sauce
½ teaspoon hot sauce
1 small bay leaf

• Stir together all ingredients; cover and let stand 8 hours. Remove bay leaf. (Sauce is intended for basting ribs only.) Yield: 4½ cups.

Sweet Sauce

Prep: 10 min.　**Cook:** 30 min.

1 cup ketchup
1 cup red wine vinegar
1 (8-ounce) can tomato sauce
½ cup spicy honey mustard
½ cup Worcestershire sauce
¼ cup butter or margarine
2 tablespoons brown sugar
2 tablespoons hot sauce

1 tablespoon seasoned salt
1 tablespoon paprika
1 tablespoon lemon juice
1½ teaspoons garlic powder
⅛ teaspoon chili powder
⅛ teaspoon ground red pepper
⅛ teaspoon ground black
    pepper

• Bring all ingredients to a boil in a Dutch oven. Reduce heat, and simmer sauce, stirring occasionally, 30 minutes. Yield: 1 quart.

Baked Meatballs

Prep: 20 min.   **Cook:** 30 min.

Make these ahead and then freeze them for superfast meatballs anytime. They're also great as appetizers and in sandwiches.

1½ pounds ground beef
1 large egg, lightly beaten
¾ cup quick-cooking oats, uncooked
¾ cup milk
1 teaspoon salt

1 teaspoon Italian seasoning
¼ teaspoon pepper
3 tablespoons all-purpose flour
1½ teaspoons paprika
½ teaspoon salt

• Combine first 7 ingredients; shape into 1-inch balls.
• Combine all-purpose flour, paprika, and salt. Gently roll meatballs in flour mixture, and place on a lightly greased rack in a foil-lined 13- x 9-inch pan.
• Bake at 400° for 25 to 30 minutes. Drain on paper towels. Serve with your favorite sauce. Yield: 4 dozen.

Note: To freeze, cool completely, and seal in an airtight container. To serve, place in a single layer on a baking sheet; bake at 400° for 10 to 15 minutes.

Baked Linguine with Meat Sauce

Prep: 40 min.   **Cook:** 30 min.   **Other:** 5 min.

2 pounds lean ground beef
2 garlic cloves, minced
1 (28-ounce) can crushed tomatoes
1 (8-ounce) can tomato sauce
1 (6-ounce) can tomato paste
2 teaspoons sugar
1 teaspoon salt

8 ounces uncooked linguine
1 (16-ounce) container sour cream
1 (8-ounce) package cream cheese, softened
1 bunch green onions, chopped
2 cups (8 ounces) shredded sharp Cheddar cheese

• Cook beef and garlic in a Dutch oven, stirring until beef crumbles and is no longer pink. Stir in tomatoes and next 4 ingredients; simmer 30 minutes. Set mixture aside.

• Cook pasta according to package directions; drain. Place pasta in a lightly greased 13- x 9-inch baking dish.
• Stir together sour cream, cream cheese, and green onions. Spread over pasta. Top with meat sauce.
• Bake at 350° for 20 to 25 minutes or until thoroughly heated. Sprinkle with Cheddar cheese, and bake 5 more minutes or until cheese melts. Let stand 5 minutes. Serve with a salad and bread, if desired. Yield: 8 servings.

Note: To lighten dish, use no-salt-added tomato products, light sour cream, light cream cheese, and reduced-fat Cheddar cheese.

Baked Linguine with Meat Sauce

Pork Chops with Caramelized Onions and Peppers

Prep: 20 min. **Cook:** 1 hr.

It's easy to caramelize onions: Simply stir onion slices over medium heat in a skillet until the natural sugars in them turn golden brown.

¼ cup butter or margarine
3 medium onions, thinly sliced
2 tablespoons bourbon (optional)
1 (15-ounce) jar roasted red bell peppers, drained and chopped
1 teaspoon fresh thyme, chopped

½ teaspoon salt, divided
½ teaspoon pepper, divided
6 (1¼-inch-thick) boneless pork loin chops
⅔ cup all-purpose flour
2 tablespoons butter or margarine
½ cup chicken broth

• Melt ¼ cup butter in a large skillet over medium heat; add onions, and sauté 15 minutes or until golden and tender. Add bourbon, if desired, and stir occasionally 5 minutes or until onions caramelize or begin to turn golden brown. Remove from heat; stir in red peppers, thyme, ¼ teaspoon salt, and ¼ teaspoon pepper.
• Remove mixture from skillet, and set aside.
• Sprinkle pork chops with remaining salt and pepper; dredge in flour.
• Melt 2 tablespoons butter in skillet over medium-high heat; add pork chops, and cook 4 minutes on each side or until browned. Remove from skillet, and place in a lightly greased 13- x 9-inch baking dish.
• Add chicken broth to skillet, and cook over high heat 2 minutes, stirring to loosen particles from bottom of skillet. Spoon onion mixture and remaining pan juices over meat.
• Bake, covered, at 375° for 25 to 30 minutes. Yield: 6 servings.

Note: For testing purposes only, we used Woodford Reserve Distiller's Select Bourbon.

Pork Chops and Gravy

Prep: 8 min.   **Cook:** 2 hrs., 30 min.

½ cup all-purpose flour
1½ teaspoons dry mustard
½ teaspoon salt
½ teaspoon garlic powder
6 (1-inch-thick) lean pork
    chops

1 (10½-ounce) can condensed
    chicken broth, undiluted
2 tablespoons vegetable oil

• Combine first 4 ingredients in a shallow dish; dredge chops in flour mixture, and set aside.
• Combine remaining flour mixture and chicken broth in a 3½-quart electric slow cooker.
• Pour oil into a large skillet; place over medium-high heat until hot. Cook chops in hot oil just until browned on both sides; place in slow cooker.
• Cover and cook at HIGH 2 to 2½ hours or until tender. Serve with hot rice or mashed potatoes. Yield: 6 servings.

Garlic-Parmesan Pork Chops

Prep: 5 min.   **Cook:** 37 min.

6 (½-inch-thick) boneless pork
    loin chops
½ teaspoon salt
½ teaspoon pepper
¼ cup milk
2 tablespoons Dijon mustard
1 cup Italian-seasoned
    breadcrumbs
¼ cup butter or margarine,
    divided

1½ teaspoons bottled minced
    garlic
¾ cup whipping cream
⅓ cup white wine or chicken
    broth
½ cup grated Parmesan cheese

• Sprinkle pork chops evenly with salt and pepper.
• Stir together milk and mustard. Dip pork chops in milk mixture, and dredge in breadcrumbs. Place pork chops on a rack in a broiler pan.
• Bake pork chops at 375° for 30 minutes or until done.
• Melt 1 tablespoon butter in a saucepan over medium-high heat; add garlic, and sauté 2 to 3 minutes. Stir in cream, wine, and cheese; reduce heat, and simmer 3 to 4 minutes (do not boil). Whisk in remaining 3 tablespoons butter until melted. Serve with chops. Yield: 4 to 6 servings.

Slow-Roasted Pork

Prep: 15 min.   **Cook:** 7 hrs.   **Other:** 4 hrs.

Serve this tender shredded pork over Caribbean Rice and Peas (page 321).

1 medium onion, finely chopped
4 garlic cloves, peeled and crushed
½ cup fresh orange juice
½ cup fresh grapefruit juice
⅓ cup fresh lemon juice
2 tablespoons brown sugar
3 bay leaves, crumbled
2 teaspoons salt
2 teaspoons chili powder
1 teaspoon ground allspice
1 teaspoon ground black pepper
1 (5- to 6-pound) Boston butt pork roast or pork shoulder
1 tablespoon vegetable oil
Garnishes: lemon slices, grated lemon rind, fresh parsley sprigs

• Combine first 11 ingredients in a large bowl. Add pork roast, turning to coat with marinade. Cover and refrigerate roast at least 4 hours or overnight.
• Remove roast from marinade, reserving marinade. Brown all sides of roast in hot oil in a Dutch oven. Add reserved marinade.
• Bake, covered, at 275° for 6 to 7 hours or until meat can be shredded. Garnish, if desired. Yield: 8 servings.

PARTY PLEASER

Cooks Chat

"This pork was very moist and flavorful. Great with Caribbean Rice and Peas. Excellent!"

Orange-Cranberry Glazed Pork Tenderloins

Prep: 35 min.   **Cook:** 40 min.

Prepare cranberry basting sauce up to
8 hours ahead, and chill.

1 (16-ounce) can whole-berry cranberry sauce
1 teaspoon grated orange rind
⅔ cup fresh orange juice
2 teaspoons balsamic vinegar
½ teaspoon pepper
¼ teaspoon ground allspice
⅛ teaspoon salt
⅛ teaspoon ground cinnamon
⅛ teaspoon ground cloves
1½ pounds pork tenderloins, trimmed
Garnishes: fresh rosemary sprigs, whole cranberries

• Bring first 9 ingredients to a boil in a large saucepan. Reduce heat, and simmer mixture, stirring occasionally, 20 minutes.
• Place pork in a lightly greased shallow roasting pan.
• Bake at 425° for 40 minutes or until a meat thermometer inserted into thickest portion registers 160°, basting occasionally with half of cranberry mixture. Slice pork; serve with remaining cranberry mixture. Garnish, if desired. Yield: 6 servings.

Honey-Garlic Pork Tenderloin

Prep: 5 min.   **Cook:** 26 min.   **Other:** 1 hr.

6 tablespoons lemon juice
6 tablespoons honey
2½ tablespoons soy sauce
1½ tablespoons dry sherry or chicken broth
3 garlic cloves, pressed
¾ pound pork tenderloin

• Stir together first 5 ingredients in a shallow dish or zip-top freezer bag; remove ½ cup mixture, and set aside. Prick pork several times with a fork, and place in remaining mixture. Cover or seal, and chill 1 hour.
• Remove pork, discarding marinade.
• Grill pork, covered with grill lid, over medium heat (300° to 350°) 11 to 13 minutes on each side or until a meat thermometer inserted into thickest portion registers 160°, basting with reserved ½ cup mixture. Yield: 2 servings.

Note: To serve 4, double all ingredients, and proceed as directed.

Festive Pork Roast

Prep: 30 min.   **Cook:** 2 hrs., 30 min.   **Other:** 8 hrs., 10 min.

A blend of Asian spices, red wine, and sugar create a
delectable taste bud sensation.

1½ cups dry red wine
⅔ cup firmly packed brown
    sugar
½ cup ketchup
½ cup water
¼ cup vegetable oil
4 garlic cloves, minced

3 tablespoons soy sauce
2 teaspoons curry powder
1 teaspoon ground ginger
½ teaspoon pepper
1 (5-pound) boneless rolled
    pork roast
4 teaspoons cornstarch

• Combine first 10 ingredients in a large shallow dish or zip-top
freezer bag; add pork. Cover or seal, and chill 8 hours, turning
occasionally.
• Remove pork from marinade, reserving 2½ cups marinade.
Bring reserved marinade to a boil in a small saucepan; whisk in
cornstarch, and cook, stirring constantly, 2 to 3 minutes or until
thickened. Cool.
• Pat pork dry, and place on a rack in a shallow roasting pan.
• Bake pork at 325° for 2½ hours or until a meat thermometer
inserted into thickest portion registers 170°, basting with ¼ cup
reserved sauce during the last 15 minutes. Allow roast to stand
10 minutes before slicing. Serve with reserved sauce. Yield: 8 to
10 servings.

"My family loves this recipe, especially the Gingered Jezebel Sauce. It's easy enough for everyday but elegant enough for company."

Grilled Pork Tenderloin with Gingered Jezebel Sauce

Prep: 5 min.   **Cook:** 25 min.   **Other:** 30 min.

½ cup lite soy sauce
2 tablespoons dark brown sugar
2 green onions, chopped
2 tablespoons sherry (optional)

3 pounds pork tenderloins
Gingered Jezebel Sauce
Garnish: fresh rosemary

• Combine first 3 ingredients and, if desired, sherry in a shallow dish or large zip-top freezer bag; add pork. Cover or seal, and chill 20 minutes.
• Remove pork from marinade, discarding marinade. Grill pork, covered with grill lid, over medium-high heat (350° to 400°) 25 minutes or until a meat thermometer inserted into thickest portion registers 155°, turning once and basting with ½ cup Gingered Jezebel Sauce the last 5 to 10 minutes. Let stand 10 minutes or until thermometer registers 160°. Slice and serve with remaining ¾ cup Gingered Jezebel Sauce. Garnish, if desired. Yield: 6 servings.

Gingered Jezebel Sauce

Prep: 5 min.   **Cook:** 2 min.

Ginger replaces dry mustard in this version of Jezebel sauce.

⅔ cup pineapple preserves
⅓ cup apple jelly
2 tablespoons prepared
    horseradish

1 tablespoon grated fresh ginger

• Microwave pineapple preserves and apple jelly in a glass bowl at HIGH 2 minutes or until melted. Stir in remaining ingredients. Yield: 1¼ cups.

Baked Glazed Ham

Prep: 10 min.   **Cook:** 1 hr., 30 min.   **Other:** 15 min.

By preparing this ham at the beginning of the month, you'll have enough left over to use in two casserole recipes and two sandwich recipes.

2 tablespoons sugar
1 tablespoon paprika
1 tablespoon chili powder
1 teaspoon ground cumin
¾ teaspoon ground cinnamon
½ teaspoon ground cloves
1 (8-pound) smoked fully
    cooked ham half, trimmed
1 (12-ounce) can cola soft
    drink
1 (8-ounce) jar plum or apricot
    preserves
⅓ cup orange juice

• Combine first 6 ingredients. Score fat on ham in a diamond pattern. Sprinkle ham with sugar mixture, and place in a lightly greased shallow roasting pan. Pour cola into pan.
• Bake, covered, at 325° for 1 hour. Uncover and bake 15 more minutes.
• Stir together preserves and orange juice. Spoon ¾ cup glaze over ham, and bake 15 more minutes or until a meat thermometer inserted into thickest portion registers 140°. Let stand 15 minutes before slicing. Serve with remaining glaze. Yield: 16 servings.

Asian Pork Tenderloin

Prep: 20 min.   **Cook:** 25 min.   **Other:** 8 hrs., 5 min.

⅓ cup packed light brown
    sugar
⅓ cup lite soy sauce
¼ cup sesame oil
2 tablespoons Worcestershire
    sauce
2 tablespoons lemon juice
4 garlic cloves, crushed
1 tablespoon dry mustard
1½ teaspoons pepper
1½ to 2 pounds pork
    tenderloin

• Whisk together first 8 ingredients. Place pork in a shallow dish; add marinade, turning pork to coat. Cover and chill 8 hours. Remove pork from marinade, discarding marinade. Place in a foil-lined roasting pan.
• Bake at 450° for 25 minutes or until a meat thermometer registers 160°. Let pork stand 5 minutes. Yield: 6 servings.

Tandoori Chicken

Prep: 20 min.　**Cook:** 35 min.　**Other:** 8 hrs.

This spicy chicken dish calls for quite a few ingredients, but it's well worth it. High-heat roasting makes for a short cooking time.

6 tablespoons fresh lime juice (about 3 limes)
3 tablespoons plain yogurt
1 to 2 small jalapeño or serrano chile peppers, seeded and minced
1½ teaspoons salt
1 teaspoon ground turmeric
1 teaspoon ground coriander
1 teaspoon ground cumin
½ teaspoon ground ginger

½ teaspoon garlic powder
½ teaspoon ground red pepper
¼ teaspoon ground cinnamon
¼ teaspoon ground cloves
2 tablespoons vegetable oil, divided
3 pounds mixed chicken pieces
Garnishes: lime wedges, jalapeño or serrano chile peppers

• Stir together first 12 ingredients and 1 tablespoon vegetable oil in a large bowl until blended.
• Skin chicken breasts. Remove breast bones by inserting a sharp knife tip between bone and meat, cutting gently to remove as much meat as possible. Cut breasts into thirds. Cut deep slits, 1 inch apart, in remaining chicken pieces (do not skin pieces). Place chicken in a large bowl with spice mixture. Thoroughly rub spice mixture into slits. Cover and chill 8 hours.
• Drizzle remaining 1 tablespoon oil in a large aluminum foil-lined roasting pan. Arrange chicken in a single layer in pan.
• Bake chicken at 450° for 35 minutes or until done.
• Arrange chicken on a serving platter. Garnish, if desired. Yield: 8 servings.

Note: For testing purposes only, we used Butterball Best of the Fryer, a cut-up mix of chicken breasts, thighs, legs, and wings.

Cooks Chat

"Excellent recipe—easy to make and very tasty. This has become a family favorite!"

"This recipe is easy and yummy. My family loves Indian food, and we loved this! I served it with saffron rice."

Cooks Chat

"Simply delicious. Your guests will love this recipe."

"Terrific recipe! The only ingredient I didn't have on hand was plums, and I may consider substituting dried tomatoes next time. Very easy to prepare and a hit with my family and guests—one of them owns a restaurant and asked for the recipe!"

Chicken Marbella

Prep: 10 min.   **Cook:** 1 hr.   **Other:** 8 hrs.

This recipe is always a hit, even with kids. Choose a mixture of everyone's favorite cuts of chicken—such as 1 package each of bone-in breasts, legs, thighs, and wings—or purchase pick-of-the-chick packages or chicken quarters to equal 8 pounds.

1 (12-ounce) package pitted, bite-size dried plums
1 (3.5-ounce) jar capers
1 (0.5-ounce) bottle dried oregano
6 bay leaves
1 garlic bulb, minced (about 1 tablespoon)
1 cup pimiento-stuffed olives

½ cup red wine vinegar
½ cup olive oil
1 tablespoon coarse sea salt
2 teaspoons pepper
8 pounds mixed chicken pieces
1 cup brown sugar
1 cup dry white wine
¼ cup fresh parsley, chopped

- Combine first 10 ingredients in a large zip-top freezer bag or a large bowl. Add chicken pieces, turning to coat well; seal or cover and chill for at least 8 hours (overnight is best), turning chicken occasionally.
- Arrange chicken in a single layer in 1 or 2 (13- x 9-inch) baking pan(s). Pour marinade evenly over chicken, and sprinkle evenly with brown sugar; pour wine around pieces.
- Bake at 350° for 50 minutes to 1 hour, basting frequently.
- Remove chicken, dried plums, olives, and capers to a serving platter. Drizzle with ¾ cup pan juices; sprinkle parsley evenly over top. Serve with remaining pan juices. Yield: 8 to 10 servings.

Mama's Fried Chicken

Prep: 30 min.　**Cook:** 30 min. per batch　**Other:** 2 hrs.

Pair this Southern favorite with Layered Potato Salad (page 122) for the ultimate in traditional comfort food.

1 (3- to 4-pound) whole chicken, cut into pieces	2 cups buttermilk Self-rising flour
1 teaspoon salt	Vegetable oil
1 teaspoon pepper	

- Sprinkle chicken with salt and pepper. Place chicken in a shallow dish or zip-top freezer bag, and add buttermilk. Cover or seal, and chill at least 2 hours.
- Remove chicken from buttermilk, discarding buttermilk. Dredge chicken in flour.
- Pour oil to a depth of 1½ inches into a deep skillet or Dutch oven; heat to 360°. Add chicken, a few pieces at a time; cover and cook 6 minutes. Uncover chicken; cook 9 minutes. Turn chicken; cover and cook 6 minutes. Uncover and cook 5 to 9 minutes, turning chicken the last 3 minutes for even browning, if necessary. Drain on paper towels. Yield: 4 to 6 servings.

SOUTHERN CLASSIC

Cooks Chat

"This chicken is tender and juicy on the inside and crunchy on the outside. It truly has a down-home taste. This recipe is ideal for family reunions or just as a Sunday dish."

"This is a wonderful Southern-style recipe. All my loved ones enjoyed it."

Buttermilk Baked Chicken

Prep: 10 min.　　**Cook:** 45 min.

¼ cup butter or margarine*
4 bone-in chicken breasts, skinned
½ teaspoon salt
½ teaspoon pepper
1½ cups buttermilk, divided*

¾ cup all-purpose flour
1 (10¾-ounce) can cream of mushroom soup, undiluted*
Hot cooked rice

• Melt butter in a lightly greased 13- x 9-inch baking dish in a 425° oven.
• Sprinkle chicken with salt and pepper. Dip chicken in ½ cup buttermilk, and dredge in flour. Arrange chicken, breast side down, in dish.
• Bake at 425° for 25 minutes. Turn chicken, and bake 10 more minutes. Stir together remaining 1 cup buttermilk and soup; pour over chicken, and bake 10 more minutes, shielding with aluminum foil to prevent excessive browning, if necessary. Serve over rice. Yield: 4 servings.

*Substitute light butter; nonfat buttermilk; and reduced-sodium, reduced-fat cream of mushroom soup, if desired.

Cola-Can Chicken

Prep: 20 min.　　**Cook:** 1 hr., 15 min.　　**Other:** 5 min.

The cola can serves as a poultry rack to hold the chicken upright, and the cola left in the can moistens the chicken from the inside out as it grills.

2 tablespoons Barbecue Rub, divided
1 (3½- to 4-pound) whole chicken

3 tablespoons vegetable oil
1 (12-ounce) can cola soft drink
Cola Barbecue Sauce

• Sprinkle 1 teaspoon Barbecue Rub inside body cavity and ½ tea-spoon inside neck cavity of chicken.
• Rub oil over skin. Sprinkle with 1 tablespoon Barbecue Rub, and rub over skin.
• Pour out ¾ cup of cola, and reserve for Cola Barbecue Sauce, leaving remaining cola in can. Make 2 additional holes in top of can. Spoon remaining 1½ teaspoons rub into cola can. Cola will start to foam.

- Place chicken upright onto cola can, fitting can into cavity. Pull legs forward to form a tripod, allowing chicken to stand upright.
- Prepare a hot fire by piling charcoal or lava rocks on 1 side of grill, leaving other side empty. (For gas grills, light only 1 side.) Place a drip pan on unlit side, and place food rack on grill. Place chicken upright over drip pan. Grill, covered with grill lid, 1 hour and 15 minutes or until golden and a meat thermometer inserted in meaty part of thigh registers 180°.
- Remove chicken from grill; let stand 5 minutes. Carefully remove can. Serve with Cola Barbecue Sauce. Yield: 2 to 4 servings.

Barbecue Rub

Prep: 5 min.

"This rub makes the best baby back ribs I've ever tasted!"

1 tablespoon mild chili powder	1 teaspoon ground cumin
2 teaspoons salt	½ teaspoon garlic powder
2 teaspoons light brown sugar	¼ teaspoon ground red
1 teaspoon black pepper	pepper

- Combine all ingredients. Yield: 3 tablespoons.

Cola Barbecue Sauce

Prep: 15 min.   Cook: 8 min.

1 tablespoon butter	2 tablespoons fresh lemon juice
½ small onion, minced	2 tablespoons Worcestershire
1 tablespoon minced fresh ginger	sauce
1 garlic clove, minced	2 tablespoons steak sauce
¾ cup reserved cola	½ teaspoon pepper
¾ cup ketchup	½ teaspoon liquid smoke
½ teaspoon grated lemon rind	Salt to taste

- Melt butter in a heavy saucepan over medium heat. Add onion, ginger, and garlic; sauté 3 minutes or until tender.
- Stir in reserved cola; bring mixture to a boil. Stir in ketchup and remaining ingredients; bring to a boil. Reduce heat, and simmer 5 minutes. Yield: about 1½ cups.

Note: For testing purposes only, we used A.1. Steak Sauce.

Chicken in Lemon Marinade

Prep: 15 min. **Cook:** 24 min. **Other:** 2 hrs.

Cooks Chat

"Wow! This marinade was so incredible. I started to grill the chicken, but then decided I would follow the recipe and broil it. That was definitely the right choice. The chicken remained incredibly moist, and broiling made it easy to brown it just as much as I wanted. This is definitely going to be a staple dish in my house. Both of my young children loved it."

⅔ cup vegetable oil
½ cup lemon juice
1 tablespoon Worcestershire sauce
⅛ teaspoon hot sauce
1 small onion, grated
1 teaspoon salt
1 teaspoon pepper
1 teaspoon celery salt
6 skinned and boned chicken breasts
Garnishes: lemon rind strips, parsley

• Process first 8 ingredients in a blender until smooth, stopping to scrape down sides. Reserve ¼ cup lemon mixture, and chill.
• Place chicken in a shallow dish or zip-top freezer bag; pour remaining lemon mixture over chicken. Cover or seal, and chill 2 hours, turning chicken occasionally.
• Remove chicken from marinade, discarding marinade; place chicken on a lightly greased rack in a broiler pan.
• Broil 7 inches from heat 11 to 12 minutes on each side or until tender, basting chicken frequently with reserved ¼ cup lemon mixture. Garnish, if desired. Yield: 6 servings.

Chicken Fingers with Honey-Horseradish Dip

Prep: 25 min. **Cook:** 20 min.

16 saltine crackers, finely
    crushed
¼ cup pecans, toasted and
    ground
½ teaspoon salt
½ teaspoon pepper

2 teaspoons paprika
4 (6-ounce) skinned and boned
    chicken breasts
1 egg white
Honey-Horseradish Dip

• Stir together first 5 ingredients.
• Cut each chicken breast into 4 strips. Whisk egg white until frothy;
dip chicken strips into egg white, and dredge in saltine mixture.
• Place a rack coated with cooking spray in a broiler pan. Coat
chicken strips on each side with cooking spray; arrange on pan.
• Bake at 425° for 18 to 20 minutes or until golden brown. Serve
with Honey-Horseradish Dip. Yield: 8 servings.

Honey-Horseradish Dip

Prep: 5 min.

½ cup plain nonfat yogurt
¼ cup coarse-grained mustard
¼ cup honey

2 tablespoons prepared
    horseradish

• Stir together all ingredients. Yield: 1 cup.

Cooks Chat

*"This is one of the first recipes
everyone in my family loved—from
my 'everything spicy' son to my
'everything sweet' son. I made the
dip and mixed the dry ingredients
the night before, so it was quick and
easy at dinnertime, too."*

*"The dip is very good if you like
things spicy! This recipe is easy to
make, but I didn't have enough
coating mix to cover all of the strips
of chicken, so I doubled the coating
ingredients. Great for appetizers!"*

Peppery Chicken Fried Chicken

Prep: 30 min.   **Cook:** 42 min.

Cut leftover chicken into strips, and serve over salad greens. Drizzle with creamy Ranch or blue cheese dressing.

8 (6-ounce) skinned and boned chicken breasts
4½ teaspoons salt, divided
2½ teaspoons freshly ground black pepper, divided
76 saltine crackers (2 sleeves), crushed
2½ cups all-purpose flour, divided
1 teaspoon baking powder
1 teaspoon ground red pepper
8 cups milk, divided
4 large eggs
Peanut oil

• Place chicken breasts between 2 sheets of heavy-duty plastic wrap, and flatten to ¼-inch thickness using a meat mallet or rolling pin.
• Sprinkle ½ teaspoon salt and ½ teaspoon black pepper evenly over chicken. Set aside.
• Combine cracker crumbs, 2 cups flour, baking powder, 1½ teaspoons salt, 1 teaspoon black pepper, and ground red pepper.
• Whisk together 1½ cups milk and eggs. Dredge chicken in cracker crumb mixture; dip in milk mixture. Dredge in cracker mixture again.
• Pour oil to a depth of ½ inch into a 12-inch skillet (do not use a nonstick skillet). Heat to 360°. Fry chicken, in batches, 10 minutes, adding oil as needed. Turn and fry 4 to 5 more minutes or until golden brown. Remove to a wire rack in a jellyroll pan. Keep chicken warm in a 225° oven. Carefully drain hot oil, reserving cooked bits and 2 tablespoons drippings in skillet.
• Whisk together remaining ½ cup flour, remaining 2½ teaspoons salt, remaining 1 teaspoon black pepper, and remaining 6½ cups milk. Pour mixture into reserved drippings in skillet; cook over medium-high heat, whisking constantly, 10 to 12 minutes or until thickened. Serve gravy with chicken. Yield: 8 to 10 servings.

Apple-Bacon Stuffed Chicken Breasts

Prep: 30 min.   **Cook:** 22 min.

2 bacon slices, diced
½ cup peeled, chopped Granny Smith apple
½ cup dried cranberries, divided
1 tablespoon fine, dry breadcrumbs
½ teaspoon poultry seasoning
½ teaspoon ground cinnamon
4 skinned and boned chicken breasts

2 tablespoons butter or margarine
1 cup apple juice
2 tablespoons apple brandy or apple juice
¼ teaspoon salt
2 teaspoons cornstarch
1 tablespoon water
¼ cup coarsely chopped pecans
2 tablespoons chopped fresh parsley

• Cook bacon in a large skillet over medium heat until crisp; remove bacon, reserving 1 tablespoon drippings in skillet.
• Sauté chopped apple in reserved drippings over medium-high heat 4 minutes. Remove from heat; stir in bacon, ¼ cup cranberries, and next 3 ingredients.
• Cut a 3½-inch-long horizontal slit through the thickest portion of each chicken breast, cutting to, but not through, other side, forming a pocket. Stuff apple mixture evenly into each pocket. Wipe skillet clean.
• Melt butter in skillet over medium heat. Add chicken, and cook 8 to 10 minutes on each side or until done. Remove chicken, and keep warm.
• Add remaining ¼ cup cranberries, apple juice, apple brandy, and salt to skillet. Stir together cornstarch and 1 tablespoon water until smooth; stir into juice mixture, and cook, stirring constantly, 1 minute or until thickened. Spoon over chicken, and sprinkle with pecans and parsley. Yield: 4 servings.

Chicken Mediterranean

Prep: 8 min. **Cook:** 15 min. **Other:** 2 hrs., 5 min.

½ pound skinned and boned chicken breasts, cut into cubes
4 garlic cloves, minced
2 tablespoons olive oil
1 (14½-ounce) can diced tomatoes, undrained
¼ cup kalamata olives, pitted and chopped
½ teaspoon dried parsley flakes
½ teaspoon dried basil
½ teaspoon dried oregano
⅓ cup crumbled feta cheese
4 ounces penne pasta, cooked

• Combine first 3 ingredients in a zip-top freezer bag. Seal and chill 2 hours.
• Cook chicken mixture in a large skillet over medium-high heat 8 minutes or until chicken is done; remove from skillet. Add tomatoes and next 4 ingredients to skillet. Reduce heat, and simmer, stirring often, 7 minutes.
• Return chicken to skillet. Sprinkle with feta cheese, and remove from heat. Cover and let stand 5 minutes. Serve immediately over hot cooked pasta. Yield: 2 servings.

Note: For 4 servings, use 1 (14½-ounce) can diced tomatoes, and double all other ingredients. Cook chicken mixture 8 to 10 minutes or until done; remove from skillet. Add tomatoes and next 4 ingredients to skillet. Reduce heat, and simmer, stirring often, 7 to 8 minutes. Proceed as directed.

KITCHEN COMFORT
★★★★★

Cooks Chat

"My boyfriend loved this. He said it was better than anything we have ever eaten in a restaurant."

"This is a quick dish to make. It's easy enough to make for a week-night dinner or when friends come to visit. The kalamata olives make this dish. I also use tomato-and-basil feta cheese; it adds some great extra flavor."

"This recipe is simple and tastes awesome. Everyone loves it, from my husband to my 2-year-old."

Chicken Picante Pasta

Prep: 10 min.

1 cup picante sauce
½ cup light sour cream
½ cup light cream cheese, softened
¼ teaspoon ground cumin
3 cups chopped cooked chicken
8 ounces penne pasta, cooked
1 (4.5-ounce) can chopped green chiles
3 small green onions, chopped

• Stir together first 4 ingredients in a large bowl. Add chopped chicken and remaining ingredients, tossing gently to coat. Serve pasta chilled or heated. Yield: 6 servings.

Chicken Chimichangas

Prep: 20 min.   **Cook:** 38 min.

1 (16-ounce) jar picante sauce or salsa, divided
7 cups chopped cooked chicken
1 small onion, diced
2 to 2½ teaspoons ground cumin
1½ teaspoons dried oregano
1 teaspoon salt
20 (8-inch) flour tortillas
2½ cups (10 ounces) shredded Cheddar cheese
Toppings: guacamole, sour cream, shredded lettuce, diced tomato

• Combine 1½ cups picante sauce and next 5 ingredients in a Dutch oven; cook over medium-low heat, stirring often, 25 minutes or until most of liquid evaporates. Spoon ⅓ cup mixture below center of each tortilla; top with 2 tablespoons cheese.
• Fold in 2 sides of tortillas to enclose filling. Fold over top and bottom edges of tortillas, making rectangles. Secure with wooden picks. Place, folded side down, on greased baking sheets. Coat chimichangas with cooking spray.
• Bake at 425° for 8 minutes; turn and bake 5 more minutes. Remove picks; top with remaining picante sauce and desired toppings. Yield: 20 servings.

Chicken Cakes with Creole Sauce

Prep: 20 min.   **Cook:** 12 min.   **Other:** 15 min.

½ medium-size red bell pepper, diced
4 green onions, thinly sliced
1 garlic clove, pressed
3 cups chopped cooked chicken breast
1 cup soft breadcrumbs
1 large egg, lightly beaten
2 tablespoons light mayonnaise
1 tablespoon Creole mustard
1 teaspoon Creole seasoning
Creole Sauce

• Sauté first 3 ingredients in a nonstick skillet coated with cooking spray 4 minutes or until vegetables are tender. Wipe skillet clean.
• Stir together bell pepper mixture, chicken, and next 5 ingredients in a bowl. Shape chicken mixture into 8 (3½-inch) patties. Cover and chill 15 minutes.
• Cook patties, in 2 batches, in skillet coated with cooking spray over medium heat 3 minutes on each side or until golden. Serve immediately with Creole Sauce. Yield: 8 servings.

Creole Sauce

Prep: 5 min.

1 cup mayonnaise
3 green onions, sliced
2 tablespoons Creole mustard
2 garlic cloves, pressed
1 tablespoon chopped fresh parsley
¼ teaspoon ground red pepper

• Stir together all ingredients until well blended. Yield: 1¼ cups.

Cooks Chat

"This recipe is easy to make and simply delicious! If you didn't know better, you might think you were eating crab rather than chicken—my husband did! The Creole Sauce really makes the dish. This has become a favorite standby for using leftover chicken."

"My family begs me to make this recipe. It's quick and delicious. When time is short, I use a prepared chicken from the market."

"This is an easy and wonderful dish that tastes like you worked much harder on it than you really did. I use a roasted chicken from my grocery store deli to make it even quicker."

Hickory-Smoked Bourbon Turkey

Prep: 30 min.   **Cook:** 6 hrs.   **Other:** 2 days, 45 min.

We gave this succulent recipe our highest rating.

1 (11-pound) whole turkey,
    thawed
2 cups maple syrup
1 cup bourbon
1 tablespoon pickling spice
Hickory wood chunks
1 large carrot, scraped
1 celery rib
1 medium onion, peeled and
    halved
1 lemon
1 tablespoon salt
2 teaspoons pepper
Garnishes: mixed greens, lemon
    wedges

• Remove giblets and neck from turkey; reserve for other uses, if desired. Rinse turkey thoroughly with cold water, and pat dry. Add water to a large stockpot, filling half full; stir in maple syrup, bourbon, and pickling spice. Add turkey and, if needed, additional water to cover. Cover and chill turkey 2 days.
• Soak hickory wood chunks in fresh water at least 30 minutes. Prepare charcoal fire in smoker; let burn 20 to 30 minutes.
• Remove turkey from water, discarding water mixture; pat dry. Cut carrot and celery in half crosswise. Stuff cavity with carrot, celery, and onion. Pierce lemon with a fork; place in neck cavity. Combine salt and pepper; rub mixture over turkey. Fold wings under, and tie legs together with string, if desired.
• Drain wood chunks, and place on coals. Place water pan in smoker, and add water to depth of fill line. Place turkey in center of lower food rack; cover with smoker lid.
• Cook 6 hours or until a meat thermometer inserted into thickest portion of turkey thigh registers 180°, adding additional water, charcoal, and wood chunks as needed. Remove from smoker, and let stand 15 minutes before slicing. Garnish, if desired. Yield: 12 to 14 servings.

FOR THE HOLIDAYS

Cooks Chat

"Wow . . . I mean WOW . . . this was the most tender, juicy, flavorful turkey I have ever prepared. I made it for Thanksgiving and then ended up making it for a Christmas party at our home. Everyone enjoyed it. The kids even loved it, and if you are a parent, that should tell you something. I served it with sweet potatoes, green bean casserole, broccoli-cheese-rice casserole, corn, and rolls."

"This was our first time using a smoker (a 'practice run' for Thanksgiving), and this turned out fabulous—moist and richly flavorful. We used maple wood chips and added maple syrup to the water. We will definitely make this dish for our Thanksgiving feast this year—and probably for years to come."

"Friends had us over to try this fabulous dish. It had such a wonderful flavor that I had to get the recipe so I could cook it myself one day."

Sesame-Crusted Turkey Mignons

Prep: 20 min. **Cook:** 24 min.

½ cup sesame seeds, toasted
¼ cup olive oil
1 garlic clove, minced
1 tablespoon chopped fresh
  chives
1 tablespoon soy sauce
2 teaspoons lemon juice
1 teaspoon grated fresh ginger

½ teaspoon sesame oil
2 (11-ounce) packages turkey
  mignons*
Creamy Wine Sauce
Hot cooked noodles
Garnishes: lemon slices and
  parsley

• Stir together first 8 ingredients; dredge turkey in sesame seed mixture. Place on a lightly greased rack in a broiler pan.
• Broil 5½ inches from heat 12 minutes on each side or until done. Serve with Creamy Wine Sauce over hot cooked noodles. Garnish, if desired. Yield: 4 servings.

*Substitute 2 turkey tenderloins, cut in half, for turkey mignons, if desired.

Creamy Wine Sauce

Prep: 5 min. **Cook:** 15 min.

1 cup fruity white wine*
2 teaspoons lemon juice
¼ cup whipping cream

2 tablespoons soy sauce
⅓ cup butter or margarine

• Bring wine and lemon juice to a boil in a saucepan over medium-high heat. Boil 6 to 8 minutes or until mixture is reduced by half. Whisk in whipping cream. Cook 3 to 4 minutes, whisking constantly, until thickened.
• Reduce heat to simmer, and whisk in soy sauce and butter until butter is melted. Yield: about ¾ cup.

*Substitute white grape juice for wine, if desired.

Catfish Pecan with Lemon-Thyme-Pecan Butter

Prep: 25 min.   **Cook:** 28 min.

This is one of our favorite catfish dishes ever. Keep the cooked fish warm in a low oven for up to 30 minutes.

1½ cups pecan halves, divided
¾ cup all-purpose flour
1½ teaspoons Creole seasoning, divided
1 large egg
1 cup milk
8 (6-ounce) catfish, flounder, redfish, or bass fillets

1 cup butter, divided
2 large lemons, halved
1 tablespoon Worcestershire sauce
6 large fresh thyme sprigs
Kosher salt and pepper to taste
Garnishes: fresh thyme, lemon slices

• Process ¾ cup pecans, flour, and 1 teaspoon Creole seasoning in a food processor until finely ground; place pecan mixture in a large shallow bowl, and set aside.
• Whisk together egg and milk in a large bowl, and set aside.
• Sprinkle both sides of fillets evenly with remaining ½ teaspoon Creole seasoning.
• Dip catfish fillets in egg mixture, draining off excess; dredge fillets in pecan mixture, coating both sides, and shake off excess.
• Melt 2 tablespoons butter in a large nonstick skillet over medium heat until butter starts to bubble. Place 2 fillets in skillet, and cook 2 to 3 minutes on each side or until golden. Drain on a wire rack in a jellyroll pan, and keep warm in a 200° oven. Wipe skillet clean, and repeat procedure with remaining fillets.
• Wipe skillet clean. Melt remaining ½ cup butter in skillet over high heat; add remaining ¾ cup pecans, and cook, stirring occasionally, 2 to 3 minutes or until toasted. Squeeze juice from lemon halves into skillet; place halves, cut side down, in skillet. Stir in Worcestershire sauce, thyme, salt, and pepper, and cook 30 seconds or until thyme wilts and becomes very aromatic. Remove and discard lemon halves and wilted thyme.
• Place fish on a serving platter; spoon pecan mixture over fish. Garnish, if desired. Yield: 8 servings.

Spicy Skillet Fish

Prep: 10 min.   **Cook:** 10 min. per batch   **Other:** 30 min.

For a different variation, prepare this recipe as directed, and make fish soft tacos with warmed flour or corn tortillas. Drizzle with fresh lime juice, and serve with your favorite rice.

2 garlic cloves
1 (2-inch) piece fresh ginger, peeled and chopped (about 2 tablespoons chopped)
1/2 cup chopped fresh cilantro
1 small jalapeño pepper, seeded
1 teaspoon salt
1/2 teaspoon ground paprika
1/2 teaspoon ground turmeric
1/2 teaspoon ground coriander
2 teaspoons vegetable oil
2 pounds catfish, grouper, or flounder fillets (about 6 fillets)
2 tablespoons vegetable oil
Fresh lemon or lime wedges (optional)

• Process first 9 ingredients in a food processor until finely chopped.
• Spread 2 teaspoons spice mixture evenly over both sides of each fillet. Cover and chill 30 minutes.
• Cook fish, in batches, in hot vegetable oil in a large nonstick skillet over medium-high heat 5 minutes on each side or until fish flakes with a fork. Serve with fresh lemon or lime wedges, if desired. Yield: 6 servings.

Barbecue Baked Catfish

Prep: 20 min.   **Cook:** 12 min.

¾ cup ketchup
¼ cup butter or margarine
1 tablespoon balsamic vinegar
1 tablespoon Worcestershire
  sauce
1 teaspoon Dijon mustard

½ teaspoon Jamaican Jerk
  seasoning
1 garlic clove, minced
10 (3- to 4-ounce) catfish fillets
⅛ teaspoon pepper
Garnish: chopped fresh parsley

• Stir together ketchup and next 6 ingredients in a small saucepan over medium-low heat; cook ketchup mixture 10 minutes, stirring occasionally.
• Sprinkle catfish with pepper; arrange in an even layer in a lightly greased aluminum foil-lined broiler pan. Pour sauce over catfish. Bake catfish at 400° for 10 to 12 minutes or until fish flakes with a fork. Garnish, if desired. Yield: 5 servings.

Classic Fried Catfish

Prep: 10 min.   **Cook:** 6 min.

¾ cup yellow cornmeal
¼ cup all-purpose flour
2 teaspoons salt
1 teaspoon ground red pepper
¼ teaspoon garlic powder

4 catfish fillets (about 1½
  pounds)
¼ teaspoon salt
Vegetable oil

• Combine first 5 ingredients in a large shallow dish.
• Sprinkle catfish fillets with salt, and dredge in cornmeal mixture, coating evenly.
• Pour vegetable oil to a depth of 3 inches into a Dutch oven; heat to 350°. Fry fillets 5 to 6 minutes or until golden; drain on paper towels. Yield: 4 servings.

Battered Catfish and Chips

Prep: 15 min.   **Cook:** 20 min.

Take a shortcut—your food processor's 1-millimeter slicing blade will quickly snip potatoes into perfect chips.

4 large baking potatoes
2 cups all-purpose flour
1 tablespoon baking powder
1 teaspoon kosher salt
¼ teaspoon ground red pepper
1 (12-ounce) bottle dark beer

Vegetable oil
1¼ teaspoons salt, divided
¾ teaspoon black pepper, divided
4 (6-ounce) catfish fillets
Malt vinegar

• Cut potatoes into paper-thin slices. Combine potato and water to cover in a large bowl; set aside.
• Combine flour and next 3 ingredients. Add beer, whisking until smooth. Cover and chill 1 hour, if desired.
• Drain potato well. Pour oil to a depth of 1½ inches into a heavy skillet; heat to 375°. Fry potato, in 4 batches, 2 to 3 minutes or until golden. Drain on paper towels; sprinkle with 1 teaspoon salt and ½ teaspoon black pepper. Keep warm.
• Sprinkle fish with remaining ¼ teaspoon each salt and black pepper. Dip fish in batter; carefully add to skillet, and fry, 2 fillets at a time, 1½ to 2 minutes on each side or until golden. Serve with chips and malt vinegar. Yield: 4 servings.

Jack's Fried Catfish

Prep: 10 min.   **Cook:** 8 min. per batch   **Other:** 1 hr., 10 min.

Cooks Chat

"Very tasty and easy to fix. I especially liked the crispy texture. I would make this again for family or for a party. I used additional salt for my family because they love salty fish. Also, I placed the excess meal mixture in a freezer bag for the next time I make this recipe."

Jack says the catfish fillets are done when "most of the bubbling stops, and the fillets begin to float."

6 (4- to 6-ounce) catfish fillets
2 cups milk
2 cups yellow cornmeal
1 tablespoon seasoned salt
2 teaspoons pepper

½ teaspoon onion powder
½ teaspoon garlic powder
1 teaspoon salt
Vegetable oil
Garnish: lemon wedges

• Place catfish fillets in a single layer in a shallow dish; cover with milk. Cover and chill 1 hour.
• Combine cornmeal and next 4 ingredients in a shallow dish.
• Remove catfish fillets from refrigerator, and let stand at room temperature 10 minutes. Remove from milk, allowing excess to drip off. Sprinkle evenly with 1 teaspoon salt.
• Dredge catfish fillets in cornmeal mixture, shaking off excess.
• Pour oil to a depth of 1½ inches into a large skillet, and heat to 350°. Fry fillets, in batches, about 3 to 4 minutes on each side or until golden brown. Drain fish on wire racks over paper towels. Garnish, if desired. Yield: 6 servings.

Baked Fish with Parmesan-Sour Cream Sauce

Prep: 10 min.   **Cook:** 25 min.

Tilapia, flounder, or any other white fish works in place of orange roughy.

1½ pounds orange roughy fillets
1 (8-ounce) container sour
  cream
¼ cup shredded Parmesan
  cheese
½ teaspoon paprika

½ teaspoon salt
¼ teaspoon pepper
2 tablespoons Italian-seasoned
  breadcrumbs
2 tablespoons butter or
  margarine, melted

• Place fillets in a single layer in a lightly greased 13- x 9-inch pan. Stir together sour cream and next 4 ingredients; spread mixture evenly over fillets. Sprinkle with breadcrumbs; drizzle with butter.
• Bake at 350° for 20 to 25 minutes or until fish flakes with a fork. Yield: 4 to 6 servings.

Grilled Salmon with Mustard-Molasses Glaze

Prep: 10 min.   **Cook:** 10 min.

½ cup coarse-grained mustard
½ cup molasses
¼ cup red wine vinegar

6 (4- to 5-ounce) salmon fillets
⅛ teaspoon salt
⅛ teaspoon pepper

• Whisk together first 3 ingredients in a medium bowl.
• Sprinkle fillets with salt and pepper. Brush with half of mustard mixture.
• Grill, covered with grill lid, over high heat (400° to 500°) 4 to 5 minutes on each side or until fish flakes with a fork. Baste with remaining mustard mixture. Yield: 6 servings.

Mediterranean Swordfish

Prep: 20 min.   **Cook:** 30 min.

Grouper makes a terrific substitute, but it cooks more quickly than swordfish. Check to see if it flakes with a fork after 15 to 20 minutes.

1 medium onion, chopped
2 teaspoons olive oil
1 garlic clove, minced
½ teaspoon salt, divided
½ teaspoon pepper, divided
½ cup dry white wine or chicken broth
¼ cup chopped pimiento-stuffed olives
1 tablespoon small capers, drained
4 (8-ounce) swordfish steaks (about ¾ to 1 inch thick)
2 plum tomatoes, seeded and diced
¼ cup chopped fresh parsley

• Sauté onion in hot oil in an ovenproof skillet or pan over medium heat 3 minutes or until tender. Add garlic, ¼ teaspoon salt, and ¼ teaspoon pepper; sauté 1 minute. Reduce heat to low; stir in wine, olives, and capers.
• Sprinkle fish evenly with remaining salt and pepper. Place fish over onion mixture.
• Bake, covered, at 400° for 26 minutes or until fish flakes with a fork. Sprinkle with diced tomato and parsley. Yield: 4 servings.

Asian Shrimp with Pasta

Prep: 25 min.   **Cook:** 7 min.

It may seem like this recipe calls for a lot of ingredients, but you'll make this often, so keep these items on hand.

1 pound unpeeled, medium-size shrimp
1 (9-ounce) package refrigerated angel hair pasta
¼ cup lite soy sauce
¼ cup seasoned rice wine vinegar
2 teaspoons sesame oil
6 green onions, chopped
1 cup frozen sweet green peas, thawed
¾ cup shredded carrots
1 (8-ounce) can sliced water chestnuts, drained
¼ cup chopped fresh cilantro
2 tablespoons minced fresh ginger
2 garlic cloves, minced
1 teaspoon vegetable oil
2 tablespoons fresh lime juice
½ teaspoon freshly ground pepper
2 tablespoons chopped unsalted dry-roasted peanuts

• Peel shrimp, and devein, if desired. Set shrimp aside.
• Prepare pasta according to package directions, omitting salt and fat. Drain and place in a large bowl or on a platter.
• Stir together soy sauce, vinegar, and sesame oil. Drizzle over pasta. Add green onions and next 4 ingredients to pasta; toss.
• Sauté ginger and garlic in hot vegetable oil 1 to 2 minutes (do not brown). Add shrimp, lime juice, and pepper; cook 3 to 5 minutes or just until shrimp turn pink. Add shrimp mixture to pasta mixture, and toss. Sprinkle with nuts, and serve immediately.
Yield: 6 servings.

KIDS LOVE IT

Cooks Chat

"This will be a new favorite! I'll be sure to have these ingredients on hand for a speedy, delicious dinner."

"Wow, my family gobbled up every bit of this! My kids, ages 9 and 11, declared this recipe a keeper and asked when we could have it again. I added extra cilantro and peanuts."

Coconut Fried Shrimp

Prep: 25 min.   **Cook:** 2 min. per batch

1 pound unpeeled, medium-
      size fresh shrimp
¾ cup biscuit mix
1 tablespoon sugar
¾ cup beer

¾ cup all-purpose flour
2½ cups flaked coconut
Vegetable oil
Orange-Lime Dip

• Peel shrimp, leaving the tails intact; devein, if desired, and set shrimp aside.
• Combine biscuit mix, sugar, and beer, stirring until smooth; set mixture aside.
• Coat shrimp with flour; dip into beer mixture, allowing excess to drain. Gently roll coated shrimp in flaked coconut.
• Pour vegetable oil to a depth of 3 inches into a large saucepan; heat to 350°. Cook shrimp, a few at a time, 1 to 2 minutes or until golden; drain on paper towels, and serve immediately with Orange-Lime Dip. Yield: about 3 dozen.

Orange-Lime Dip

Prep: 3 min.   **Cook:** 5 min.

1 (10-ounce) jar orange
      marmalade
3 tablespoons spicy brown
      mustard

1 tablespoon fresh lime juice

• Combine all ingredients in a small saucepan; cook over medium heat, stirring constantly, until marmalade melts. Remove from heat; cool. Dip may be stored in refrigerator up to 1 week. Yield: about 1¼ cups.

Shrimp Oriental

Prep: 40 min.   **Cook:** 10 min.

This dish is shrimp-turned-irresistible with its spicy-sweet flavor and colorful appeal.

2 pounds unpeeled, large fresh shrimp
1 (15½-ounce) can pineapple chunks, undrained
½ cup sugar
2 tablespoons cornstarch
1 teaspoon salt
¼ cup rice wine vinegar
2 tablespoons chili sauce
⅓ cup ketchup
1 teaspoon soy sauce
1 green bell pepper, cubed
1 red bell pepper, cubed
Garnish: green onion slivers

• Peel shrimp, and devein, if desired. Set shrimp aside.
• Drain pineapple, reserving juice. Stir together pineapple juice, sugar, and next 6 ingredients.
• Cook juice mixture in a large skillet or wok over high heat, stirring constantly, 15 to 30 seconds or until thickened. Add cubed bell pepper, and cook 3 to 4 minutes. Add pineapple chunks and shrimp. Cover and cook, stirring often, 3 to 5 minutes or just until shrimp turn pink. Serve over rice, if desired. Garnish, if desired. Yield: 4 servings.

Chicken Oriental: Substitute 4 skinned and boned chicken breasts, cubed, for shrimp. Cook for 10 minutes or until chicken is done.

Mexican-Grilled Shrimp with Smoky Sweet Sauce

Prep: 25 min.   **Cook:** 6 min.

If you use wooden skewers for this recipe, soak them in water for at least an hour to keep them from burning.

2 pounds unpeeled, large fresh shrimp
20 (12-inch) skewers
½ cup firmly packed dark brown sugar
6 garlic cloves, pressed
1 canned chipotle pepper in adobo sauce, minced

1 tablespoon adobo sauce
2 tablespoons rum
2 tablespoons water
1 tablespoon tamarind paste
¼ teaspoon salt
1 tablespoon olive oil
Smoky Sweet Sauce

• Peel shrimp, leaving tails on; devein, if desired. Thread 4 shrimp onto each skewer. Set aside.
• Cook brown sugar in a small heavy saucepan over low heat until melted. Add garlic and next 6 ingredients. Cook 5 minutes or until tamarind paste melts. Remove from heat.
• Brush shrimp with olive oil. Grill, without grill lid, over medium-high heat (350° to 400°) 4 to 6 minutes or until shrimp turn pink, turning once, and basting with tamarind glaze. Serve with Smoky Sweet Sauce. Yield: 4 servings.

Note: Tamarind is a tree-growing fruit. Its long pods contain a sweet-and-sour pulp from which a paste is made. Look for tamarind paste in the Mexican or Asian section of your grocery store.

Smoky Sweet Sauce

Prep: 8 min.   **Cook:** 6 min.

1 cup low-sodium fat-free chicken broth
½ cup chopped refrigerated mango slices
¼ cup loosely packed chopped fresh cilantro

2 teaspoons adobo sauce
¾ teaspoon salt
⅓ cup whipping cream
2½ tablespoons butter

• Process first 5 ingredients in a blender 1 minute. Pour mixture into a saucepan, and bring to a boil over medium-high heat. Add cream, and cook, whisking often, 6 minutes or until slightly thick. Remove from heat; whisk in butter until melted. Yield: 1¾ cups.

Shrimp and Scallops Mornay

Prep: 35 min. **Cook:** 30 min.

1 cup butter or margarine,
  divided
¼ cup minced shallots
2 (8-ounce) packages fresh
  mushrooms, sliced
1 tablespoon lemon juice
1½ pounds unpeeled, large
  fresh shrimp
1½ pounds sea scallops
2½ cups half-and-half

⅓ cup all-purpose flour
⅔ cup grated Parmesan cheese
3 tablespoons dry sherry
1 teaspoon Dijon mustard
½ teaspoon salt
¼ teaspoon ground white
  pepper
Pinch ground nutmeg
⅔ cup shredded Swiss cheese

• Melt 6 tablespoons butter in a Dutch oven over low heat; add shallots, and sauté 1 minute. Increase heat to high. Add mushrooms and lemon juice, and cook, stirring constantly, just until mushrooms are tender. Transfer to a bowl.
• Peel shrimp; devein, if desired.
• Melt 4 tablespoons butter in Dutch oven over medium heat; add shrimp, and sauté 3 to 5 minutes or just until shrimp turn pink. Add to mushroom mixture.
• Bring scallops and half-and-half to a boil in a saucepan over medium-high heat. Reduce heat, and simmer, stirring often, 3 to 5 minutes or until scallops are opaque. Pour through a wire-mesh strainer into a small bowl; add scallops to mushroom mixture. Reserve half-and-half.
• Drain any liquid from mushroom mixture. Add liquid to reserved half-and-half.
• Melt remaining 6 tablespoons butter in Dutch oven over low heat; whisk in flour until smooth. Cook, whisking constantly, 1 minute. Gradually add half-and-half mixture; cook over medium heat, whisking constantly, until mixture is thickened and bubbly. Add Parmesan cheese and next 5 ingredients; cook, whisking constantly, 3 minutes or until cheese melts and sauce is smooth. Remove from heat; stir in mushroom mixture.
• Spoon into 10 lightly greased shell-shaped baking dishes or individual serving bowls, and sprinkle evenly with shredded Swiss cheese. Place on 2 (15- x 10-inch) jellyroll pans.
• Broil 5½ inches from heat 8 minutes or until Swiss cheese is golden and mixture is bubbly. Serve immediately. Yield: 10 servings.

Note: Mixture may be prepared a day ahead and chilled. Broil just before serving.

Marinated Shrimp

Prep: 20 min.   **Cook:** 3 min.   **Other:** 8 hrs.

2 pounds unpeeled, medium-size fresh shrimp
6 cups salted water
½ cup sugar
1½ cups white vinegar
1 cup vegetable oil

¼ cup capers, undrained
1½ teaspoons celery salt
½ to 1 teaspoon salt
1 medium-size white or red onion, sliced and separated into rings

• Peel shrimp, leaving tails on. Devein, if desired.
• Bring 6 cups salted water to a boil; add shrimp, and cook 3 minutes or just until shrimp turn pink. Drain and rinse with cold water. Chill 2 hours.
• Combine sugar and next 5 ingredients in a shallow dish; add shrimp alternately with onion. Cover and chill at least 6 hours, turning often.
• Drain shrimp, and discard marinade before serving. Yield: 8 to 10 servings.

Fried Oysters

Prep: 20 min.   **Cook:** 20 min.

A trick of the trade from our Test Kitchens is to use cracker crumbs in breading mixtures—they'll make these fried oysters extra crispy.

1 quart fresh oysters, rinsed and drained
1 large egg, lightly beaten
1½ cups saltine crumbs (1 sleeve crackers)

1 cup ketchup
1 tablespoon prepared horseradish
⅛ teaspoon hot sauce (optional)
Canola oil

• Dip oysters in egg, and dredge in cracker crumbs. Place on a pan, and chill 2 hours, if desired.
• Stir together ketchup, horseradish, and, if desired, hot sauce; chill.
• Pour oil to a depth of 1 inch into a Dutch oven, and heat to 350°. Fry oysters, in batches, 3 to 4 minutes or until golden brown. Drain on paper towels. Serve immediately with desired sauce. Yield: 6 to 8 servings.

salads

★★★★★

Round out
tonight's meal
or create a fresh
main dish with
these crisp green
salads, pasta
salads, and tasty
dressings.

*Strawberry-Chicken Salad,
page 254*

"I make this all of the time. It is so easy and so very good. I use bagged slaw mix rather than chopping cabbage, carrot, and onions."

"I've made this by omitting the carrot and green onions and adding sunflower seeds and sliced roasted chicken. It was fabulous!"

"I've been looking for a good slaw recipe without mayonnaise, and this is it! This is a big hit at family get-togethers!"

"This recipe was so easy and so different. I made this for a family gathering. Everyone wrinkled their noses when I said that I made coleslaw, but this was a smash! The dill in this gave it a very unique, mild flavor. I was told that this had better show up at the next family picnic!"

"Dill adds just the right flavor to make this different from ordinary slaw. It was the talk of the 4th of July party!"

Crunchy Cabbage Slaw

Prep: 30 min.   **Cook:** 10 min.   **Other:** 1 hr.

1 (3-ounce) package ramen noodle soup mix
¼ cup sliced almonds
⅓ cup canola oil*
¼ cup cider vinegar
2½ tablespoons sugar
1 small green cabbage, shredded
1 small carrot, grated
3 green onions, sliced

• Remove flavor packet from soup mix, and reserve. Break ramen noodles into pieces, and place on 1 side of a lightly greased baking sheet. Place sliced almonds on other side of baking sheet.
• Bake at 350°, stirring occasionally, 5 to 10 minutes or until toasted. Set aside.
• Whisk together reserved flavor packet, oil, vinegar, and sugar in a bowl until blended. Chill 1 hour.
• Toss together cabbage, carrot, onions, and dressing in a large bowl. Place noodles around outside edge of cabbage mixture, and top with almonds. Yield: 7½ cups.

*Substitute ⅓ cup vegetable oil for canola oil, if desired.

Creamy Dill Slaw

Prep: 10 min.   **Other:** 8 hrs.

4 green onions, sliced
1 (8-ounce) container sour cream*
1 cup mayonnaise*
2 tablespoons sugar
2 tablespoons chopped fresh dill
2 tablespoons white vinegar
1 teaspoon salt
½ teaspoon pepper
1 (16-ounce) package shredded coleslaw mix
1 (10-ounce) package finely shredded cabbage
Garnish: chopped fresh dill

• Stir together first 8 ingredients in a large bowl until mixture is blended; stir in coleslaw mix and cabbage. Cover and chill 8 hours. Garnish, if desired. Yield: 8 servings.

*Substitute 1 (8-ounce) container light sour cream and 1 cup light mayonnaise, if desired.

Almond-Citrus Salad

Prep: 15 min.

⅔ cup vegetable oil
2 teaspoons grated grapefruit
    rind
½ cup fresh grapefruit juice
1 (0.7-ounce) envelope Italian
    salad dressing mix
1 grapefruit
2 oranges
1 avocado, peeled and sliced

3 cups torn spinach
3 cups torn leaf lettuce
3 cups torn iceberg lettuce
½ cup sliced celery
½ cup chopped green
    bell pepper
¼ cup Sweet-and-Spicy
    Almonds

• Combine oil and next 3 ingredients in a jar; cover tightly, and shake vigorously.
• Peel and section grapefruit and oranges, and place in a large bowl. Add avocado and next 5 ingredients. Add dressing, tossing to coat. Sprinkle with Sweet-and-Spicy Almonds. Yield: 8 servings.

Sweet-and-Spicy Almonds

Prep: 5 min.　　**Cook:** 15 min.

1 cup sliced almonds
1 tablespoon butter or
    margarine, melted
1½ teaspoons sugar
¼ teaspoon ground cumin

¼ teaspoon chili powder
⅛ teaspoon dried crushed red
    pepper
Pinch of salt

• Combine almonds and butter, stirring well. Combine sugar and next 4 ingredients. Sprinkle over almonds; toss to coat. Spread on a lightly greased baking sheet.
• Bake at 325°, stirring occasionally, 15 minutes; cool. Yield: 1 cup.

PARTY PLEASER

Cooks Chat

"My daughter made this salad for our family using orange juice and orange rind. It was refreshing and delicious. We also tried it with baked chicken added, which made a great combination for a main dish."

Fruit Salad with Blackberry-Basil Vinaigrette

Prep: 10 min.

Look for refrigerated jars of sliced mango and pink grapefruit segments in the produce section of the supermarket.

8 cups gourmet mixed salad greens
1½ cups sliced mango
1½ cups pink grapefruit segments
1½ cups sliced fresh strawberries
1 cup fresh blackberries
1 large avocado, sliced
Blackberry-Basil Vinaigrette

• Place salad greens and next 5 ingredients in a large bowl, and gently toss. Serve immediately with Blackberry-Basil Vinaigrette. Yield: 6 servings.

Blackberry-Basil Vinaigrette

Prep: 5 min.

½ (10-ounce) jar seedless blackberry preserves
¼ cup red wine vinegar
6 fresh basil leaves
1 garlic clove, sliced
½ teaspoon salt
½ teaspoon seasoned pepper
¾ cup vegetable oil

• Pulse blackberry preserves, red wine vinegar, and next 4 ingredients in a blender 2 or 3 times until blended. With blender running, pour vegetable oil through food chute in a slow, steady stream; process until smooth. Yield: 1 cup.

Spinach-and-Cranberry Salad with Warm Chutney Dressing

Prep: 20 min. **Cook:** 3 min.

2 tablespoons butter or
  margarine
1½ cups coarsely chopped
  pecans
1 teaspoon salt
1 teaspoon freshly ground
  pepper
2 (6-ounce) packages fresh baby
  spinach

6 bacon slices, cooked and
  crumbled
1 cup dried cranberries
2 hard-cooked eggs, finely
  chopped
Warm Chutney Dressing

• Melt butter in a nonstick skillet over medium-high heat; add pecans, and cook, stirring constantly, 2 minutes or until toasted. Remove from heat; add salt and pepper, tossing to coat. Drain pecans on paper towels.
• Toss together pecans, spinach, bacon, and next 2 ingredients. Drizzle with Warm Chutney Dressing, gently tossing to coat. Serve immediately. Yield: 8 servings.

Warm Chutney Dressing

Prep: 5 min. **Cook:** 4 min.

6 tablespoons balsamic vinegar
⅓ cup bottled mango chutney
2 tablespoons Dijon mustard

2 tablespoons honey
2 garlic cloves, minced
¼ cup olive oil

• Cook first 5 ingredients in a saucepan over medium heat, stirring constantly, 3 minutes. Stir in olive oil, blending well; cook 1 minute. Yield: 1 cup.

Cooks Chat

"Unusual ingredients combine to make a scrumptious salad that's a meal in itself. This is a great special-occasion salad."

"The pepper on the pecans is the hidden secret."

Cooks Chat

"One of my friends made this salad for a Christmas dinner. Oh my gosh, it was fabulous! The tartness of the dressing, the sweetness of the pecans, and the bite of the blue cheese all combined to make perfection! The tender spinach was terrific in this yummy salad."

"I made this for Valentine's dinner, and everyone thought it was excellent. The sweetness from the brown sugar and apple combined with the blue cheese to create a wonderful flavor."

Cooks Chat

"This salad was absolutely delicious—especially the dressing. If you're serving more than two people, though, you might want to increase the measurements; my husband and I easily finished it in one sitting."

Spinach-Pecan Salad

Prep: 10 min.   **Cook:** 3 min.

1 tablespoon butter or margarine
½ cup pecan halves
1 tablespoon brown sugar
1 (6-ounce) package fresh baby spinach

1 large Granny Smith apple, thinly sliced
½ cup crumbled blue cheese
2 tablespoons olive oil
2 tablespoons white vinegar

• Melt butter in a small skillet over low heat; add pecans and brown sugar. Cook, stirring constantly, 2 to 3 minutes or until caramelized. Cool on wax paper.
• Place spinach in a large serving bowl. Toss in pecans, apple, and blue cheese. Add oil and vinegar, and toss gently to coat. Yield: 4 servings.

Fresh Pear Salad with Asian Sesame Dressing

Prep: 15 min.

2 cups shredded red cabbage
2 cups shredded romaine lettuce
3 red Bartlett pears, sliced
2 medium carrots, shredded (about 1 cup)

1 green onion, chopped
Asian Sesame Dressing
2 teaspoons sesame seeds, toasted (optional)

• Toss together first 5 ingredients in a large bowl, and drizzle with Asian Sesame Dressing, tossing gently to coat. Sprinkle with sesame seeds, if desired. Serve immediately. Yield: 6 servings.

Asian Sesame Dressing

Prep: 5 min.

¼ cup vegetable oil
2 tablespoons white wine vinegar
1 tablespoon soy sauce

2 teaspoons sugar
½ teaspoon sesame oil
¼ teaspoon dried crushed red pepper

• Whisk together all ingredients. Yield: ½ cup.

*Fresh Pear Salad
with Asian Sesame Dressing*

Potato Cobb Salad

Prep: 30 min. **Cook:** 30 min. **Other:** 2 hrs.

Cooks Chat

"Everyone loved this salad. I served it with barbecued steak and corn on the cob. There was none left! Definitely a keeper. It could even be a meal in itself."

"I served this salad for a Labor Day lunch, and everyone raved about it. This is one of the best salads I have had in a long time. The addition of the potatoes is really a great idea—they add a lot to the flavor. This salad's easy to make and can be prepared ahead of time."

3 pounds Yukon gold potatoes
¾ teaspoon salt
1 (16-ounce) bottle olive oil-and-vinegar dressing, divided
8 cups mixed salad greens
2 large avocados
1 tablespoon fresh lemon juice
3 large tomatoes, seeded and diced
12 small green onions, sliced
2 cups (8 ounces) shredded sharp Cheddar cheese
4 ounces crumbled blue cheese
6 to 8 bacon slices, cooked and crumbled
Freshly ground pepper to taste

• Cook potatoes in boiling salted water to cover 30 minutes or until tender. Drain and cool slightly. Peel and cut into cubes.
• Sprinkle potatoes evenly with ¾ teaspoon salt. Pour 1 cup dressing over potatoes; gently toss. Set aside remaining dressing. Cover potato mixture; chill at least 2 hours or overnight.
• Arrange salad greens evenly on a large serving platter. Peel and chop avocados; toss with lemon juice.
• Arrange potatoes, avocados, tomatoes, and next 4 ingredients in rows over salad greens. Sprinkle with pepper. Serve with remaining dressing. Yield: 8 to 10 servings.

Bok Choy Salad

Prep: 15 min. **Cook:** 10 min.

Cooks Chat

"This is excellent! I used 2 tablespoons toasted sesame oil and 2 tablespoons vegetable oil in place of the ¼ cup olive oil listed. Also, I have used all almonds and substituted regular cabbage—still fantastic."

2 (3-ounce) packages ramen noodle soup mix
½ cup sunflower seeds
3 tablespoons slivered almonds, chopped
½ cup sugar
¼ cup olive oil
¼ cup cider vinegar
2 tablespoons soy sauce
1 bok choy, shredded
6 green onions, chopped

• Remove flavor packets from soup mixes; reserve for another use. Crumble noodles.
• Combine noodles, sunflower seeds, and almonds. Spread on a 15- x 10-inch jellyroll pan.
• Bake at 350° for 8 to 10 minutes or until golden brown; set aside. Bring sugar and next 3 ingredients to a boil in a saucepan over medium heat. Remove from heat; cool.
• Place bok choy and green onions in a large bowl. Drizzle with sugar mixture. Add ramen noodle mixture, tossing well. Serve immediately. Yield: 6 to 8 servings.

Bok Choy Salad

Ramen Noodle Salad

Prep: 25 min.   **Cook:** 5 min.

1 (3-ounce) package ramen
   noodle soup mix
¼ cup butter or margarine
1 cup walnuts or pecans,
   chopped

1 (16-ounce) package fresh
   broccoli florets
1 head romaine lettuce, torn
4 green onions, chopped
Sweet-and-Sour Dressing

• Remove seasoning packet from ramen noodles, and reserve for another use. Break noodles into pieces.
• Melt butter in a large skillet over medium-high heat; add ramen noodles and walnuts, and sauté until lightly browned. Drain on paper towels.
• Toss together noodle mixture, broccoli, lettuce, and green onions in a large bowl; add ¼ cup Sweet-and-Sour Dressing, tossing to coat. Serve with remaining dressing. Yield: 8 to 10 servings.

Sweet-and-Sour Dressing

Prep: 5 min.

½ cup vegetable oil
¼ cup sugar
¼ cup red wine vinegar

1 tablespoon soy sauce
½ teaspoon salt
¼ teaspoon pepper

• Whisk together all ingredients. Yield: 1 cup.

Black Bean-and-Rice Salad

Prep: 25 min.   **Other:** 2 hrs.

½ cup canola oil
¼ cup lime juice
2 cups canned black beans,
    rinsed and drained*
2 cups cooked long-grain rice
½ cup chopped onion

¼ cup chopped fresh cilantro
1 (4-ounce) jar diced pimiento,
    drained
2 garlic cloves, pressed
½ teaspoon salt
¼ teaspoon pepper

• Whisk together oil and lime juice in a large bowl.
• Add remaining ingredients, and toss mixture to coat. Cover and chill salad 2 hours. Yield: 4 to 6 servings.

*Substitute 2 cups cooked black beans for canned, if desired.

Cooks Chat

"My entire family loves this salad! What a hit with the relatives! It tastes even better the second day."

Wild Rice Salad

Prep: 10 min.   **Cook:** 10 min.   **Other:** 8 hrs.

1 (6-ounce) package fast-
    cooking long-grain and
    wild rice mix
2 cups chopped cooked
    chicken
½ cup dried cranberries
1 Granny Smith apple, peeled
    and diced

1 medium carrot, grated
⅓ cup white balsamic vinegar*
4 tablespoons olive oil
¼ teaspoon salt
¼ teaspoon pepper
2 green onions, chopped
1 (2.25-ounce) package sliced
    almonds, toasted

• Cook rice according to package directions; cool.
• Stir together chicken, next 8 ingredients, and rice in a large bowl. Cover and chill 8 hours. Sprinkle with almonds just before serving. Yield: 6 servings.

*Substitute red wine vinegar for white balsamic vinegar, if desired.

Note: For testing purposes only, we used Uncle Ben's Long-Grain & Wild Rice Fast Cook Recipe.

Cooks Chat

"All who try this salad love it! To make this even quicker and easier, I use precooked chicken and don't bother peeling the apple. This salad's light, nutty tasting, and perfect for summer. I even serve it warm as a side dish!"

Lentil-and-Orzo Salad

Prep: 15 min.   **Other:** 2 hrs.

¼ cup vinaigrette dressing
2 tablespoons fresh lemon juice
½ teaspoon ground cumin
½ teaspoon salt
½ teaspoon ground black
    pepper
¼ teaspoon dried crushed red
    pepper

2 cups cooked lentils
1 cup cooked orzo
½ red bell pepper, diced
½ small red onion, diced
1½ tablespoons chopped fresh
    cilantro

• Whisk together first 6 ingredients in a large bowl; add lentils and remaining ingredients, tossing gently to coat.
• Cover and chill 2 hours. Yield: 4 servings.

Chilled Vegetable Salad

Prep: 20 min.   **Cook:** 5 min.   **Other:** 8 hrs., 30 min.

1 cup sugar
¾ cup cider vinegar
½ cup vegetable oil
1 medium-size green bell
    pepper, chopped
1 medium onion, chopped
3 celery ribs, sliced
1 (7-ounce) jar diced pimiento,
    undrained

1 (15¼-ounce) can small sweet
    green peas, drained
1 (14½-ounce) can French-cut
    green beans, drained
1 (11-ounce) can white
    shoepeg corn, drained
½ teaspoon salt
¼ teaspoon pepper

• Bring first 3 ingredients to a boil in a small saucepan over medium heat; cook, stirring often, 5 minutes or until sugar dissolves. Remove dressing from heat, and cool 30 minutes.
• Stir together chopped bell pepper and next 8 ingredients in a large bowl; gently stir in dressing. Cover and chill salad 8 hours. Serve with a slotted spoon. Yield: 8 cups.

Note: Salad may be stored in an airtight container in the refrigerator for several days.

Green Bean Salad with Feta

Prep: 5 min. **Cook:** 8 min. **Other:** 2 hrs.

1½ pounds fresh green beans,
    trimmed
1 small red onion, chopped
    (about ½ cup)
½ cup Lemon Vinaigrette
½ cup crumbled feta cheese
½ cup walnuts, toasted and
    coarsely chopped
Garnish: lemon slices

• Cook green beans in boiling salted water to cover 8 minutes or until crisp-tender. Drain and plunge into ice water to stop the cooking process; drain and pat dry. Place in a serving bowl; cover and chill at least 2 hours.
• Add chopped onion and Lemon Vinaigrette to beans, tossing to coat. Sprinkle with feta and walnuts. Garnish, if desired. Yield: 6 to 8 servings.

Lemon Vinaigrette

Prep: 5 min.

Use leftover vinaigrette to marinate artichoke hearts or chicken breasts, or serve over salad niçoise.

3 tablespoons fresh lemon juice
3 tablespoons white wine
    vinegar
1 tablespoon Dijon mustard
½ teaspoon sugar
¼ teaspoon salt
⅛ teaspoon freshly ground
    pepper
½ cup vegetable oil

• Whisk together first 6 ingredients in a small bowl; gradually whisk in oil until blended. Yield: about 1 cup.

Cooks Chat

"This recipe is so easy, and it's absolutely wonderful with a summer meal. I use precut, trimmed green beans, which makes the recipe even easier. I also use dried tomato-flavored low-fat feta. The walnuts really make the dish."

"The crunchy texture of the beans is fabulous, and the walnuts and feta are wonderful. All who tried this dish at my dinner party enjoyed it. I served it with corn casserole and pork."

"I made this recipe for a party, and everyone loved it. I'll definitely make it again."

Green Bean-Potato Salad

Prep: 20 min.   **Cook:** 20 min.   **Other:** 2 hrs.

2 pounds red potatoes
1 pound fresh green beans
¼ cup red wine vinegar
4 green onions, sliced
2 tablespoons chopped fresh
    tarragon

2 tablespoons Dijon mustard
2 tablespoons olive oil
2 teaspoons salt
1 teaspoon pepper
Garnish: fresh tarragon sprig

• Combine potatoes and water to cover in a large saucepan; bring to a boil over medium heat, and cook 13 minutes. Add green beans, and cook 7 minutes or until potatoes are tender. Drain and rinse with cold water. Cut each potato into 8 wedges.
• Whisk together vinegar and next 6 ingredients in a large bowl; add potato wedges and green beans, tossing gently to coat. Cover and chill 2 hours. Garnish, if desired. Yield: 8 servings.

Joy's Potato Salad

Prep: 30 min.   **Cook:** 20 min.   **Other:** 8 hrs.

2 pounds small new potatoes
2 teaspoons salt, divided
1 medium-size green bell
    pepper, diced
12 cherry tomatoes, halved
½ small red onion, diced

3 tablespoons minced fresh basil
⅓ cup red wine vinegar
½ teaspoon pepper
2 teaspoons sugar
½ cup olive oil
Red Leaf lettuce

• Cook potatoes in boiling water to cover and 1 teaspoon salt 15 to 20 minutes or until tender; drain. Plunge into ice water to stop the cooking process; drain. Peel potatoes, and cut in half. Place potato, bell pepper, and next 3 ingredients in a large bowl.
• Process remaining 1 teaspoon salt, vinegar, pepper, and sugar in a blender until smooth. Turn blender on high; add oil in a slow, steady stream. Pour over potato mixture; toss gently to coat.
• Cover and chill 8 hours. Drain; serve on a lettuce-lined dish. Yield: 6 to 8 servings.

New Potato Salad

Prep: 15 min. **Cook:** 30 min. **Other:** 8 hrs.

Bacon adds the final touch to this classic salad.

4 pounds new potatoes
¼ cup white vinegar
2 garlic cloves
1 teaspoon sugar
½ teaspoon salt
½ teaspoon pepper
¾ cup olive oil

2 tablespoons chopped fresh
  basil
2 pints grape tomatoes*
⅓ cup chopped red onion
8 bacon slices, cooked and
  crumbled

• Cook potatoes in boiling water to cover 25 to 30 minutes or just until tender; drain and cool. Cut potatoes in half, and set aside.
• Process vinegar and next 4 ingredients in a blender, stopping to scrape down sides. Turn blender on high, and gradually add oil in a slow, steady stream. Stir in chopped basil.
• Place potato, tomatoes, and onion in a large bowl. Drizzle with dressing; toss gently. Cover and chill 8 hours. Top with crumbled bacon just before serving. Yield: 8 servings.

*Substitute 2 large tomatoes, seeded and chopped, for grape tomatoes, if desired.

Cooks Chat

"I have used this recipe many times, and the results have always been delicious! Using red potatoes in it is especially good."

Roasted New Potato Salad

Prep: 15 min.   **Cook:** 35 min.

If you like your potatoes crispier, bake them about 10 minutes longer, stirring once. Don't forget to schedule the extra time when planning your meal.

2 tablespoons olive oil
2 pounds small red potatoes, diced
½ medium-size sweet onion, chopped
2 teaspoons minced garlic
1 teaspoon coarse salt
½ teaspoon freshly ground pepper

8 to 10 cooked crisp bacon slices, crumbled
1 bunch green onions, chopped
¾ cup prepared Ranch-style dressing
Salt and pepper to taste

• Place oil in a 15- x 10-inch jellyroll pan; add potatoes and next 4 ingredients, tossing to coat. Arrange potato mixture in a single layer.
• Bake at 425° for 30 to 35 minutes or until potatoes are tender, stirring occasionally. Transfer to a large bowl.
• Toss together potatoes, bacon, green onions, and dressing. Add salt and pepper to taste. Serve immediately, or cover and chill until ready to serve. Yield: 4 to 6 servings.

Dianne's Southwestern Cornbread Salad

Prep: 30 min.   **Cook:** 15 min.   **Other:** 2 hrs.

This salad's a great choice for a
covered-dish dinner. It's attractive, it travels well,
and it always has folks asking for the recipe.

1 (6-ounce) package Mexican
   cornbread mix
1 (1-ounce) envelope
   Ranch-style buttermilk
   salad dressing mix
1 small head romaine lettuce,
   shredded
2 large tomatoes, chopped
1 (15-ounce) can black beans,
   rinsed and drained

1 (15¼-ounce) can whole
   kernel corn with red and
   green peppers, drained
1 (8-ounce) package shredded
   Mexican four-cheese blend
6 bacon slices, cooked and
   crumbled
5 green onions, chopped

• Prepare cornbread according to package directions; cool and
crumble. Set aside.
• Prepare salad dressing according to package directions.
• Layer a large bowl with half each of cornbread, lettuce, and next
6 ingredients; spoon half of dressing evenly over top. Repeat layers
with remaining ingredients and dressing. Cover and chill at least
2 hours. Yield: 10 to 12 servings.

Spicy Beef Salad

Prep: 15 min. **Cook:** 12 min. **Other:** 1 hr., 5 min.

Lemon grass is an essential herb in Thai cooking. It tastes like fresh citrus, has long gray-green leaves, and looks like a stiff green onion.

1 large tomato, cut into thin wedges
1 large sweet onion, cut in half and thinly sliced
1 cucumber, diced
2 green onions, chopped
1 pound flank steak
1½ teaspoons salt, divided
2 teaspoons ground coriander, divided
2 small fresh Thai peppers or serrano peppers
1 stalk lemon grass, coarsely chopped*
2 garlic cloves
1 tablespoon chopped fresh ginger
2 tablespoons fresh lemon juice
1 tablespoon rice wine vinegar
¼ cup fish sauce
1 tablespoon vegetable oil
1 teaspoon sugar
Mixed salad greens
Garnish: sliced green onions

• Combine first 4 ingredients; set aside.
• Rub steak with ½ teaspoon salt and 1 teaspoon coriander.
• Process remaining 1 teaspoon salt, remaining 1 teaspoon coriander, and next 9 ingredients in a food processor or blender until smooth. Chill dressing 1 hour.
• Grill steak, covered with grill lid, over medium-high heat (350° to 400°) 6 minutes on each side or to desired degree of doneness. Let stand 5 minutes. Thinly slice steak.
• Place steak and vegetable mixture in a large bowl, and drizzle with dressing, tossing to coat. Serve over salad greens. Garnish, if desired. Yield: 4 to 6 servings.

*Substitute 2 teaspoons grated lemon rind for lemon grass, if desired.

Broccoli-Chicken Salad

Prep: 20 min.   **Cook:** 15 min.   **Other:** 1 hr.

4 skinned and boned chicken
    breasts
4 cups water
¼ cup soy sauce
2 garlic cloves, minced
1 (16-ounce) package fresh
    broccoli florets

4 green onions, chopped
1 medium-size red bell pepper,
    chopped
1 cup sweetened dried
    cranberries
Chutney Dressing
¼ cup chopped peanuts

• Bring first 4 ingredients to a boil in a medium saucepan. Boil 15 minutes or until chicken is done; drain. Cool chicken, and cut into bite-size pieces.
• Toss together chicken, broccoli, and next 4 ingredients. Chill 1 hour. Sprinkle with peanuts before serving. Yield: 6 servings.

Chutney Dressing

Prep: 5 min.

1 (9-ounce) jar mango chutney
½ cup mayonnaise
2 garlic cloves, minced

¼ teaspoon dried crushed
    red pepper

• Stir together all ingredients. Yield: 1¾ cups.

Note: For testing purposes only, we used Major Grey Chutney.

Honey Chicken Salad

Prep: 20 min.

The dressing mixture is reminiscent of poppy seed dressing.

4 cups chopped cooked chicken
3 celery ribs, diced (about
    1½ cups)
1 cup sweetened dried
    cranberries
½ cup chopped pecans, toasted

1½ cups mayonnaise
⅓ cup orange blossom honey
¼ teaspoon salt
¼ teaspoon pepper
Garnish: chopped toasted
    pecans

• Stir together first 4 ingredients.
• Whisk together mayonnaise and next 3 ingredients. Add to chicken mixture, stirring gently until combined. Garnish, if desired. Yield: 4 servings.

Strawberry-Chicken Salad

Prep: 30 min.   **Cook:** 8 min.   **Other:** 1 hr., 10 min.

4 skinned and boned chicken breasts
Raspberry Vinaigrette, divided
8 cups mixed salad greens
1 quart strawberries, sliced

2 pears, sliced
2 avocados, peeled and sliced
½ small sweet onion, diced
½ cup pecan halves, toasted

- Combine chicken and ½ cup Raspberry Vinaigrette in a large zip-top freezer bag. Seal and chill 1 hour.
- Remove chicken from marinade, discarding marinade.
- Grill, covered with grill lid, over medium-high heat (350° to 400°) 4 minutes on each side or until done. Let chicken stand 10 minutes; slice.
- Place salad greens and next 5 ingredients in a large bowl, and gently toss. Divide mixture evenly between 4 serving plates; top with grilled chicken slices. Serve with remaining Raspberry Vinaigrette. Yield: 4 servings.

Raspberry Vinaigrette

Prep: 5 min.

¾ cup pear nectar
⅓ cup vegetable oil
⅓ cup raspberry vinegar
3 tablespoons chopped fresh basil

1 tablespoon Dijon mustard
1 tablespoon sesame oil
½ teaspoon freshly ground pepper
¼ teaspoon salt

- Place all ingredients in a screw-top jar; cover tightly, and shake vigorously until blended. Store in refrigerator for up to 2 weeks, shaking before serving. Yield: 1½ cups.

Breadstick Basket

- Unroll the dough from 2 (11-ounce) cans of refrigerated soft breadsticks, and separate at perforations. Reserve and set aside 6 strips. Gently press and stretch each of the remaining 18 strips to a length of 12 inches.
- Wrap the outside of a 4-quart stainless steel mixing bowl with nonstick aluminum foil, and invert onto a lightly greased baking sheet. Arrange strips in a lattice pattern over the top and sides of the bowl, trimming excess as needed. (To weave a lattice pattern, place 4 to 5 strips of dough across the bowl in one direction; fold back alternating strips as each crisscross strip is added.)
- Whisk together 1 large egg and 1 tablespoon water; brush lightly over strips, reserving remaining egg mixture.

• Roll each of the 6 reserved strips into a 20-inch rope; pinch 3 of the ropes together at 1 end to seal, and braid. Repeat procedure with remaining 3 ropes. Gently press the 2 braided ropes around the rim of the bowl, pinching together at both ends to seal. Brush lightly with reserved egg mixture, discarding any remaining mixture.
• Bake at 375° for 30 minutes or until evenly browned. Shield top of bowl with aluminum foil after 20 minutes to prevent excessive browning. Remove from oven, and cool completely on a wire rack. Gently remove basket from bowl. (The inside of the basket will be pale in color.)

Sherried Chicken-and-Grape Salad

Prep: 20 min.

6 cups chopped cooked chicken
3 cups sliced green grapes
1 cup toasted slivered almonds
2 celery ribs, diced
3 green onions, minced

¾ cup mayonnaise
¼ cup sour cream
2 tablespoons sherry
½ teaspoon seasoned salt
½ teaspoon seasoned pepper

• Stir together all ingredients. Yield: 6 to 8 servings.

Note: For a special occasion, serve chicken salad in small grapefruit halves with pulp removed. (Line grapefruit halves with leaf lettuce.) Create a handle for the grapefruit with florist wire, florist tape, and small silk flowers. Bend wire to form handle, insert into citrus shell, and tape flowers to handle.

Bacon-Mandarin Salad

Prep: 20 min.

½ cup olive oil
¼ cup red wine vinegar
¼ cup sugar
1 tablespoon chopped fresh basil
⅛ teaspoon hot sauce
2 (15-ounce) cans mandarin oranges, drained and chilled*

1 bunch Red Leaf lettuce, torn
1 head romaine lettuce, torn
1 (16-ounce) package bacon, cooked and crumbled
1 (4-ounce) package sliced almonds, toasted

• Whisk together first 5 ingredients in a large bowl, blending well. Add oranges and lettuces, tossing gently to coat. Sprinkle with crumbled bacon and sliced almonds. Serve immediately. Yield: 12 servings.

*Substitute fresh orange segments for canned mandarin oranges, if desired.

Shrimp Pasta Salad with Green Goddess Dressing

Prep: 30 min. **Cook:** 5 min.

3 cups water
1 pound unpeeled, medium-size fresh shrimp
1 (8-ounce) package small shell pasta, cooked, rinsed, and drained
2 teaspoons champagne or white wine vinegar
⅛ teaspoon salt

⅛ teaspoon pepper
1 small head Green Leaf lettuce, separated into leaves
2 medium tomatoes, cut into wedges
1 yellow bell pepper, cut into strips
Green Goddess Dressing

• Bring 3 cups water to a boil, and add shrimp; cook 3 to 5 minutes or just until shrimp turn pink. Drain and rinse with cold water.
• Peel shrimp, and devein, if desired.
• Toss together pasta, vinegar, salt, and pepper. Line a large platter with lettuce leaves; spoon pasta in center, and top with shrimp. Arrange tomato and bell pepper around pasta. Serve salad with Green Goddess Dressing. Yield: 6 to 8 servings.

Green Goddess Dressing

Prep: 10 min.

1⅓ cups mayonnaise
½ cup fresh parsley leaves
2 tablespoons chopped fresh chives
2 teaspoons champagne or white wine vinegar

1 teaspoon anchovy paste
1 teaspoon grated lemon rind
2 tablespoons fresh lemon juice
¼ teaspoon pepper

• Process all ingredients in a food processor until smooth, stopping to scrape down sides. Cover and chill. Yield: about 1⅓ cups.

PARTY PLEASER

Cooks Chat

"*Purchase fresh/frozen precooked shrimp to cut down on time. Don't skip the dressing that goes with this salad. This is an absolutely fabulous dish with easy directions and excellent flavors!*"

"*The dressing had a really good flavor. I will make this again.*"

"*I loved this, and so did my mom. She asked me to make it for Mother's Day dinner this year.*"

Salad Niçoise

Prep: 20 min.   **Cook:** 18 min.   **Other:** 30 min.

You can prepare and chill each component of this super salad ahead of time and assemble it when ready to serve.

2 pounds unpeeled small red potatoes
1½ pounds fresh green beans
Herb Dressing
2 heads romaine lettuce
6 (3-ounce) packages albacore tuna, flaked

1 (2-ounce) can anchovy fillets, drained (optional)
5 hard-cooked eggs, quartered
5 plum tomatoes, cut into wedges or 1 (8-ounce) container grape tomatoes
1 cup sliced ripe olives

• Cook potatoes in boiling water to cover 15 minutes or until tender; drain. Cool slightly; cut into slices. Set aside.
• Cook green beans in boiling water to cover 3 minutes; drain. Plunge into ice water to stop the cooking process.
• Toss together potato slices, green beans, and ½ cup Herb Dressing in a large bowl. Chill at least 30 minutes.
• Tear 1 head romaine lettuce into bite-size pieces. Line a platter with leaves of remaining head of romaine lettuce. Arrange potato mixture over lettuce leaves. Top with torn lettuce pieces.
• Mound tuna in center of greens. Arrange anchovies around tuna, if desired. Place eggs and tomato wedges on salad. Sprinkle with sliced olives. Serve with remaining Herb Dressing. Yield: 8 servings.

Herb Dressing

Prep: 10 min.

1 cup olive oil
½ cup red wine vinegar
¼ cup drained capers
2 green onions, chopped
2 teaspoons dried basil
2 teaspoons dried marjoram

2 teaspoons dried oregano
2 teaspoons dried thyme
½ teaspoon dry mustard
½ teaspoon salt
½ teaspoon freshly ground pepper

• Whisk together all ingredients. Yield: 1½ cups.

Sesame Noodle Salad

Prep: 20 min.

This simple side can become a main dish if you add meat or vegetable stir-ins. Try finely diced fresh tomato, squash, and green pepper; chopped cooked chicken; leftover grilled shrimp or flank steak; or fried tofu cubes.

1 (8-ounce) package linguine
¼ cup rice vinegar
¼ cup soy sauce
¼ cup dark sesame oil

1 teaspoon sugar
5 green onions, sliced
Toasted sesame seeds (optional)

• Cook linguine according to package directions; drain and rinse linguine with cold water.
• Stir together vinegar and next 3 ingredients in a large bowl. Stir in linguine and onions; sprinkle with sesame seeds, if desired. Serve immediately. Yield: 4 servings.

Pasta Salad

Prep: 35 min.

1 pound uncooked fusilli
¼ cup white wine vinegar
2 tablespoons chopped fresh parsley
1½ teaspoons dried Italian seasoning
1 teaspoon salt
½ teaspoon garlic powder

½ teaspoon pepper
¾ cup olive oil
1 cup grated Parmesan cheese
⅓ cup diced onion
1 (4-ounce) can chopped pimiento, drained
1 (2¼-ounce) can sliced ripe olives, drained

• Cook pasta according to package directions; drain.
• Whisk together vinegar and next 5 ingredients in a large bowl. Add olive oil in a slow, steady stream, whisking constantly until blended. Add pasta, cheese, and remaining ingredients, tossing to coat. Serve immediately, or cover and chill 8 hours. Yield: 10 cups.

Honey-Pecan Dressing

Prep: 5 min.

This tangy-sweet dressing works nicely for a
green salad or fruit salad.

3 tablespoons sugar
1 tablespoon chopped sweet
 onion
½ teaspoon dry mustard
¼ teaspoon salt

½ cup honey
¼ cup red wine vinegar
1 cup vegetable oil
1 cup chopped pecans, toasted

• Pulse first 6 ingredients in a blender 2 to 3 times until blended.
With blender running, pour oil through food chute in a slow,
steady stream; process until smooth. Stir in pecans. Yield: 2½ cups.

Fruit Salad with Honey-Pecan Dressing: Arrange fresh
orange and grapefruit sections, sliced avocado, and sliced strawberries over Bibb lettuce leaves; drizzle with dressing.

Cooks Chat

*"The combination of ingredients
sounds strange, but the end result is
very delicious!"*

Raspberry Salad Dressing

Prep: 5 min.

1 (10-ounce) jar seedless
 raspberry fruit spread or
 preserves

½ cup seasoned rice wine
 vinegar
¼ cup olive oil

• Microwave raspberry spread in a microwave-safe bowl at
MEDIUM LOW (30%) power 1 minute or until melted. Whisk
in vinegar and olive oil until blended; let cool. Serve at room
temperature. Yield: about 2 cups.

Romaine Salad with Raspberry Dressing: Combine 1 head
romaine lettuce, torn; 1 small red onion, sliced; 1 cup crumbled feta
cheese; ½ cup chopped toasted pecans; and 4 bacon slices, cooked
and crumbled. Serve with Raspberry Salad Dressing.

Cooks Chat

*"This dressing is fabulous! Along
with green leafy lettuce, lots of gorgonzola cheese, bacon, toasted
pecans, and onions, it made the best
salad we've had in a long time. It's
also great with sliced chicken on top
as a main dish."*

*"My sister-in-law brought this salad
over for dinner, and we all loved the
fresh raspberry taste combined with
the creaminess of the feta. I liked
the recipe so much that I had to go
online and find it for myself! Enjoy."*

Blue Cheese-Buttermilk Dressing

Prep: 5 min.

1 (4-ounce) package crumbled blue cheese
1 cup nonfat buttermilk
½ to ⅔ cup reduced-fat mayonnaise

3 to 4 tablespoons lemon juice
1 garlic clove, minced

• Stir together all ingredients in a bowl. Serve over salad. Yield: 1¾ cups.

Mustard Vinaigrette

Prep: 5 min.

Drizzle this dressing over salad greens or over a meaty po'boy sandwich.

2 tablespoons coarse-grained Dijon mustard
¾ cup vegetable oil
¼ cup white vinegar

½ teaspoon sesame oil
¼ teaspoon freshly ground pepper

• Whisk together all ingredients; serve with mixed salad greens. Yield: 1⅓ cups.

sandwiches & soups

★★★★★

Cozy up to a warm cup of soup or indulge in a gourmet sandwich from this scrumptious selection.

Fiesta Chowder, page 282

Philly Firecrackers

Prep: 20 min.   **Other:** 8 hrs.

½ cup sour cream*
½ cup mayonnaise*
1 green onion, chopped
2 tablespoons prepared
    horseradish
½ teaspoon salt
½ teaspoon pepper

8 (12-inch) flour tortillas
1 pound roast beef, cut into
    24 thin slices
2 (6-ounce) packages deli-style
    sharp Cheddar cheese
    slices (optional)
2 cups shredded iceberg lettuce

• Stir together first 6 ingredients until blended. Spread evenly on 1 side of each tortilla; top each with 3 beef slices and, if desired, 2 cheese slices. Sprinkle evenly with shredded lettuce.
• Roll up tortillas tightly; wrap in parchment paper or plastic wrap. Chill 8 hours. Yield: 8 servings.

Note: For testing purposes only, we used Sargento Deli Style Sharp Cheddar Cheese slices.

*Substitute ½ cup light sour cream and ½ cup light mayonnaise, if desired.

Sweet-and-Savory Burgers

Prep: 15 min.   **Cook:** 10 min.   **Other:** 4 hrs.

¼ cup soy sauce
2 tablespoons corn syrup
1 tablespoon lemon juice
½ teaspoon ground ginger
¼ teaspoon garlic powder
2 green onions, thinly sliced

2 pounds ground beef
¼ cup chili sauce
¼ cup jalapeño jelly
8 hamburger buns
Toppings: grilled sweet onions,
    grilled pineapple slices

• Stir together first 6 ingredients, and pour into a shallow pan or baking dish.
• Shape beef into 8 patties, and place in a single layer in marinade, turning to coat both sides. Cover and chill 4 hours. Drain, reserving marinade.
• Grill patties over medium-high heat (350° to 400°) 5 minutes on each side or until beef is no longer pink, brushing several times with reserved marinade. Stir together chili sauce and jalapeño jelly. Serve patties on buns with chili sauce mixture and toppings. Yield: 8 servings.

Debate Barbecue Sandwiches

Prep: 15 min.   **Cook:** 8 hrs.

1 (3-pound) boneless pork loin
    roast, trimmed
1 cup water
1 (18-ounce) bottle barbecue
    sauce
¼ cup firmly packed brown
    sugar

2 tablespoons Worcestershire
    sauce
1 to 2 tablespoons hot sauce
1 teaspoon salt
1 teaspoon pepper
Hamburger buns
Coleslaw

• Place roast in a 4-quart electric slow cooker; add 1 cup water.
• Cover and cook at HIGH 7 hours or until meat is tender; stir
with a fork, shredding meat. Add barbecue sauce and next 5 ingredients; reduce setting to LOW, and cook, covered, 1 hour. Serve
barbecue on buns with coleslaw. Yield: 20 servings.

Hot Ham-and-Cheese Rollup

Prep: 20 min.   **Cook:** 25 min.   **Other:** 5 min.

To enjoy for lunch, reheat a rollup in the microwave at HIGH
1 minute or until thoroughly heated.

1 (13.8-ounce) refrigerated
    pizza crust dough
2 tablespoons chopped fresh or
    2 teaspoons dried basil
6 ounces thinly sliced maple-
    glazed ham

1 cup (4 ounces) shredded
    part-skim mozzarella
    cheese
Pasta sauce or mustard (optional)

• Roll out dough to a 12-inch square. Sprinkle with basil to
½ inch from edges. Top with ham slices, and sprinkle with cheese
to ½ inch from edges.
• Roll up dough, beginning at 1 end; place, seam side down, on an
aluminum foil-lined baking sheet coated with cooking spray.
• Bake at 400° for 20 to 25 minutes or until golden brown. Cool
5 minutes. Cut into 1½-inch slices. Serve rollups with pasta sauce
or mustard, if desired. Yield: 4 servings.

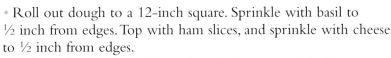

Ham-Swiss-and-Asparagus Sandwiches

Prep: 20 min. **Cook:** 1 min.

Purchase ¾ pound sliced deli ham instead of baking your own ham, if you'd rather.

¾ pound fresh asparagus
3 tablespoons light butter or
    margarine, softened
1 small garlic clove, minced
4 (6-inch) French bread loaves,
    split

3 tablespoons light mayonnaise
8 Baked Glazed Ham slices
    (page 200)
4 Swiss cheese slices*
Green Leaf lettuce
3 plum tomatoes, sliced

• Snap off tough ends of asparagus. Cook in boiling water to cover 3 minutes or until crisp-tender; drain. Plunge into ice water to stop the cooking process; drain and chill.
• Stir together butter and garlic.
• Spread butter mixture evenly over bottom halves of bread. Spread mayonnaise evenly over top halves of bread. Layer bottom halves evenly with ham, asparagus, and cheese; place on a baking sheet.
• Broil 2 inches from heat 1 minute or just until cheese melts. Top evenly with lettuce, tomato, and top halves of bread. Yield: 4 servings.

*Substitute 6 ounces thinly sliced Brie with rind removed for Swiss cheese slices, if desired.

KITCHEN COMFORT

Cooks Chat

"Simply one of the best sandwiches I've ever had!"

"For a gourmet twist, I add arugula in place of the lettuce and pickled asparagus instead of the fresh asparagus. Magnifique!"

Smoked Turkey Wraps

Prep: 15 min.

2 (6.5-ounce) packages buttery garlic-and-herb spreadable cheese, softened*
8 (10-inch) whole-grain pita wraps or flour tortillas
Caramelized Onions
1½ pounds thinly sliced smoked turkey

16 bacon slices, cooked and crumbled
4 cups loosely packed arugula or gourmet mixed baby salad greens

• Spread softened cheese evenly over whole-grain pita wraps; top cheese evenly with Caramelized Onions and remaining ingredients. Roll up, and wrap in parchment paper; chill. Cut in half to serve. Yield: 8 servings.

*For testing purposes only, we used Alouette Garlic et Herbes Gourmet Spreadable Cheese for garlic-and-herb spreadable cheese.

Caramelized Onions

Prep: 5 min.   **Cook:** 20 min.

2 large sweet onions, diced
1 tablespoon sugar

2 tablespoons olive oil
2 teaspoons balsamic vinegar

• Cook diced onion and sugar in hot oil in a large skillet over medium-high heat, stirring often, 20 minutes or until onion is caramel-colored. Stir in balsamic vinegar. Yield: 2 cups.

Shrimp Po'boys

Prep: 32 min.   **Cook:** 16 min.

2 pounds unpeeled, large fresh
   shrimp
1¼ cups all-purpose flour
½ teaspoon salt
½ teaspoon pepper
½ cup milk
1 large egg

Peanut oil
⅓ cup butter
1 teaspoon minced garlic
4 French bread rolls, split
Rémoulade Sauce
1 cup shredded lettuce

• Peel shrimp, and devein, if desired.
• Combine flour, salt, and pepper. Stir together milk and egg until smooth. Toss shrimp in milk mixture; dredge in flour mixture.
• Pour oil to a depth of 2 inches into a Dutch oven; heat to 375°. Fry shrimp, in batches, 1 to 2 minutes or until golden; drain on wire racks.
• Melt butter; add garlic. Spread cut sides of rolls evenly with butter mixture; place on a large baking sheet.
• Bake at 450° for 8 minutes. Spread cut sides of rolls evenly with Rémoulade Sauce. Place shrimp and lettuce on bottom halves of rolls; cover with roll tops. Yield: 4 sandwiches.

Rémoulade Sauce

Prep: 5 min.

1 cup mayonnaise
3 green onions, sliced
2 tablespoons Creole mustard
2 garlic cloves, pressed
1 tablespoon chopped fresh
   parsley

¼ teaspoon ground red
   pepper
Garnish: sliced green onions

• Stir together first 6 ingredients until well blended. Garnish, if desired. Yield: about 1¼ cups.

Cooks Chat

"These gyros were easy, and they had a very good flavor combination. The shrimp were terrific even by themselves. I had a few leftover shrimp, and they were just as good the next day as part of a cold sandwich."

"This recipe is very simple and is great for a good summer dinner with friends. Kids love it, too!"

Grilled-Shrimp Gyros with Herbed Yogurt Spread

Prep: 25 min.   **Cook:** 10 min.   **Other:** 30 min.

Chill wraps until ready to serve.

1½ pounds unpeeled, medium-size fresh shrimp
2 tablespoons Greek seasoning
2 tablespoons olive oil
6 (12-inch) wooden skewers
4 (8-inch) pita rounds or gyro rounds

Herbed Yogurt Spread
½ cup crumbled feta cheese
1 large tomato, chopped
1 cucumber, thinly sliced

• Peel shrimp, and devein, if desired.
• Combine seasoning and olive oil in a zip-top freezer bag; add shrimp. Seal and chill 30 minutes.
• Soak skewers in water 30 minutes while shrimp marinates; thread shrimp onto skewers.

• Grill, covered with grill lid, over medium heat (300° to 350°) about 5 minutes on each side or just until shrimp turn pink.
• Wrap each pita round in a damp cloth; microwave at HIGH 10 to 15 seconds or until soft. Spread 1 side of each pita round with Herbed Yogurt Spread. Top evenly with shrimp, cheese, tomato, and cucumber; roll up. Yield: 4 servings.

Herbed Yogurt Spread

Prep: 5 min.

½ cup low-fat yogurt
1 garlic clove, minced
1 tablespoon chopped fresh or
    ¾ teaspoon dried oregano

1 teaspoon chopped fresh mint
2 teaspoons lemon juice
¼ teaspoon pepper

• Whisk together all ingredients; chill until ready to serve or up to 8 hours. Yield: about ½ cup.

Rolled Olive Sandwiches

Prep: 20 min.   **Other:** 4 hrs.

24 thin sandwich bread slices
1 (8-ounce) package cream
    cheese, softened
1 cup diced salad olives

½ cup chopped pecans, toasted
½ cup mayonnaise
¼ teaspoon pepper

• Remove crusts from bread; reserve crusts for another use. Flatten bread slices with a rolling pin.
• Stir together cream cheese and next 4 ingredients. Spread 2 tablespoons cream cheese mixture on 1 side of each bread slice. Roll up tightly; cover and chill at least 4 hours. To serve, cut each roll into 4 slices. Yield: 96 appetizers.

MAKE AHEAD

Cooks Chat

"These are excellent and easy to make. I make them ahead of time, slice them, and cover them with a damp paper towel and plastic wrap. They are always a hit! A friend of mine who hates olives loves these."

Chunky Italian Soup

Chunky Italian Soup

Prep: 20 min.   **Cook:** 45 min.

1 pound lean ground beef or
   beef tips
1 medium onion, chopped
2 (14½-ounce) cans Italian-
   style stewed tomatoes
1 (11-ounce) can Cream of
   Tomato Bisque soup,
   undiluted
4 cups water
2 garlic cloves, minced
2 teaspoons dried basil
2 teaspoons dried oregano

1 teaspoon salt
½ teaspoon pepper
1 tablespoon chili powder
   (optional)
1 (16-ounce) can kidney beans,
   drained
1 (16-ounce) can Italian-style
   green beans, drained
1 carrot, chopped
1 zucchini, chopped
8 ounces rotini noodles, cooked
Grated Parmesan cheese

• Cook beef and onion in a Dutch oven over medium heat, stirring until beef crumbles and is no longer pink; drain. Return mixture to pan. Stir in tomatoes, next 7 ingredients, and, if desired, chili powder; bring to a boil. Reduce heat; simmer, stirring occasionally, 30 minutes. Stir in kidney beans and next 3 ingredients; simmer, stirring occasionally, 15 minutes. Stir in pasta. Sprinkle each serving with cheese. Yield: 10 cups.

Cooks Chat

"Incredible! This family favorite is very easy and filling. I serve it with garlic bread. It's great prepared in the slow cooker, too!"

"Great! I will make this again and again. I used sirloin tip strips, which were really tender and hearty, for the beef."

Easy Chili

Prep: 15 min.   **Cook:** 6 hrs.

Top with shredded Cheddar cheese and corn chips. If you want to thicken this saucy chili, stir in finely crushed saltine crackers until you achieve the desired thickness. Complete the meal with sliced apples and grapes.

1½ pounds lean ground beef
1 onion, chopped
1 small green bell pepper,
   chopped
2 garlic cloves, minced
2 (16-ounce) cans red kidney
   beans, rinsed and drained

2 (14½-ounce) cans diced
   tomatoes
2 to 3 tablespoons chili powder
1 teaspoon salt
1 teaspoon pepper
1 teaspoon ground cumin

• Cook first 4 ingredients in a large skillet over medium-high heat, stirring until beef crumbles and is no longer pink; drain. Place mixture in a 5-quart slow cooker; stir in beans and remaining ingredients. Cook at HIGH 3 to 4 hours or at LOW 5 to 6 hours. Yield: 6 to 8 servings.

Cooks Chat

"Terrific! If your taste is like mine (the hotter the better!), nothing cuts the Asheville, North Carolina, snow like adding a couple of dashes of Texas Pete and 1 more teaspoon of chili powder. I also added a little more onion. As easy as this recipe is, you can make it to suit your own taste."

"Just the right size for a family of four. I wanted mine a little thinner, so the second time I made it, I added half a jar of home-canned tomato juice, and it was just right."

Cooks Chat

"This recipe was easy to follow, and the stew was amazing! It made a lot, and the leftovers were great! I served it with some warm rolls from the bakery at the grocery store, which were definitely a great touch."

Beef Stew

Prep: 30 min.   **Cook:** 2 hrs., 31 min.

Chock-full of beef and veggies, this stew is a must-have recipe for cold winter nights.

1 (2¾-pound) boneless chuck roast*
¼ cup all-purpose flour
2 tablespoons vegetable oil
4 cups water
1 tablespoon Worcestershire sauce
2 teaspoons salt
1 teaspoon garlic salt
¾ teaspoon pepper
¼ teaspoon ground allspice
2 bay leaves
4 carrots, scraped
2 celery ribs
4 medium-size red potatoes
3 small onions
2 green bell peppers
3 tablespoons all-purpose flour
3 tablespoons water

• Trim fat from roast; cut roast into 1-inch cubes. Place cubes and ¼ cup flour in a plastic bag; seal bag, and shake vigorously to coat.
• Pour oil into a large Dutch oven; place over medium-high heat until hot. Add beef, and cook, stirring occasionally, until browned.
• Add 4 cups water and next 6 ingredients; bring to a boil. Cover, reduce heat, and simmer 2 hours or until tender.
• Cut carrots and celery into 2-inch lengths. Peel potatoes, and cut potatoes and onions into eighths. Cut bell peppers into 1-inch pieces.
• Add carrots, celery, potatoes, onions, and bell peppers to beef mixture; cover and simmer 30 minutes or until vegetables are tender.
• Combine 3 tablespoons flour and 3 tablespoons water, stirring well; stir into stew. Bring to a boil; boil, stirring constantly, 1 minute or until thickened and bubbly. Remove bay leaves. Yield: 6 to 8 servings.

*Substitute 2 pounds stew meat for roast, if desired.

Witches' Brew Chicken Soup

Prep: 15 min.   **Cook:** 40 min.

Make a hauntingly delicious meal for your kids with this hearty soup.

1 tablespoon butter or
　　margarine
4 skinned and boned chicken
　　breasts, chopped
1 large onion, chopped
3 carrots, chopped
2 garlic cloves, minced
2 (14-ounce) cans low-sodium
　　chicken broth
1 tablespoon chicken bouillon
　　granules
1 teaspoon ground cumin
¼ teaspoon ground red
　　pepper

3 (15.8-ounce) cans great
　　Northern beans, rinsed,
　　drained, and divided
1 (4.5-ounce) can chopped
　　green chiles
2 tablespoons all-purpose flour
½ cup milk
¼ cup chopped fresh cilantro
Toppings: shredded Cheddar
　　cheese, sour cream, sliced
　　green onions, cooked and
　　crumbled bacon

• Melt butter in a large Dutch oven over medium-high heat; add chicken and next 3 ingredients, and sauté 10 minutes. Stir in broth and next 3 ingredients.
• Bring to a boil; reduce heat, and simmer, stirring occasionally, 20 minutes. Stir in 2 cans of beans and chiles.
• Mash remaining can of beans in a small bowl. Whisk together flour and milk, and stir into beans. Gradually add bean mixture to soup mixture, stirring constantly. Cook 10 minutes or until thickened. Remove from heat, and stir in cilantro. Serve with desired toppings. Yield: 12 cups.

Cooks Chat

"I have given out this recipe to everyone! This amazing soup is a meal in itself! Take it to potlucks, serve it to guests, or dish it up as a family meal. I buy rotisserie chicken already cooked when I am in a hurry. This soup freezes well, too."

"The best soup ever! Extremely flavorful—with a bit of a kick. This is great for fun fall occasions."

White Christmas Chili

Prep: 10 min.   **Cook:** 1 hr., 30 min.

4 skinned and boned chicken breasts
5 cups water
1 large onion, chopped and divided
2 tablespoons butter or margarine
2 celery ribs, chopped (about ⅓ cup)
3 (16-ounce) cans great Northern beans, rinsed, drained, and divided
3 (4.5-ounce) cans chopped green chiles
1 cup canned chicken broth
1 teaspoon ground cumin
1 bay leaf
1 teaspoon salt
⅛ teaspoon ground red pepper
1 tablespoon chopped fresh cilantro
Toppings: tortilla chips, shredded Colby-Jack cheese, salsa, sour cream

• Place chicken, 5 cups water, and half of onion in a large Dutch oven over medium-high heat, and cook 15 to 18 minutes or until chicken is tender. Remove chicken, reserving broth in Dutch oven. Cut chicken into bite-size pieces; set aside.
• Melt butter in a skillet; add celery and remaining onion, and sauté until tender.
• Stir chicken, celery mixture, 2 cans beans, and next 6 ingredients into broth in Dutch oven, and bring to a boil. Reduce heat to medium-low, and cook 1 hour, stirring frequently, until thickened.
• Process remaining 1 can beans in a blender until smooth, stopping to scrape down sides. Stir bean puree into chili.
• Remove and discard bay leaf; stir in cilantro just before serving with desired toppings. Yield: 6 to 8 servings.

Tortilla Soup

Prep: 10 min.   **Cook:** 6 hrs., 10 min.

2 (4-ounce) skinned and boned
    chicken breasts, cubed
2 cups frozen whole kernel
    corn, thawed
1 large onion, chopped
2 garlic cloves, pressed
2 (14-ounce) cans low-sodium
    fat-free chicken broth
1 (10¾-ounce) can tomato
    puree
1 (10-ounce) can diced
    tomatoes and green chiles

2 teaspoons ground cumin
1 teaspoon salt
1 teaspoon chili powder
⅛ teaspoon ground red pepper
⅛ teaspoon ground black
    pepper
1 bay leaf
4 (5½-inch) corn tortillas
Garnish: chopped fresh cilantro

• Combine first 13 ingredients in a 4-quart slow cooker.
• Cover and cook at HIGH 6 hours. Discard bay leaf.
• Cut tortillas into ¼-inch-wide strips; place on a baking sheet.
• Bake at 375° for 5 minutes. Stir and bake 5 more minutes or
until crisp. Serve with soup. Garnish, if desired. Yield: 10 cups.

Cooks Chat

*"This soup is wonderfully authentic
(I am originally from San Antonio,
Texas), and it's so easy to make! The
only addition I made is to top the
soup with shredded Monterey Jack
cheese after pouring it into serving
bowls. Try it once, and it will
become a staple in your household."*

*"I love this recipe! It's extremely
easy to make and is ideal for those
of us who are always on the go. It
also freezes quite well."*

*"My husband and I love this recipe!
Great soup to come home to after a
long day."*

Hot Brown Soup

Prep: 10 min.   **Cook:** 15 min.

¼ cup butter or margarine
¼ cup minced onion
¼ cup all-purpose flour
½ teaspoon garlic salt
⅛ teaspoon hot sauce
4 cups milk
1 cup (4 ounces) shredded
    sharp Cheddar cheese

½ cup chopped cooked ham
½ cup chopped cooked turkey
Toppings: crumbled bacon,
    chopped tomato, chopped
    fresh parsley

• Melt butter in a Dutch oven over medium heat. Add onion; sauté
until tender. Add flour, garlic salt, and hot sauce; cook, stirring constantly, 1 minute. Gradually stir in milk; cook until thickened and
bubbly. Reduce heat; stir in cheese until melted. Add ham and
turkey; cook, stirring occasionally, until heated (do not boil). Serve
with desired toppings. Yield: 5 cups.

Cooks Chat

*"This is one of the best recipes for
using Thanksgiving leftovers. I look
forward to making this one every
year. I make it with just turkey (no
ham), and it is great."*

Quick Chicken and Dumplings

Prep: 10 min.   **Cook:** 25 min.

One roasted whole chicken or 6 skinned and boned cooked chicken breasts yield about 3 cups chopped meat.

4 cups water
3 cups chopped cooked chicken
2 (10¾-ounce) cans cream of chicken soup, undiluted
2 teaspoons chicken bouillon granules

1 teaspoon seasoned pepper
1 (7.5-ounce) can refrigerated buttermilk biscuits

• Bring first 5 ingredients to a boil in a Dutch oven over medium-high heat, stirring often.
• Separate biscuits in half, forming 2 rounds; cut each round in half. Drop biscuit pieces, 1 at a time, into boiling mixture; stir gently. Cover, reduce heat to low, and simmer, stirring occasionally, 15 to 20 minutes. Yield: 4 to 6 servings.

To lighten: Use reduced-sodium, reduced-fat cream of chicken soup; reduced-fat biscuits; and chopped, cooked chicken breasts.

Mexican Chicken-Corn Chowder

Prep: 20 min.   **Cook:** 30 min.

3 tablespoons butter or margarine
4 skinned and boned chicken breasts, cut into bite-size pieces (1½ pounds)
1 small onion, chopped
2 garlic cloves, minced
2 cups half-and-half
2 cups (8 ounces) shredded Monterey Jack cheese
2 (14¾-ounce) cans cream-style corn

1 (4.5-ounce) can chopped green chiles, undrained
½ teaspoon hot sauce
¼ teaspoon salt
½ to 1 teaspoon ground cumin
2 tablespoons chopped fresh cilantro
Garnishes: chopped fresh cilantro, Anaheim chile

• Melt butter in a Dutch oven over medium-high heat; add chicken, onion, and garlic, and sauté 10 minutes. Stir in next 7 ingredients; cook over low heat, stirring often, 15 minutes. Stir in 2 tablespoons cilantro. Garnish, if desired. Yield: 2 quarts.

Chicken-Corn Chowder

Prep: 10 min.   **Cook:** 20 min.

This soup can be made ahead and thinned with
milk when reheating.

1 tablespoon butter or
    margarine
1 (8-ounce) package sliced
    fresh mushrooms
1 medium onion, chopped
2 (14-ounce) cans chicken
    broth
1 (16-ounce) package frozen
    shoepeg white corn
2 cups cubed cooked chicken
    breast

1 (10¾-ounce) can condensed
    cream of chicken soup
½ cup uncooked orzo
1 tablespoon sugar
½ teaspoon dried basil
½ teaspoon dried rosemary or
    thyme
½ teaspoon salt
½ teaspoon pepper
1 cup milk
2 tablespoons all-purpose flour

• Melt butter in a large Dutch oven over medium-high heat; add
mushrooms and onion, and sauté 5 minutes or until tender.
• Add chicken broth and next 9 ingredients; simmer 10 minutes or
until orzo is tender.
• Stir together milk and flour in a small bowl; gradually stir into
chowder, and simmer 5 minutes. Yield: 6 servings.

Cooks Chat

*"This is a great recipe for active
families. I serve it with hot French
bread, and my three boys love it. It
freezes and reheats well and seems
to take the chill right out of our
bones after being outside at football
practice in the fall."*

*"We just had this wonderful soup
for supper. It was very easy to prepare, and the flavor was great. My
husband and children loved it! I
didn't add the mushrooms, and
instead of orzo, I used potatoes.
This is a keeper for those days
when you need something that is
tasty and filling but doesn't take a
lot of time."*

*"This has an excellent blend of
flavors. I use Yukon Gold potatoes
instead of orzo."*

Fiesta Chowder

Prep: 15 min.   **Cook:** 15 min.

3 tablespoons all-purpose flour
1 (1.4-ounce) package fajita seasoning, divided
4 skinned and boned chicken breasts, cubed
3 tablespoons vegetable oil
1 medium onion, chopped
1 teaspoon minced garlic
1 (15¼-ounce) can whole kernel corn with red and green peppers, drained
1 (15-ounce) can black beans, rinsed and drained
1 (14½-ounce) can Mexican-style stewed tomatoes
1 (4.5-ounce) can chopped green chiles
3 cups water
1 cup uncooked instant brown rice
1 (2¼-ounce) can sliced ripe olives (optional)
1 (10¾-ounce) can condensed nacho cheese soup
3 tablespoons chopped fresh cilantro
1 tablespoon lime juice
Garnish: chopped fresh cilantro
Breadsticks (optional)

• Combine flour and 2 tablespoons fajita seasoning in a zip-top freezer bag; add chicken. Seal and shake to coat.
• Cook chicken in hot oil in a large Dutch oven over high heat, stirring often, 4 minutes or until browned. Reduce heat to medium-high; add onion and garlic. Sauté 5 minutes. Stir in remaining fajita seasoning, corn, next 5 ingredients, and, if desired, olives. Bring mixture to a boil; reduce heat to medium-low, cover, and simmer 5 minutes. Remove lid, and stir in nacho cheese soup, chopped cilantro, and lime juice. Garnish, if desired, and serve with breadsticks, if desired. Yield: 8 to 10 servings.

She-Crab Soup

Prep: 10 min.   **Cook:** 1 hr., 20 min.

1 quart whipping cream	⅓ cup all-purpose flour
⅛ teaspoon salt	2 tablespoons lemon juice
⅛ teaspoon pepper	¼ teaspoon ground nutmeg
2 fish bouillon cubes	1 pound fresh crabmeat
2 cups boiling water	Garnish: chopped parsley
¼ cup unsalted butter	⅓ cup sherry (optional)

• Combine first 3 ingredients in a heavy saucepan; bring to a boil over medium heat. Reduce heat, and simmer 1 hour. Set aside. Stir together fish bouillon cubes and 2 cups boiling water until bouillon dissolves.
• Melt butter in a large heavy saucepan over low heat; add flour, stirring until smooth. Cook 1 minute, stirring constantly. Gradually add hot fish broth; cook over medium heat until thickened. Stir in cream mixture, and cook until thoroughly heated. Add lemon juice, nutmeg, and crabmeat. Ladle into individual serving bowls. Garnish, if desired. Add a spoonful of sherry to each serving, if desired. Yield: about 6 cups.

Note: For testing purposes only, we used Knorr Fish Bouillon Cubes. It is important to use good-quality sherry, not cooking sherry, for this soup.

Frogmore Stew

Prep: 10 min.   **Cook:** 30 min.

5 quarts water	6 ears fresh corn, halved
¼ cup Old Bay seasoning	4 pounds unpeeled, large fresh
4 pounds small red potatoes	shrimp
2 pounds kielbasa or hot	Old Bay seasoning
smoked link sausage, cut	Cocktail sauce
into 1½-inch pieces	

• Bring 5 quarts water and ¼ cup Old Bay seasoning to a rolling boil in a large covered stockpot.
• Add potatoes; return to a boil, and cook, uncovered, 10 minutes.
• Add sausage and corn, and return to a boil. Cook 10 minutes or until potatoes are tender. Add shrimp to stockpot; cook 3 to 4 minutes or until shrimp turn pink. Drain. Serve with Old Bay seasoning and cocktail sauce. Yield: 12 servings.

Note: For testing purposes only, we used Hillshire Farm Kielbasa.

Frogmore Stew

Cheesy Vegetable Chowder

Cheesy Vegetable Chowder

Prep: 15 min. **Cook:** 30 min.

3½ cups chicken broth
8 celery ribs, sliced
4 carrots, sliced
2 medium potatoes, peeled
   and cubed
1 large onion, chopped
½ teaspoon pepper
2 cups frozen whole kernel
   corn, thawed

¼ cup butter or margarine
¼ cup all-purpose flour
2 cups milk
2 cups (8 ounces) shredded
   sharp Cheddar cheese
Garnish: chopped fresh parsley

• Bring first 6 ingredients to a boil in a Dutch oven. Cover, reduce heat, and simmer 15 to 20 minutes or until vegetables are tender. Remove from heat, and stir in corn.
• Melt butter in a heavy saucepan over low heat; add flour, whisking until smooth. Cook 1 minute, whisking constantly. Gradually whisk in milk; cook over medium heat, whisking constantly, until mixture is thickened and bubbly. Add cheese, stirring until blended.
• Stir cheese mixture gradually into vegetable mixture. Cook over medium heat, stirring constantly, until thoroughly heated. Serve immediately. Garnish, if desired. Yield: 10 cups.

Full-of-Veggies Chili

Prep: 20 min. **Cook:** 30 min.

1 large sweet onion, diced
1 large green bell pepper, diced
2 garlic cloves, minced
2 tablespoons vegetable oil
1 (12-ounce) package ground
   beef substitute
1 large zucchini, diced
1 (11-ounce) can whole kernel
   corn, undrained
4 (8-ounce) cans no-salt-added
   tomato sauce

2 (10-ounce) cans diced tomato
   and green chiles, undrained
1 (15-ounce) can black beans,
   rinsed and drained
1 (15-ounce) can pinto beans,
   rinsed and drained
1 teaspoon sugar
1 (1¾-ounce) envelope Texas-
   style chili seasoning mix

• Sauté first 3 ingredients in hot oil in a large stockpot over medium-high heat 5 minutes or until tender. Stir in beef substitute and remaining ingredients. Bring to a boil; reduce heat. Simmer, uncovered, stirring often, 20 minutes. Yield: about 4 quarts.

Note: Chili may be frozen up to 3 months, if desired.

Cream of Curried Peanut Soup

Prep: 15 min.   **Cook:** 35 min.

2 tablespoons butter or margarine
1 small onion, minced
3 celery ribs, minced
1 garlic clove, minced
2 tablespoons all-purpose flour
2 tablespoons curry powder

⅛ to ¼ teaspoon ground red pepper
3½ cups chicken broth
1 cup creamy peanut butter
2 cups half-and-half
Garnish: chopped peanuts

• Melt butter in a large saucepan over medium heat; add onion and celery, and sauté 5 minutes. Add garlic; sauté 2 minutes. Stir in flour, curry powder, and red pepper until smooth; cook, stirring constantly, 1 minute. Add broth, and bring to a boil; reduce heat to low, and simmer 20 minutes.
• Stir in peanut butter and half-and-half; cook, stirring constantly, 3 to 4 minutes or until thoroughly heated. Cool slightly.
• Process mixture, in batches, in a food processor or blender until smooth. Garnish, if desired. Serve immediately. Yield: 6 cups.

Baked Potato Soup

Prep: 30 min.   **Cook:** 30 min.

To bake potatoes in the microwave, prick each several times with a fork. Microwave 1 inch apart on paper towels at HIGH 14 minutes or until done, turning and rearranging after 5 minutes. Let cool.

5 large baking potatoes, baked
¼ cup butter or margarine
1 medium onion, chopped
⅓ cup all-purpose flour
1 quart half-and-half
3 cups milk
1 teaspoon salt

⅛ teaspoon ground white pepper
2 cups (8 ounces) shredded Cheddar cheese
8 bacon slices, cooked and crumbled

• Peel potatoes, and coarsely mash with a fork.
• Melt butter in a Dutch oven over medium heat; add onion, and sauté until tender. Add flour, stirring until smooth. Stir in potatoes, half-and-half, and next 3 ingredients; cook over low heat until thoroughly heated. Top each serving with cheese and bacon. Yield: about 12 cups.

*Cream of Curried
Peanut Soup*

Wildest Rice Soup

Prep: 25 min.   **Cook:** 20 min.

1 (6.2-ounce) package long-grain and wild rice mix
1 pound bacon, diced
2 cups chopped fresh mushrooms
1 large onion, diced
3¾ cups half-and-half

2½ cups chicken broth
2 (10¾-ounce) cans cream of potato soup, undiluted
1 (8-ounce) loaf pasteurized prepared cheese product, cubed

• Cook wild rice mix according to package directions, omitting seasoning packet; set aside.
• Cook bacon in a Dutch oven until crisp; remove bacon and drain on paper towels, reserving 2 tablespoons drippings in Dutch oven. Sauté mushrooms and onion in drippings until tender; stir in rice, bacon, half-and-half, and remaining ingredients. Cook over medium-low heat, stirring constantly, until soup is thoroughly heated and cheese melts. Yield: 10 cups.

Note: To lighten, decrease bacon to ¼ pound, reserve 2 teaspoons drippings, and use fat-free half-and-half, fat-free chicken broth, reduced-fat cream of potato soup, and light cheese product.

Oven-Baked Split Pea-and-Lentil Soup

Prep: 20 min.   **Cook:** 2 hrs.

This hearty one-dish meal is high in iron as well as soluble fiber.

2 (32-ounce) containers low-sodium fat-free chicken broth
1 cup dried split peas
1 cup dried lentils
4 carrots, sliced
4 celery ribs, sliced
2 medium-size red bell peppers, seeded and chopped

2 onions, chopped
2 bay leaves
½ teaspoon salt
1½ teaspoons ground cumin
1 teaspoon pepper
¼ cup plain fat-free yogurt
¼ cup chopped cucumber

• Combine first 11 ingredients in an ovenproof Dutch oven.
• Bake, covered, at 350° for 2 hours or until peas and lentils are tender. Remove and discard bay leaves. Serve with yogurt and cucumber. Yield: 8 cups.

Greek Garbanzo Stew

Prep: 10 min.   **Cook:** 30 min.

Serve this zesty side over couscous for a hearty
vegetarian entrée.

1 medium onion, diced
1 tablespoon olive oil
2 garlic cloves, minced
1 (28-ounce) can diced
　tomatoes
1 (15-ounce) can garbanzo
　beans, rinsed and
　drained
1 (14-ounce) can vegetable
　broth
2 tablespoons tomato paste

½ teaspoon dried rosemary
2 teaspoons dried oregano
1 teaspoon Greek seasoning
¼ teaspoon salt
½ teaspoon pepper
1 (6-ounce) package fresh baby
　spinach
2 tablespoons chopped fresh
　parsley
Crumbled feta cheese (optional)

• Sauté onion in hot oil in a Dutch oven over medium-high heat
4 to 5 minutes or until tender. Add garlic, and cook 1 minute. Stir
in tomatoes and next 8 ingredients. Bring to a boil; reduce heat to
low, and simmer, stirring occasionally, 15 minutes. Stir in spinach
and chopped parsley; cook 5 minutes. Top with crumbled feta
cheese, if desired. Yield: 8 side-dish servings or 3 to 4 main-dish
servings.

Potato Chowder with Green Chiles

Prep: 30 min.   **Cook:** 30 min.   **Other:** 10 min.

1 large red bell pepper
4 large poblano chile peppers
5 cups chicken broth
1 large potato, peeled and cubed
1 large onion, chopped
1 jalapeño pepper, seeded and chopped
1 teaspoon salt
¼ to ½ teaspoon freshly ground pepper
¼ cup butter or margarine

⅓ cup all-purpose flour
1 teaspoon salt
1 teaspoon dry mustard
¼ to ½ teaspoon freshly ground pepper
2 cups half-and-half
1 cup milk
1 cup (4 ounces) shredded Cheddar cheese
6 bacon slices, cooked and crumbled
1 bunch green onions, chopped

• Broil bell pepper and chile peppers on an aluminum foil-lined baking sheet 5 inches from heat about 5 minutes on each side or until peppers look blistered.
• Place peppers in a zip-top freezer bag; seal and let stand 10 minutes to loosen skins. Peel peppers; remove and discard seeds. Coarsely chop peppers.
• Bring chopped roasted peppers, chicken broth, and next 5 ingredients to a boil in a Dutch oven over medium heat. Reduce heat, and simmer 15 minutes or until potato is tender.
• Melt butter in a heavy saucepan over low heat; whisk in flour and next 3 ingredients until smooth. Cook, whisking constantly, 1 minute. Gradually whisk in half-and-half.
• Stir white sauce and milk into chicken broth mixture, and cook over medium heat 8 to 10 minutes or until thickened and bubbly. Sprinkle each serving evenly with cheese, bacon, and green onions. Yield: 9 cups.

Spinach-Tortellini Soup

Prep: 10 min.　**Cook:** 20 min.

1 (14-ounce) can chicken broth
4 cups water
2 extra-large vegetable bouillon
　　cubes
1 (10-ounce) package frozen
　　chopped spinach,
　　unthawed
2 (14½-ounce) cans stewed
　　tomatoes, undrained

1 garlic clove, minced
2 (9-ounce) packages
　　refrigerated cheese-filled
　　tortellini
½ cup shredded Parmesan
　　cheese

• Bring first 3 ingredients to a boil in a Dutch oven over medium-high heat.
• Add spinach, stewed tomatoes, and garlic, and return mixture to a boil.
• Stir in tortellini, and cook 5 minutes. Sprinkle each serving evenly with shredded Parmesan cheese. Yield: 16 cups.

Note: For testing purposes only, we used Knorr Vegetable Bouillon Cubes.

Cooks Chat

"Very tasty and great in a pinch when guests visit. I substituted ravioli once, and it was very good. I've made it three times so far. It's my husband's special dish."

Curried Butternut-Shrimp Bisque

Prep: 25 min.   **Cook:** 31 min.

1 pound unpeeled, medium-size fresh shrimp
3 tablespoons unsalted butter
1 large yellow onion, chopped
1 (3-pound) butternut squash, peeled, seeded, and cut into ½-inch cubes
3 (14-ounce) cans chicken broth, divided

2 teaspoons curry powder
1 teaspoon dried thyme
1 cup whipping cream
¼ teaspoon salt
¼ teaspoon ground red pepper
Garnishes: whipping cream, paprika

• Peel shrimp, and devein, if desired. Set aside.
• Melt butter in a 4-quart heavy saucepan over medium-high heat; add onion, and sauté 7 to 8 minutes or until tender. Reduce heat to medium; add squash, and cook, stirring occasionally, 15 minutes or until tender.
• Add 1 can broth, shrimp, curry, and thyme, and cook 2 to 3 minutes or just until shrimp turn pink. Let cool slightly.
• Process mixture in a blender or food processor until smooth, stopping to scrape down sides.
• Return mixture to saucepan; add remaining broth, and bring to a boil. Stir in 1 cup whipping cream, salt, and pepper; reduce heat to low, and simmer 5 minutes. Garnish, if desired. Yield: 9½ cups.

side dishes

★★★★★

Dress up a holiday meal or round out your favorite weeknight entrée with these mouthwatering side dishes.

Fried Green Tomatoes,
page 316

Lemon-Marinated Asparagus

Prep: 20 min.   **Cook:** 3 min.   **Other:** 10 hrs.

We limited the marinating time for the asparagus to 2 hours because lemon juice tends to discolor asparagus.

½ cup fresh lemon juice
3 tablespoons olive oil
2 tablespoons sugar
¼ teaspoon salt
¼ teaspoon pepper
1 garlic clove, minced

1 (14-ounce) can quartered artichoke hearts, drained
1 (4-ounce) jar diced pimiento, drained
2 pounds fresh asparagus
Garnish: lemon rind strips

• Whisk together lemon juice and next 5 ingredients in a large bowl; add artichoke and diced pimiento, and gently toss. Cover and chill 8 hours or overnight.
• Snap off tough ends of asparagus; cook in boiling salted water to cover 3 minutes or until crisp-tender.
• Plunge asparagus into ice water to stop the cooking process; drain. Place cooked asparagus in a large zip-top freezer bag, and store overnight in refrigerator, if desired.
• Add asparagus to artichoke mixture, and gently toss. Cover and chill 2 hours. Garnish, if desired. Yield: 10 to 12 servings.

Chilled Sesame Asparagus

Prep: 5 min.   **Cook:** 5 min.   **Other:** 2 hrs.

1½ to 2 pounds fresh asparagus, trimmed
2 tablespoons plus 2 teaspoons dark sesame oil
1 tablespoon plus 1 teaspoon rice vinegar

1 tablespoon plus 1 teaspoon soy sauce
1 teaspoon sugar
1 tablespoon sesame seeds, toasted

• Cook asparagus in boiling water about 4 to 5 minutes or until crisp-tender. Plunge asparagus into ice water to stop the cooking process; drain, cover, and chill 2 hours.
• Whisk together sesame oil and next 3 ingredients. Chill 2 hours.
• Arrange asparagus on a serving dish; spoon dressing evenly over top. Sprinkle with sesame seeds. Yield: 4 to 6 servings.

Five-Bean Bake

Prep: 20 min.   **Cook:** 1 hr., 40 min.

8 bacon slices, chopped
1 large onion, diced
1 (28-ounce) can pork and beans
1 (19.75-ounce) can black beans, rinsed and drained
1 (16-ounce) can chickpeas, rinsed and drained
1 (15.5-ounce) can kidney beans, rinsed and drained
1 (15.25-ounce) can lima beans, rinsed and drained
1 cup ketchup
½ cup firmly packed brown sugar
½ cup water
¼ cup cider vinegar

• Cook chopped bacon slices in a large skillet over medium-high heat until crisp; remove bacon, reserving 2 tablespoons drippings in skillet. Add diced onion, and sauté in hot drippings 5 minutes or until tender.
• Combine bacon, onion, pork and beans, black beans, chickpeas, kidney beans, lima beans, ketchup, brown sugar, ½ cup water, and cider vinegar in a lightly greased 13- x 9-inch baking dish.
• Bake, covered, at 350° for 1 hour; uncover and bake 30 more minutes. Yield: 8 servings.

Cooks Chat

"I made this for our neighborhood's Labor Day barbecue. It was awesome! Everyone demanded the recipe, and many said it was the best baked bean dish they'd ever had. I concur!"

"Absolutely the best recipe for baked beans I've found since I tasted my grandma's! Wonderful! Thank you!"

"Two words—big hit! I didn't know that beans could be 'to die for,' as a family member put it. So easy and so good. A definite must!"

Smashed Pinto Beans

Prep: 15 min.   **Cook:** 20 min.

Keep these slightly spicy, fiber-rich beans on hand for quick breakfast burritos or soft veggie tacos.

1 medium onion, chopped
1 teaspoon olive oil
2 garlic cloves, minced
½ cup tomato sauce
2 (15-ounce) cans pinto beans, rinsed and drained
1 cup beef broth
1 tablespoon hot sauce
¼ teaspoon salt
¼ teaspoon ground cumin
½ teaspoon pepper
1 to 2 tablespoons red wine vinegar

• Sauté chopped onion in hot olive oil in a Dutch oven over medium-high heat 5 minutes or until onion is tender. Add minced garlic, and sauté 1 minute. Stir in tomato sauce and remaining ingredients.
• Bring to a boil; reduce heat, and simmer 8 minutes.
• Mash bean mixture with a potato masher until thickened, leaving some beans whole. Yield: 14 servings.

Cooks Chat

"Excellent on soft tacos with cheese. My children, traditionally not bean lovers, adore this recipe. We use this recipe in many ways—in place of canned refried beans or as a dip. Another added plus is it's quick!"

"Never use canned refried beans again. This recipe is ten times better and has got to be equal in price if you buy store-brand beans."

Delta Red Beans and Rice

Prep: 15 min. **Cook:** 4 hrs. **Other:** 16 hrs.

Cooks Chat

"This dish was wonderful. My entire family loved it, and I plan to make it again. Very, very flavorful. I served it with rice, but it really doesn't need it—you can just serve it in a bowl by itself. I boiled the beans in about 4 more cups of water than the recipe called for so that the mixture would have a soupier texture. It was outstanding."

"I think this dish is very good, and it doesn't need anything in it or on it—the flavor is perfect!"

1 pound dried red beans
6 cups water
1½ pounds smoked sausage, sliced
½ pound cooked ham, cubed
1 large sweet onion, chopped
2 garlic cloves, pressed
2 tablespoons olive oil
1 bunch green onions, chopped
1 cup chopped fresh parsley
1 teaspoon salt

1 teaspoon ground black pepper
½ teaspoon sugar
½ teaspoon dried oregano
½ teaspoon dried thyme
⅛ teaspoon ground red pepper
1 tablespoon Worcestershire sauce
¼ teaspoon hot sauce
Hot cooked rice

• Place beans in a large Dutch oven. Cover with water 2 inches above beans; soak 8 hours. Drain.
• Bring beans, 6 cups water, sausage, and ham to a boil in a Dutch oven. Cover, reduce heat, and simmer 3 hours.
• Sauté onion and garlic in hot oil in a large skillet until tender. Add to bean mixture. Stir in green onions and next 9 ingredients. Cover and chill 8 hours.
• Bring bean mixture to a simmer; cover and cook, stirring often, 1 hour. Serve over rice. Yield: 8 to 10 servings.

Spicy Red Beans and Rice

Prep: 30 min.   **Cook:** 3 hrs., 30 min.   **Other:** 8 hrs.

This hearty sausage-decked rice can serve double duty as a side dish or a main dish. Either way, it will bring the wonderful flavors of New Orleans to your table.

2 pounds dried red kidney
    beans
5 bacon slices, chopped
1 pound smoked sausage, cut
    into ¼-inch-thick slices
½ pound salt pork, quartered
6 garlic cloves, minced
5 celery ribs, sliced
2 green bell peppers, chopped

1 large onion, chopped
2 (32-ounce) containers
    chicken broth
2 cups water
1 teaspoon salt
1 teaspoon ground red pepper
1 teaspoon black pepper
Hot cooked rice

• Place kidney beans in a Dutch oven. Cover with water 2 inches above beans, and let soak 8 hours. Drain beans; rinse thoroughly, and drain again.
• Sauté bacon in Dutch oven over medium-high heat 5 minutes. Add smoked sausage and salt pork; sauté 5 minutes or until sausage is golden brown. Add garlic and next 3 ingredients; sauté 5 minutes or until vegetables are tender.
• Stir in beans, broth, 2 cups water, and next 3 ingredients; bring to a boil. Boil 15 minutes; reduce heat, and simmer, stirring occasionally, 3 hours or until beans are tender. Remove salt pork before serving. Serve over rice. Yield: 2 quarts.

Note: For quick soaking, place kidney beans in a Dutch oven; cover with water 2 inches above beans, and bring to a boil. Boil 1 minute; cover, remove from heat, and let stand 1 hour. Drain and proceed with recipe.

Cooks Chat

"Absolutely wonderful. I felt like I was dining in the French Quarter."

"This recipe is outta sight! I threw in some smoked neck bones for good measure and cooked everything until it was nice and thick."

"I made this recipe, and everyone loved it—even those who said they didn't like red beans and rice. I limited the ground red pepper because we don't like things too spicy."

Garlic Green Beans

Prep: 10 min.   **Cook:** 10 min.

4 garlic cloves, minced
3 tablespoons olive oil
2 pounds fresh green beans, trimmed

½ cup chicken broth
1 teaspoon sugar
1¼ teaspoons salt
¼ teaspoon pepper

• Sauté garlic in hot oil in a large skillet over medium-high heat; add beans, tossing to coat.
• Add broth and remaining ingredients. Cover, reduce heat, and simmer 10 minutes or until green beans are crisp-tender. Yield: 4 to 6 servings.

Marinated Green Beans with Tomatoes, Olives, and Feta

Prep: 30 min.   **Cook:** 9 min.   **Other:** 3 hrs.

2 pounds fresh green beans, trimmed
1½ teaspoons salt, divided
2 garlic cloves, minced
¼ cup olive oil
1 cup kalamata olives, sliced
2 tomatoes, seeded and chopped

2 tablespoons red wine vinegar
1 tablespoon fresh oregano, finely chopped
¼ teaspoon pepper
2 (4-ounce) packages crumbled feta cheese
Garnish: fresh oregano sprigs

• Place beans in boiling water seasoned with 1 teaspoon salt; cook 6 to 8 minutes or until crisp-tender. Drain. Plunge beans into ice water to stop the cooking process. Place in a shallow serving dish.
• Cook garlic in hot oil in a skillet over medium heat 30 seconds or just until fragrant; remove from heat. Stir in olives, next 4 ingredients, and remaining ½ teaspoon salt. Pour mixture over beans, tossing to coat. Chill at least 3 hours or overnight. Sprinkle with feta cheese. Garnish, if desired. Yield: 8 to 10 servings.

Carrot-Pecan Casserole

Prep: 15 min.   **Cook:** 1 hr., 5 min.

3 pounds baby carrots, sliced
⅔ cup sugar
½ cup butter or margarine, softened
½ cup chopped pecans, toasted
¼ cup milk

2 large eggs, lightly beaten
3 tablespoons all-purpose flour
1 tablespoon grated orange rind
1 teaspoon vanilla extract
¼ teaspoon ground nutmeg

• Cook carrots in boiling water to cover in a saucepan 25 minutes or until tender; drain, let cool slightly, and process in a food processor until smooth.
• Transfer carrots to a large mixing bowl; stir in sugar and remaining ingredients. Spoon into a lightly greased 11- x 7-inch baking dish. Cover and chill 8 hours, if desired.
• Bake casserole, uncovered, at 350° for 40 minutes. Yield: 6 to 8 servings.

Carrot-Sweet Potato Puree

Prep: 20 min.   **Cook:** 17 min.

5 carrots, sliced
¾ cup water
¼ cup butter or margarine
1 (29-ounce) can sweet potatoes, drained
1 (16-ounce) can sweet potatoes, drained
1 (8-ounce) container sour cream

1 tablespoon sugar
1 teaspoon grated lemon rind
½ teaspoon ground nutmeg
¼ teaspoon salt
¼ teaspoon ground black pepper
⅛ teaspoon ground red pepper

• Microwave carrot and ¾ cup water in a glass bowl at HIGH 10 to 12 minutes or until tender. Drain.
• Process carrot and butter in a food processor until mixture is smooth, stopping to scrape down sides. Transfer to a large bowl.
• Process sweet potatoes until smooth, stopping to scrape down sides. Add to carrot mixture.
• Stir together sweet potato mixture, sour cream, and remaining ingredients. Spoon into a 1½-quart glass dish. (Cover and chill up to 2 days, if desired; let stand at room temperature 30 minutes.) Microwave at HIGH 4 to 5 minutes or until thoroughly heated. Yield: 4 servings.

Carrot Soufflé

Prep: 10 min.   **Cook:** 1 hr., 25 min.

A sprinkle of cinnamon sweetly spices this simple soufflé.

2 pounds carrots, chopped
½ cup butter or margarine, softened
1 cup sugar
3 large eggs, lightly beaten
2 tablespoons all-purpose flour
1 teaspoon baking powder
Ground cinnamon

• Cook carrot in boiling water to cover 20 to 25 minutes or until tender; drain. Mash carrot and butter with a potato masher. Add sugar and egg, and beat at medium speed with an electric mixer 2 minutes. Stir in flour and baking powder. Pour into a greased 11- x 7-inch baking dish. Sprinkle with cinnamon. Bake, uncovered, at 350° for 1 hour or until set. Yield: 8 servings.

Summer Vegetable Gratin

Prep: 30 min.   **Cook:** 55 min.   **Other:** 10 min.

If you don't have any cornbread on hand to crumble for this recipe, buy a couple of corn muffins from the deli.

2 garlic cloves, finely chopped
4 to 5 plum tomatoes, cut into ¼-inch slices
3 to 4 small red potatoes, cut into ⅛-inch slices (about ½ pound)
1 small red onion, thinly sliced
1 (7-inch) jar roasted red bell peppers, drained and chopped
2 medium zucchini, thinly sliced
1 cup sliced fresh mushrooms
¾ teaspoon salt
¾ teaspoon pepper
3 tablespoons olive oil, divided
½ cup finely crumbled cornbread
¼ cup grated Parmesan cheese
2 tablespoons Italian seasoning
1 tablespoon Dijon mustard

• Sprinkle bottom of a lightly greased 11- x 7-inch baking dish evenly with garlic. Layer with tomatoes and next 5 ingredients, sprinkling with ⅛ teaspoon each of salt and pepper between layers. Drizzle with 2 tablespoons oil.
• Bake at 350° for 45 minutes. Combine cornbread, next 3 ingredients, and remaining 1 tablespoon olive oil. Sprinkle over vegetable mixture; bake 10 more minutes or until top is golden. Let stand 10 minutes before serving. Yield: 6 servings.

Tee's Corn Pudding

Prep: 15 min.   **Cook:** 45 min.   **Other:** 5 min.

If you'd like to add Southwestern flair to this traditional recipe,
try our flavor variation, which adds spicy green chiles.

¼ cup sugar
3 tablespoons all-purpose flour
2 teaspoons baking powder
1½ teaspoons salt
6 large eggs

2 cups whipping cream
½ cup butter or margarine,
   melted
6 cups fresh corn kernels
   (about 12 ears)*

• Combine first 4 ingredients.
• Whisk together eggs, whipping cream, and butter. Gradually add
sugar mixture, whisking until smooth; stir in corn. Pour mixture
into a lightly greased 13- x 9-inch baking dish.
• Bake at 350° for 40 to 45 minutes or until deep golden and set.
Let pudding stand 5 minutes. Yield: 8 servings.

*Substitute 6 cups frozen whole kernel corn or canned shoepeg
corn, drained, for fresh corn, if desired.

Note: For testing purposes only, we used Silver Queen corn.

Southwestern Corn Pudding: Stir in 1 (4.5-ounce) can
chopped green chiles, drained, and ¼ teaspoon ground cumin.

SOUTHERN CLASSIC

Cooks Chat

*"This is a crowd-pleaser! We make
it all summer long with fresh sweet
corn. I wouldn't change a thing!"*

*"I've tried many corn pudding
recipes in an attempt to find the one
I sampled a long time ago. This is
the best! It has become a family
favorite!"*

*"A favorite with my family ever
since it ran in* Southern Living. *Of
course, fresh corn is best, but it's
still delicious with frozen corn when
in a hurry or if fresh is not available. There are never any leftovers
to be tossed out with this recipe!"*

Creamy Baked Corn

Prep: 10 min.　**Cook:** 40 min.

2 to 4 bacon slices
1 tablespoon butter or
　margarine
2 tablespoons chopped onion
2 tablespoons all-purpose flour
1 teaspoon salt
1 cup sour cream
1 (16-ounce) package frozen
　corn, thawed

• Cook bacon in a large skillet until crisp; remove bacon, and drain on paper towels, reserving 1 tablespoon drippings in skillet. Crumble bacon, and set aside.
• Melt butter in hot drippings over medium heat; add onion, and sauté until tender.
• Whisk in flour and salt until smooth and bubbly. Whisk in sour cream until smooth; cook, whisking often, 3 minutes. Stir in corn, and cook until thoroughly heated. Spoon into a lightly greased 8-inch baking dish; top with crumbled bacon.
• Bake at 350° for 15 to 20 minutes or until bubbly. Yield: 4 to 6 servings.

Creamy Fried Confetti Corn

Prep: 15 min.　**Cook:** 22 min.

8 bacon slices, chopped
4 cups fresh sweet corn kernels
　(about 8 ears)
1 medium-size white onion,
　chopped
⅓ cup chopped red bell
　pepper
⅓ cup chopped green bell
　pepper
1 (8-ounce) package cream
　cheese, cubed
½ cup half-and-half
1 teaspoon sugar
1 teaspoon salt
1 teaspoon pepper

• Cook chopped bacon in a large skillet until crisp; remove bacon, and drain on paper towels, reserving 2 tablespoons drippings in skillet. Set bacon aside.
• Sauté corn, onion, and bell peppers in hot drippings in skillet over medium-high heat 6 minutes or until tender. Add cream cheese and half-and-half, stirring until cream cheese melts. Stir in sugar, salt, and pepper. Top with bacon. Yield: 6 to 8 servings.

*Creamy Fried
Confetti Corn*

Okra Creole

Prep: 15 min. **Cook:** 25 min.

3 bacon slices
1 (16-ounce) package frozen
    sliced okra
1 (14½-ounce) can diced
    tomatoes
1 cup frozen onion seasoning
    blend

1 cup frozen corn kernels
½ cup water
1 teaspoon Creole seasoning
¼ teaspoon pepper
Hot cooked rice (optional)

• Cook bacon in a Dutch oven until crisp; remove bacon, and drain on paper towels, reserving drippings. Crumble bacon, and set aside.
• Cook okra and next 6 ingredients in hot drippings in Dutch oven over medium-high heat, stirring occasionally, 5 minutes. Reduce heat to low, cover, and simmer 15 minutes or until vegetables are tender. Top with crumbled bacon. Serve over rice, if desired. Yield: 4 servings.

Simple Stir-Fried Okra

Prep: 10 min. **Cook:** 20 min.

We prepared this recipe with frozen whole okra. The results were consistently tender, fragrant, and fresh-tasting.

1 medium-size sweet onion,
    chopped
1 teaspoon mustard seeds*
½ teaspoon ground cumin
¼ teaspoon dried crushed red
    pepper

2 tablespoons vegetable oil
1 (16-ounce) package frozen
    okra, thawed, or 1 pound
    fresh okra
¾ teaspoon salt

• Sauté first 4 ingredients in hot oil in a large skillet over medium-high heat 5 minutes or until onion is tender.
• Add okra; sauté 15 minutes or until okra is lightly browned. Stir in salt. Yield: 4 to 6 servings.

*Substitute ½ teaspoon dry mustard for 1 teaspoon mustard seeds, if desired.

Okra Creole

Sweet Onion Pudding

Prep: 1 hr.   **Cook:** 30 min.

2 cups whipping cream
1 (3-ounce) package shredded
   Parmesan cheese
6 large eggs, lightly beaten
3 tablespoons all-purpose flour
2 tablespoons sugar

2 teaspoons baking powder
1 teaspoon salt
½ cup butter or margarine
6 medium-size sweet onions,
   thinly sliced

• Stir together first 3 ingredients in a large bowl. Combine flour and next 3 ingredients; gradually stir into egg mixture. Set aside.
• Melt butter in a large skillet over medium heat; add onion, and cook, stirring often, 30 to 40 minutes or until onion is caramel-colored. Remove onion from heat.
• Stir onion into egg mixture, and spoon into a lightly greased 13- x 9-inch baking dish.
• Bake at 350° for 30 minutes or until set. Yield: 8 servings.

Beer-Battered Onion Rings

Prep: 40 min.   **Cook:** 20 min.   **Other:** 30 min.

Guests will love crunching into these sweet rings.

3 large Vidalia, Spanish, or
   Bermuda onions
2¼ cups all-purpose flour
2 teaspoons baking powder
1 teaspoon salt

¼ cup yellow cornmeal
2 cups beer
1 large egg, lightly beaten
Vegetable oil

• Peel onions; cut into ½-inch-thick slices, and separate into rings. Place rings in a large bowl of ice water; let stand 30 minutes. Drain on paper towels.
• Combine flour and next 3 ingredients; stir well. Add beer and egg, stirring until thoroughly blended and smooth. Chill batter 15 minutes.
• Dip onion rings into batter, coating both sides well. Pour oil to a depth of 2 to 3 inches into a Dutch oven; heat to 375°. Fry onion rings, a few at a time, 3 to 5 minutes or until golden on both sides. Drain well on paper towels. Serve immediately. Yield: 8 servings.

Peppery Peas O' Plenty

Prep: 15 min.   **Cook:** 40 min.

4 hickory-smoked bacon slices
1 large onion, chopped
1 cup frozen black-eyed peas
1 cup frozen purple hull peas
1 cup frozen crowder peas
1 cup frozen butter peas
1 cup frozen field peas with snaps

1 (32-ounce) container chicken
   broth
¾ to 1 teaspoon salt
1 tablespoon freshly ground
   pepper
1 tablespoon Asian garlic-chili
   sauce

• Cook bacon in a Dutch oven until crisp; remove bacon, and drain on paper towels, reserving drippings in pan. Crumble bacon.
• Sauté onion in drippings over medium-high heat 8 minutes or until translucent. Add black-eyed peas and next 8 ingredients; cook 20 minutes, uncovered. Top with bacon. Yield: 4 to 6 servings.

Note: For testing purposes only, we used Bryan Sweet Hickory Smoked Bacon and A Taste of Thai Garlic Chili Pepper Sauce.

Three-Cheese Mashed Potato Casserole

Prep: 35 min.   **Cook:** 35 min.

4 large potatoes, peeled and
   cubed*
1 cup sour cream
1 (3-ounce) package cream
   cheese, softened
¼ cup butter or margarine,
   softened

⅔ cup milk
½ cup (2 ounces) shredded
   Cheddar cheese
½ cup (2 ounces) shredded
   Muenster cheese
1½ teaspoons salt
½ teaspoon pepper

• Cook potatoes in boiling water to cover 15 minutes or until tender. Drain. Beat potatoes and next 3 ingredients at medium speed with an electric mixer until smooth. Stir in milk and remaining ingredients. Spoon into a lightly greased 2-quart baking dish. (Cover and chill 8 hours, if desired; let stand at room temperature 30 minutes before baking.)
• Bake, uncovered, at 400° for 15 to 20 minutes or until thoroughly heated. Yield: 4 servings.

*Substitute frozen mashed potatoes for cubed potatoes, if desired. Prepare according to package directions for 4 servings. For testing purposes only, we used Ore Ida Mashed Potatoes.

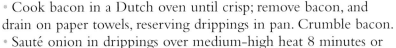

Sweet Potato Casserole

Prep: 20 min.   **Cook:** 1 hr., 40 min.   **Other:** 20 min.

We started with a mouthwatering casserole and modified the toppings to satisfy lovers of crunchy pecans and cornflakes as well as marshmallow fans.

4½ pounds sweet potatoes
1 cup granulated sugar
¼ cup milk
½ cup butter, softened
2 large eggs
1 teaspoon vanilla extract
¼ teaspoon salt

1¼ cups cornflakes cereal, crushed
¼ cup chopped pecans
1 tablespoon brown sugar
1 tablespoon butter, melted
1½ cups miniature marshmallows

• Bake sweet potatoes at 400° for about 1 hour or until tender. Let cool to touch; peel and mash sweet potatoes.
• Beat mashed sweet potatoes, granulated sugar, and next 5 ingredients at medium speed with an electric mixer until smooth. Spoon potato mixture into a greased 11- x 7-inch baking dish.
• Combine cornflakes cereal and next 3 ingredients in a small bowl. Sprinkle diagonally over casserole in rows 2 inches apart.
• Bake at 350° for 30 minutes. Remove from oven, and let casserole stand 10 minutes. Sprinkle alternate rows with marshmallows; bake 10 additional minutes. Let stand 10 minutes before serving. Yield: 6 to 8 servings.

Spinach-Stuffed Squash

Prep: 15 min.   **Cook:** 29 min.

4 large yellow squash
1½ teaspoons salt, divided
¼ cup butter or margarine, melted and divided
½ cup grated Parmesan cheese, divided
¼ teaspoon pepper
1 small onion, chopped

2 (10-ounce) packages frozen chopped spinach, cooked and well drained
1 cup sour cream
2 teaspoons red wine vinegar
¼ cup fine, dry breadcrumbs
1 tablespoon cold butter or margarine, cut up

• Combine squash, ½ teaspoon salt, and water to cover in a Dutch oven. Bring to a boil, and cook 10 minutes or until tender. Cool.
• Cut squash in half lengthwise, and remove seeds. Drizzle cut sides of squash evenly with 2 tablespoons melted butter; sprinkle evenly with 2 tablespoons cheese, ½ teaspoon salt, and pepper.

• Pour remaining 2 tablespoons melted butter in a large skillet over medium-high heat, and add onion; sauté 4 minutes or until tender. Stir in cooked spinach, sour cream, red wine vinegar, and remaining ½ teaspoon salt. Spoon spinach mixture evenly into squash halves. Place squash in a 13- x 9-inch baking dish. Sprinkle with breadcrumbs and remaining 6 tablespoons cheese, and dot with cold butter.
• Bake at 350° for 15 minutes or until thoroughly heated. Yield: 6 to 8 servings.

Spinach-Artichoke Casserole

Prep: 20 min.   **Cook:** 30 min.

2 (10-ounce) packages frozen
    chopped spinach, thawed
1 (14-ounce) can artichoke
    hearts, drained and
    chopped
1 (10¾-ounce) can fat-free
    cream of mushroom soup,
    undiluted
1 (8-ounce) container light
    sour cream
3 green onions, chopped
2 tablespoons all-purpose flour

1 tablespoon minced fresh
    parsley
¼ teaspoon Worcestershire
    sauce
1 tablespoon butter or margarine
1 cup sliced fresh mushrooms
2 garlic cloves, pressed
1 tablespoon lemon juice
½ teaspoon pepper
2 cups (8 ounces) shredded
    Monterey Jack cheese with
    peppers, divided

• Drain spinach well, pressing between layers of paper towels. Stir together spinach and next 7 ingredients.
• Melt butter in a skillet over medium-high heat. Add mushrooms and next 3 ingredients; sauté 5 minutes. Stir mushroom mixture and 1 cup cheese into spinach mixture; spoon into a lightly greased 11- x 7-inch baking dish. Sprinkle with remaining 1 cup cheese.
• Bake at 400° for 30 minutes. Yield: 8 to 10 servings.

PARTY PLEASER

Cooks Chat

"This is a fabulous recipe. It's easy, takes minimal prep time, and garners rave reviews. I made it for Thanksgiving and Christmas, and everyone wanted the recipe—plus, there were no leftovers to clean up."

"I used marinated artichoke hearts, and it added so much flavor to this casserole. I would double the recipe if serving more than four hearty eaters. This would be ideal for a dinner party because it's really good and easy to make, and it can be assembled earlier in the day."

"I made this last year both for Thanksgiving and a church Christmas dinner. It was requested for this year's upcoming holiday dinner. It is good, attractive, and a little different—a wonderful special-occasion dish! I did not use the fat-free and light ingredients."

Italian Squash Pie

Prep: 20 min.　**Cook:** 38 min.

A thin layer of Dijon mustard on the crust seals it and prevents the pie from becoming soggy.

1 (8-ounce) can refrigerated
　crescent rolls
2 teaspoons Dijon mustard
¼ cup butter or margarine
1½ pounds yellow squash
　(about 4 cups), thinly
　sliced*
1 medium onion, chopped
1 garlic clove, pressed
¼ cup chopped fresh parsley
1 tablespoon chopped fresh or
　½ teaspoon dried basil
2 teaspoons chopped fresh or
　½ teaspoon dried oregano
2 teaspoons chopped fresh or
　½ teaspoon dried thyme
½ teaspoon salt
½ teaspoon pepper
2 large eggs
¼ cup milk
2 cups (8 ounces) shredded
　mozzarella cheese
Garnishes: fresh oregano sprigs,
　sliced yellow squash

• Unroll crescent rolls; press dough on bottom and up sides of a 10-inch tart pan, pressing to seal perforations.
• Bake at 375° for 6 minutes or until lightly browned. Gently press crust down with a wooden spoon. Spread crust with mustard, and set aside.
• Melt butter in a large skillet over medium-high heat. Add squash, onion, and garlic; sauté 7 minutes or until tender. Remove from heat; stir in parsley and next 5 ingredients.
• Whisk together eggs and milk in a large bowl; stir in cheese and vegetable mixture. Pour over crust.
• Bake at 375° for 20 to 25 minutes or until a knife inserted in center comes out clean. Garnish, if desired. Yield: 6 servings.

*Substitute 1½ pounds zucchini for yellow squash, if desired.

Cooks Chat

"This cross between squash casserole and quiche is absolutely delicious! It's good with fresh sliced tomatoes."

"I served this to company, and it was a hit. The mustard is the key to the recipe. I cut back somewhat on the herbs. This one is a keeper. I love collecting squash recipes, and this one is saved in my permanent file. Thanks."

"Loved this squash pie! I used it as a side dish instead of a main dish. I used just a little less of each herb, especially the thyme."

Two-Cheese Squash Casserole

Prep: 30 min.   **Cook:** 1 hr.

4 pounds yellow squash, sliced
4 tablespoons butter or margarine, divided
1 large sweet onion, finely chopped
2 garlic cloves, minced
2½ cups soft breadcrumbs, divided
1¼ cups shredded Parmesan cheese, divided
1 cup (4 ounces) shredded Cheddar cheese
½ cup chopped fresh chives
½ cup minced fresh parsley
1 (8-ounce) container sour cream
1 teaspoon salt
1 teaspoon freshly ground pepper
2 large eggs, lightly beaten
¼ teaspoon garlic salt

• Cook squash in boiling water to cover in a large skillet 8 to 10 minutes or just until tender. Drain well; gently press between paper towels.

• Melt 2 tablespoons butter in skillet over medium-high heat; add onion and garlic, and sauté 5 to 6 minutes or until tender. Remove skillet from heat; stir in squash, 1 cup breadcrumbs, ¾ cup Parmesan cheese, and next 7 ingredients. Spoon into a lightly greased 13- x 9-inch baking dish.

• Melt remaining 2 tablespoons butter. Stir together melted butter, remaining 1½ cups soft breadcrumbs, remaining ½ cup Parmesan cheese, and garlic salt. Sprinkle mixture evenly over top of casserole.

• Bake at 350° for 35 to 40 minutes or until set. Yield: 8 to 10 servings.

Cooks Chat

*"I am a lover of fried green toma-
toes! When I saw this recipe in
Southern Living, I was overjoyed.
To say the least, my taste buds felt
the same way as I savored each
bite! These were a breeze to make,
which was a plus."*

*"I loved these! First time I ever
made or tasted a fried green tomato,
and now I see what all the fuss is
about. The batter is great and fries
up well without any trouble—just
like fried food should be!"*

*"This is a great recipe, and the
whole family enjoyed eating the
tomatoes, even my toddler. I did,
however, use my deep fryer instead
of a skillet, and it worked just fine."*

Fried Green Tomatoes

Prep: 20 min.   **Cook:** 4 min. per batch

If your family has a large appetite, you may want to
double this recipe.

1 large egg, lightly beaten
½ cup buttermilk
½ cup all-purpose flour, divided
½ cup cornmeal
1 teaspoon salt

½ teaspoon pepper
3 medium-size green tomatoes,
    cut into ⅓-inch slices
Vegetable oil
Salt to taste

• Combine egg and buttermilk; set aside.
• Combine ¼ cup all-purpose flour, cornmeal, 1 teaspoon salt, and
pepper in a shallow bowl or pan.
• Dredge tomato slices in remaining ¼ cup flour; dip in egg mixture, and dredge in cornmeal mixture.
• Pour oil to a depth of ¼ to ½ inch into a large cast-iron skillet;
heat to 375°. Drop tomatoes, in batches, into hot oil, and cook
2 minutes on each side or until golden. Drain on paper towels or a
rack. Sprinkle hot tomatoes with salt to taste. Yield: 4 to 6 servings.

Fried Green Tomato Stacks

Prep: 15 min. **Cook:** 12 min.

These stacks don't just offer a fun presentation—they also boast an incredible flavor from the fresh tomatillo dressing.

3 tomatillos, husked
2 tablespoons bacon drippings
1 garlic clove, pressed
1½ teaspoons salt, divided
1 teaspoon pepper, divided
½ teaspoon paprika
¼ cup thinly sliced fresh basil
1½ cups self-rising yellow
    cornmeal
4 large green tomatoes, cut into
    18 (¼-inch) slices

1 cup buttermilk
Peanut oil
1 (8-ounce) package cream
    cheese, softened
1 (4-ounce) package goat
    cheese, softened
⅓ cup milk
1 teaspoon sugar
Garnish: fresh basil leaf

• Bring tomatillos and water to cover to a boil in a small saucepan; reduce heat, and simmer 10 minutes. Drain tomatillos, and cool.
• Process tomatillos, bacon drippings, garlic, ½ teaspoon salt, ½ teaspoon pepper, and paprika in a food processor or blender until smooth; stir in basil. Cover and chill until ready to serve.
• Stir together cornmeal, ¾ teaspoon salt, and remaining ½ teaspoon pepper. Dip tomato slices in buttermilk, and dredge in cornmeal mixture.
• Pour oil to a depth of ½ inch into a large skillet; heat to 375°. Fry tomato slices, in batches, in hot oil 1 to 2 minutes on each side; drain on a wire rack over paper towels. Keep warm.
• Combine cream cheese, next 3 ingredients, and remaining ¼ teaspoon salt. Place 1 fried tomato slice on each of 6 salad plates; top each evenly with half of cream cheese mixture. Top each with 1 fried tomato slice and remaining cream cheese mixture. Top with remaining 6 fried tomato slices; drizzle with tomatillo dressing. Garnish, if desired. Yield: 6 servings.

Cooks Chat

"This has become a signature dish for me. My family and friends request it often. I usually serve it as the salad or vegetable course. The tomatillo dressing is wonderful on fish, too!"

"This recipe is awesome! The flavors are out of this world. The dressing is excellent, and any leftovers are great on black beans, burritos, etc. This would be a great dish with a fruit salad for a light lunch or dinner, as well as a delicious appetizer."

"I grew up eating fried green tomatoes. This is the best thing I have ever put in my mouth. What an unbelievable combination of flavors! We ate this as an entrée. Excellent!"

Creamy Macaroni and Cheese

Prep: 35 min.   **Cook:** 20 min.

The combination of sharp Cheddar and extra-sharp Cheddar makes this homemade mac 'n' cheese especially cheesy. Your kids will thank you for the extra effort.

½ cup butter or margarine
½ cup all-purpose flour
½ teaspoon salt
½ teaspoon ground black pepper
¼ teaspoon ground red pepper
¼ teaspoon garlic powder
2 cups half-and-half

2 cups milk
2 (10-ounce) blocks sharp Cheddar cheese, shredded and divided
1 (10-ounce) block extra-sharp Cheddar cheese, shredded
1 (16-ounce) package elbow macaroni, cooked

• Melt butter in a large skillet over medium-high heat. Gradually whisk in flour until smooth; cook, whisking constantly, 2 minutes. Stir in salt and next 3 ingredients. Gradually whisk in half-and-half and milk; cook, whisking constantly, 8 to 10 minutes or until mixture is thickened.
• Stir in half of sharp Cheddar cheese. Stir in extra-sharp Cheddar cheese until smooth. Remove from heat.
• Combine pasta and cheese mixture, and pour into a lightly greased 13- x 9-inch baking dish. Sprinkle with remaining sharp Cheddar cheese.
• Bake at 350° for 20 minutes (bake 15 minutes longer for a crusty top). Yield: 6 to 8 servings.

Note: For testing purposes only, we used Kraft Cracker Barrel cheeses.

Pecan, Rice, and Crawfish Dressing

Prep: 25 min.   **Cook:** 30 min.

Be sure not to drain the crawfish after thawing. The juices add lots of flavor.

1 medium onion
1 celery rib
1 green bell pepper
1 red bell pepper
1 pound lean ground beef
2 garlic cloves, minced
2 (16-ounce) packages frozen peeled, cooked crawfish tails, thawed
2 cups cooked long-grain rice
1 cup chopped pecans, toasted
¼ cup butter or margarine, cut into pieces
1 small bunch green onions, chopped
2 tablespoons Creole seasoning
½ teaspoon pepper
Chopped fresh parsley

• Chop first 4 ingredients. Cook chopped vegetables, ground beef, and garlic in a Dutch oven over medium-high heat 10 minutes, stirring until beef crumbles and is no longer pink.
• Stir in crawfish and next 6 ingredients; cook 3 minutes or until thoroughly heated, and spoon mixture into a lightly greased 13- x 9-inch baking dish.
• Bake at 350° for 25 to 30 minutes or until lightly browned. Sprinkle with parsley. Yield: 8 to 10 servings.

Cooks Chat

"This is a very flavorful recipe, although I did not use all of the garlic or chicken broth called for. My husband says this is the new family dressing! Delicious!"

Southern Rice Dressing

Prep: 1 hr.   **Cook:** 45 min.

2 garlic bulbs
2 teaspoons olive oil
2 cups cooked regular rice
1 recipe Basic Cornbread, crumbled
1 (16-ounce) package ground pork sausage
3 tablespoons butter or margarine
1 medium onion, diced
1 medium-size red or green bell pepper, diced

1 large carrot, diced
½ cup chopped fresh parsley
1½ tablespoons chopped fresh or 1 to 2 teaspoons rubbed sage
1 tablespoon poultry seasoning
½ teaspoon salt
½ teaspoon pepper
4 cups chicken broth

• Cut off pointed ends of garlic bulbs; place garlic on a piece of aluminum foil, and drizzle with olive oil. Fold foil to seal.
• Bake at 350° for 45 minutes; cool. Squeeze pulp from garlic cloves into a large bowl. Add rice and cornbread.
• Cook sausage in a large skillet over medium heat, stirring until it crumbles and is no longer pink; drain sausage on paper towels, and wipe skillet clean.
• Melt butter in skillet over medium-high heat. Add onion, bell pepper, and carrot, and sauté 3 minutes or until tender.
• Stir sausage, vegetables, parsley, and next 4 ingredients into rice mixture. Add broth; stir to moisten. Spoon into a lightly greased 13- x 9-inch baking dish. Cover and chill 8 hours, if desired; remove from refrigerator, and let stand at room temperature 30 minutes.
• Bake, covered, at 350° for 45 minutes or until thoroughly heated. Yield: 12 servings.

Basic Cornbread

Prep: 10 min.   **Cook:** 25 min.

2 cups buttermilk self-rising white cornmeal mix
½ cup all-purpose flour
¼ cup butter or margarine, melted

1 large egg, lightly beaten
2 cups buttermilk

• Heat a well-greased 9-inch ovenproof skillet at 450° for 5 minutes.
• Stir together all ingredients in a bowl. Pour batter into hot skillet.
• Bake at 450° for 20 minutes or until golden brown. Yield: 1 (9-inch) cornbread (about 5 cups crumbled).

Caribbean Rice and Peas

Prep: 10 min.   **Cook:** 30 min.

Pigeon peas, nicknamed no-eye peas, are of African origin. They're yellow-gray in color and are about the size of green peas.

1 small onion, finely chopped
2 garlic cloves, pressed
1 tablespoon olive oil
2 cups basmati rice
2½ cups water
1 (10½-ounce) can condensed chicken broth
½ cup unsweetened coconut milk
1 (15-ounce) can pigeon peas, rinsed and drained*
1 tablespoon chopped fresh parsley
2 teaspoons grated lemon rind
1 teaspoon salt
Garnish: fresh parsley sprigs

• Sauté onion and garlic in hot oil in a Dutch oven over medium-high heat 1 to 2 minutes or until translucent. Add rice and next 3 ingredients; bring to a boil. Cover, reduce heat, and simmer 25 minutes or until liquid is absorbed and rice is tender. Stir in peas, parsley, lemon rind, and salt. Garnish, if desired. Yield: 8 to 10 servings.

*Substitute 1 (15-ounce) can field peas for pigeon peas, if desired.

Cooks Chat

"Great taste. This is a nice change from plain rice. I used green peas as a substitute."

"I gave my family a taste of the tropics and paired this dish with grilled Jamaican Jerk chicken. We're talkin' good, mon."

Orphan's Rice

Orphan's Rice

Prep: 10 min.　**Cook:** 30 min.　**Other:** 10 min.

1 tablespoon butter
¾ cup pecan halves
½ cup slivered almonds
⅓ cup pine nuts
½ small onion, minced
1 garlic clove, minced
2 tablespoons vegetable oil
1 (10-ounce) package yellow
　rice

3 cups low-sodium chicken
　broth
2 bacon slices, cooked and
　crumbled
¼ cup finely chopped ham
1 tablespoon minced fresh
　parsley

• Melt butter in a skillet over medium heat. Add pecan halves, almonds, and pine nuts, and sauté, stirring often, 3 minutes or until almonds are light golden brown.
• Sauté onion and garlic in hot oil in a saucepan over medium-high heat 5 minutes or until tender. Add rice, and sauté, stirring constantly, 1 minute. Add broth, and cook rice 18 minutes. Remove from heat.
• Stir in nuts, bacon, ham, and parsley. Cover and let stand 10 minutes. Yield: 6 to 8 servings.

Note: We like to use three different nuts for this recipe; however, feel free to use all of the same variety.

Lemon Rice Pilaf

Prep: 15 min.　**Cook:** 12 min.

2 tablespoons butter or
　margarine
4 celery ribs, sliced
6 green onions, chopped
3 cups hot cooked rice

2 tablespoons grated lemon
　rind
½ teaspoon salt
¼ teaspoon pepper

• Melt butter in a large skillet over medium-high heat; add celery and green onions, and sauté until celery is tender. Stir in rice and remaining ingredients; cook over low heat 2 minutes or until thoroughly heated. Yield: 6 servings.

Cooks Chat

"Absolutely delicious! We've made this every Thanksgiving since 1996. It's become a family tradition."

"Wow! I made this recipe for my Thanksgiving dinner, along with several other surefire stunners. This was the HIT—it even beat the deep-fried Cajun turkey! People talked about this for days and insisted that it be made every year from now on. Praise doesn't get any better than that!"

Sausage-and-Wild Mushroom Stuffing

Prep: 40 min.   **Cook:** 40 min.

This plentiful stuffing filled with wild mushrooms boasts a rich, dark color. Hot sausage instead of regular adds a kick to this casserole.

½ pound ground pork sausage
½ cup butter or margarine
3 pounds mixed wild mushrooms (shiitake, portobello, enoki), sliced
1 large onion, sliced
1 bunch green onions, sliced
1 (14-ounce) can chicken broth
1 (8-ounce) package herb-seasoned stuffing mix
1 poultry herb bouquet, chopped (see Note)
½ teaspoon salt
½ teaspoon pepper

• Brown sausage in a large skillet, stirring to crumble. Drain and set aside.
• Melt butter in skillet; add mushrooms, onion, and green onions, and sauté until tender. Combine mushroom mixture, sausage, broth, and remaining ingredients in a large bowl; stir. Spoon stuffing evenly into 2 lightly greased (11- x 7-inch) baking dishes.
• Bake, uncovered, at 375° for 40 minutes or until lightly browned. Yield: 8 to 10 servings.

Note: A poultry herb bouquet contains 2 sprigs each of fresh sage, rosemary, and thyme; 1 teaspoon of each dried herb may be substituted for fresh herbs, if desired.

Cooks Chat

"You can't go wrong with this recipe! It's easy to make and is a fine recipe with any course. If you're planning to make a Mardi Gras meal, this one should definitely be a part of it!"

"I took this dish to work, and four people asked for the recipe—that's a good sign!"

Baked Cheese Grits

Prep: 20 min.   **Cook:** 45 min.

5 cups water
1 teaspoon salt
1⅓ cups uncooked quick-cooking white grits
1 (15½-ounce) can yellow hominy, drained
½ cup butter or margarine
2 cups (8 ounces) shredded sharp Cheddar cheese
½ cup grated Parmesan cheese

• Bring 5 cups water and salt to a boil in a heavy Dutch oven; gradually stir in grits. Return to a boil; reduce heat, and cook 4 to 5 minutes, stirring occasionally.
• Stir in hominy, butter, and Cheddar cheese; spoon into a lightly greased 13- x 9-inch baking dish. Sprinkle with Parmesan cheese.
• Bake at 350° for 45 minutes or until set. Yield: 12 servings.

desserts

★★★★★

Get ready to
satisfy everyone's
sweet tooth
with one of
these decadent
cakes, chewy
cookies, or juicy
cobblers.

*Buttered Rum Pound Cake
with Bananas Foster Sauce,
page 340*

Best Carrot Sheet Cake

Prep: 25 min.   **Cook:** 43 min.

2 cups all-purpose flour
2 teaspoons baking soda
2 teaspoons ground cinnamon
½ teaspoon salt
3 large eggs
2 cups sugar
¾ cup vegetable oil
¾ cup buttermilk
2 teaspoons vanilla extract

2 cups grated carrots
1 (8-ounce) can crushed pineapple, drained
1 (3½-ounce) can sweetened flaked coconut
1 cup chopped pecans or walnuts
Buttermilk Glaze
Cream Cheese Frosting

• Stir together first 4 ingredients. Beat eggs and next 4 ingredients at medium speed with an electric mixer until smooth. Add flour mixture, beating at low speed until blended. Fold in carrots and next 3 ingredients. Pour batter into a greased and floured 13- x 9-inch pan.
• Bake at 350° for 30 minutes; cover pan loosely with aluminum foil to prevent excessive browning, and bake 13 more minutes or until a wooden pick inserted in center comes out clean. Drizzle Buttermilk Glaze evenly over cake; cool completely in pan. Spread Cream Cheese Frosting evenly over cake. Yield: 10 to 12 servings.

Buttermilk Glaze

Prep: 5 min.   **Cook:** 10 min.

1 cup sugar
1½ teaspoons baking soda
½ cup butter or margarine

½ cup buttermilk
1 tablespoon light corn syrup
1 teaspoon vanilla extract

• Bring sugar, baking soda, butter, buttermilk, and corn syrup to a boil in a Dutch oven over medium-high heat. Boil, stirring often, 4 minutes or until mixture is golden brown. Remove from heat, and stir in vanilla. Yield: 1½ cups.

Cream Cheese Frosting

Prep: 5 min.

½ cup butter or margarine, softened
1 (8-ounce) package cream cheese, softened
1 (3-ounce) package cream cheese, softened

1 (16-ounce) package powdered sugar
1½ teaspoons vanilla extract

• Beat butter and cream cheese at medium speed with an electric mixer until creamy. Add powdered sugar and vanilla; beat at high speed 10 seconds or until smooth. Yield: 4 cups.

Coconut Sheet Cake

Prep: 15 min.   **Cook:** 45 min.   **Other:** 30 min.

3 large eggs
1 (8-ounce) container sour
  cream
⅓ cup water
1 (8.5-ounce) can cream of
  coconut

½ teaspoon vanilla extract
1 (18.25-ounce) package white
  cake mix
Coconut-Cream Cheese
  Frosting

• Beat eggs at high speed with an electric mixer 2 minutes. Add sour cream, ⅓ cup water, and next 2 ingredients, beating well after each addition. Add cake mix, beating at low speed just until blended. Beat at high speed 2 minutes. Pour batter into a greased and floured 13- x 9-inch baking pan.
• Bake at 325° for 40 to 45 minutes or until a wooden pick inserted in center comes out clean. Cool cake in pan on a wire rack. Cover pan with plastic wrap, and freeze cake 30 minutes. Remove cake from freezer.
• Spread Coconut-Cream Cheese Frosting on top of chilled cake. Cover and store in refrigerator. Yield: 12 servings.

Note: If desired, cake can be baked in 1 greased and floured 15- x 10-inch jellyroll pan for 30 to 32 minutes or until a wooden pick inserted in center comes out clean. Yield: 15 servings.

Coconut-Cream Cheese Frosting

Prep: 10 min.

This delectable frosting is very rich and thick.

1 (8-ounce) package cream
  cheese, softened
½ cup butter or margarine,
  softened
3 tablespoons milk

1 teaspoon vanilla extract
1 (16-ounce) package
  powdered sugar, sifted
1 (7-ounce) package sweetened
  flaked coconut

• Beat cream cheese and butter at medium speed with an electric mixer until creamy; add milk and vanilla, beating well. Gradually add sugar, beating until smooth. Stir in coconut. Yield: 4 cups.

MAKE AHEAD

Cooks Chat

"So good! I love coconut cake, and this was supereasy and supermoist. My husband, who is usually really health conscious, saw me make the icing and said that he wasn't eating it—yeah, right! He was eating it right out of the pan. Loved it!"

"Outstanding! Very simple to prepare. It was a big hit. This is a keeper."

Mississippi Mud Cake

Prep: 20 min.   **Cook:** 30 min.

The women of Huffman United Methodist Church in Birmingham, Alabama, used this recipe for the church's 125th anniversary celebration. Of the 100 cakes made, none were left over.

1 cup butter, melted
2 cups sugar
½ cup unsweetened cocoa
4 large eggs, lightly beaten
1 teaspoon vanilla extract
⅛ teaspoon salt
1½ cups all-purpose flour
1½ cups coarsely chopped pecans, toasted
1 (10.5-ounce) bag miniature marshmallows
Chocolate Frosting

• Whisk together melted butter and next 5 ingredients in a large bowl. Stir in flour and chopped pecans. Pour batter into a greased and floured 15- x 10-inch jellyroll pan.
• Bake at 350° for 20 to 25 minutes or until a wooden pick inserted in center comes out clean. Remove from oven; top warm cake evenly with marshmallows. Return to oven, and bake 5 more minutes.
• Drizzle Chocolate Frosting over warm cake. Cool completely. Yield: 15 servings.

Note: Substitute 2 (19.5-ounce) packages brownie mix, prepared according to package directions, for first 7 ingredients, if desired. Stir in chopped pecans. Bake at 350° for 30 minutes. Proceed with marshmallows and frosting as directed.

Chocolate Frosting

Prep: 10 min.

1 (16-ounce) package powdered sugar, sifted
½ cup milk
¼ cup butter, softened
⅓ cup unsweetened cocoa

• Beat all ingredients at medium speed with an electric mixer until smooth. Yield: 2 cups.

Chunky Apple Cake with Cream Cheese Frosting

Prep: 25 min.   **Cook:** 45 min.

½ cup butter, melted
2 cups sugar
2 large eggs
1 teaspoon vanilla extract
2 cups all-purpose flour
1 teaspoon baking soda
1 teaspoon salt

2 teaspoons ground cinnamon
4 Granny Smith apples, peeled and sliced
1 cup chopped walnuts, toasted
Cream Cheese Frosting
Chopped walnuts, toasted (optional)

• Stir together first 4 ingredients in a large bowl until blended. Combine flour and next 3 ingredients; add to butter mixture, stirring until blended. Stir in apple slices and 1 cup walnuts. Spread into a greased 13- x 9-inch pan.
• Bake at 350° for 45 minutes or until a wooden pick inserted in center comes out clean. Cool completely in pan on a wire rack. Spread with Cream Cheese Frosting; sprinkle with walnuts, if desired. Store in refrigerator. Yield: 12 to 15 servings.

Cream Cheese Frosting

Prep: 10 min.

1 (8-ounce) package cream cheese, softened
3 tablespoons butter or margarine, softened

1½ cups powdered sugar
⅛ teaspoon salt
1 teaspoon vanilla extract

• Beat cream cheese and butter at medium speed with an electric mixer until creamy. Gradually add sugar and salt, beating until blended. Stir in vanilla. Yield: 1⅔ cups.

Fig Cake

Prep: 20 min.   **Cook:** 35 min.

Make and freeze the cake up to 2 weeks in advance; add the glaze the day you plan to serve it.

2 cups all-purpose flour
1½ cups sugar
1 teaspoon salt
1 teaspoon baking soda
1 teaspoon ground cloves
1 teaspoon ground nutmeg
1 teaspoon ground cinnamon
3 large eggs, lightly beaten

1 cup vegetable oil
1 cup buttermilk
1 teaspoon vanilla extract
1 cup chopped fresh figs or fig preserves
1 cup chopped pecans (optional), toasted
Buttermilk Glaze

• Stir together first 7 ingredients; stir in egg, oil, and buttermilk, blending well. Stir in vanilla. Fold in figs and, if desired, pecans. Pour into a greased and floured 13- x 9-inch pan.
• Bake at 325° for 35 minutes or until a wooden pick inserted in center comes out clean. Pierce top of cake several times with a wooden pick; drizzle Buttermilk Glaze over cake. Yield: 16 servings.

Buttermilk Glaze

Prep: 10 min.   **Cook:** 3 min.

1 cup sugar
½ cup butter or margarine
½ cup buttermilk

1 tablespoon light corn syrup
1 teaspoon vanilla extract

• Bring all ingredients to a boil in a small saucepan, and cook 3 minutes. Yield: about 1½ cups.

SOUTHERN CLASSIC
★ ★ ★ ★ ★

Cooks Chat

"I used fresh figs from a coworker's tree. Everyone at the office loved the cake's moistness. The pecans added a nice crunch and flavor."

"Delicious and so moist. I opted for fresh figs and pecans. Depending on your oven, the cake can take longer than the time noted. Mine was ready in about 50 minutes. If you like carrot or spice cake, this is a good choice."

Chocolate Italian Cake

Prep: 30 min.   **Cook:** 30 min.   **Other:** 10 min.

This wonderful cake is a chocolate version of the classic Italian Cream Cake.

5 large eggs, separated	1 cup buttermilk
½ cup butter, softened	1 cup sweetened flaked coconut
½ cup shortening	⅔ cup finely chopped pecans
2 cups sugar	2 teaspoons vanilla extract
2¼ cups all-purpose flour	Chocolate-Cream Cheese
¼ cup unsweetened cocoa	Frosting
1 teaspoon baking soda	Garnish: pecan halves

• Beat egg whites at high speed with an electric mixer until stiff peaks form; set aside.
• Beat butter and shortening until creamy; gradually add sugar, beating well. Add egg yolks, 1 at a time, beating until blended after each addition.
• Combine flour, cocoa, and baking soda; add to butter mixture alternately with buttermilk, beginning and ending with flour mixture. Beat at low speed until blended after each addition. Stir in coconut, chopped pecans, and vanilla. Fold in egg whites. Pour batter into 3 greased and floured 8-inch round cakepans.
• Bake at 325° for 25 to 30 minutes or until a wooden pick inserted in center comes out clean. Cool in pans 10 minutes. Remove cake layers to wire racks, and cool completely.
• Spread Chocolate-Cream Cheese Frosting between layers and on top and sides of cake. Garnish, if desired. Store in refrigerator. Yield: 1 (3-layer) cake.

Chocolate-Cream Cheese Frosting

Prep: 10 min.

1 (8-ounce) package cream cheese, softened	1 (16-ounce) package powdered sugar
½ cup butter, softened	¼ cup unsweetened cocoa
2 teaspoons vanilla extract	¼ cup buttermilk
¼ teaspoon ground cinnamon	⅔ cup finely chopped pecans

• Beat first 4 ingredients at medium speed with an electric mixer until creamy.
• Combine powdered sugar and cocoa; gradually add to butter mixture alternately with buttermilk, beginning and ending with powdered sugar mixture. Beat at low speed until blended after each addition. Stir in pecans. Yield: 4 cups.

Blackberry-Raspberry Truffle Cake

Prep: 1 hr.　**Cook:** 55 min.　**Other:** 1 hr., 45 min.

2 (18.25-ounce) packages devil's food cake mix
6 large eggs
1 cup vegetable oil
1⅓ cups water
1¼ cups light sour cream
1 (12-ounce) package semisweet chocolate morsels
1½ cups whipping cream
½ cup seedless blackberry jam
½ cup seedless raspberry jam
¼ cup water

1 (8-ounce) package cream cheese, softened
⅓ cup powdered sugar
1 (16-ounce) container frozen whipped topping, thawed
1 teaspoon vanilla extract
3 to 3½ cups chopped pecans, toasted
Garnish: ¼ cup fresh blackberries and raspberries or blackberry and raspberry candies

• Beat first 5 ingredients at medium speed with an electric mixer 2 minutes or until blended.
• Grease 3 (9-inch) parchment or wax paper-lined round cakepans. Pour batter evenly into cakepans.
• Bake at 350° for 35 to 40 minutes or until a wooden pick inserted in center comes out clean. Cool cake layers in pans on wire racks 15 minutes. Remove from pans, and remove paper. Cool completely on wire racks.
• Combine chocolate morsels and whipping cream in a medium saucepan over medium heat, whisking constantly, 10 minutes or until mixture is smooth. Pour into a mixing bowl; cover and chill 1½ hours or until mixture begins to thicken.
• Cook jams and ¼ cup water in a small saucepan over medium heat, stirring constantly, 5 minutes or until jam melts. Brush tops of cake layers with jam mixture.
• Beat chilled chocolate mixture at medium speed with an electric mixer about 20 seconds or until stiff peaks form (do not overbeat).
• Place 1 layer, glazed side up, on a cake platter. Spread with half of chocolate mixture. Top with another cake layer, glazed side down; spread with remaining chocolate mixture. Top with remaining cake layer, glazed side down. Secure layers by inserting wooden skewers from the top layer down through the other 2 layers.
• Beat cream cheese and powdered sugar at medium speed with an electric mixer until smooth. Add whipped topping and vanilla, beating until smooth. Working quickly, frost top and sides of cake with cream cheese mixture. Press pecans around sides of cake. Garnish, if desired. Store in refrigerator. Yield: 1 (3-layer) cake.

Note: For testing purposes only, we used Betty Crocker SuperMoist Devil's Food Cake Mix.

Hummingbird Cake

Prep: 36 min.   **Cook:** 23 min.

This recipe originally ran in the magazine in 1978, and the stream of letters from readers requesting the recipe has never stopped. Online cooks share the sentiments.

3 cups all-purpose flour
2 cups sugar
1 teaspoon baking soda
½ teaspoon salt
1 teaspoon ground cinnamon
3 large eggs, lightly beaten
¾ cup vegetable oil

1½ teaspoons vanilla extract
1 (8-ounce) can crushed
    pineapple, undrained
1 cup chopped pecans
1¾ cups mashed ripe banana
    (about 4 large)
Cream Cheese Frosting

• Combine first 5 ingredients in a large bowl; add eggs and oil, stirring just until dry ingredients are moistened. Add vanilla, pineapple, pecans, and bananas, stirring just until combined.
• Pour batter into 3 greased and floured 9-inch round cakepans.
• Bake at 350° for 23 minutes or until a wooden pick inserted in center comes out clean. Cool in pans on wire racks 10 minutes; remove from pans, and cool completely on wire racks.
• Spread Cream Cheese Frosting between layers and on top and sides of cake. Store in refrigerator. Yield: 1 (3-layer) cake.

Cream Cheese Frosting

Prep: 5 min.

½ cup butter or margarine,
    softened
1 (8-ounce) package cream
    cheese, softened

1 (16-ounce) package
    powdered sugar, sifted
1 teaspoon vanilla extract
½ cup chopped pecans

• Beat butter and cream cheese at medium speed with an electric mixer until creamy. Gradually add powdered sugar, beating at low speed until blended. Beat at high speed until smooth; stir in vanilla and pecans. Yield: 3¼ cups.

Milk Chocolate Bar Cake

Prep: 20 min.   **Cook:** 25 min.

1 (18.25-ounce) package Swiss
   chocolate cake mix
1 (8-ounce) package cream
   cheese, softened
1 cup powdered sugar
½ cup granulated sugar

10 (1.45-ounce) milk chocolate
   candy bars with almonds,
   divided
1 (12-ounce) container frozen
   whipped topping, thawed

• Prepare cake batter according to package directions. Pour into 3 greased and floured 8-inch round cakepans.
• Bake at 325° for 20 to 25 minutes or until a wooden pick inserted in center comes out clean. Cool in pans on wire racks 10 minutes. Remove from pans, and cool completely on wire racks.
• Beat cream cheese, powdered sugar, and granulated sugar at medium speed with an electric mixer until mixture is creamy.
• Chop 8 candy bars finely. Fold cream cheese mixture and chopped candy into whipped topping.
• Spread icing between layers and on top and sides of cake. Chop remaining 2 candy bars. Sprinkle half of chopped candy bars over cake. Press remaining chopped candy along bottom edge of cake. Store in refrigerator. Yield: 1 (3-layer) cake.

Note: For testing purposes only, we used Duncan Hines Swiss Chocolate Cake Mix and Hershey's Milk Chocolate Bars with Almonds.

Cooks Chat

"A coworker baked this cake last week and brought it to work. It was wonderful! Several people asked for the recipe. The cake only lasted a couple of hours—it was so good that no one could resist. I plan to bake this cake for my family ASAP. (OK, OK, it's really for me!)"

"I have been making this cake for a couple of years. My friends and family love it! Everyone thinks I spend hours on this cake, and it just takes a little time and gets better each time I make it. Everyone at work requests this cake when we have an office function, which is pretty often. Plus, some of my friends have asked for the recipe. Call me selfish, but I just don't want to give it to them."

Red Velvet Cake

Prep: 15 min.   **Cook:** 22 min.

½ cup butter or margarine, softened
1½ cups sugar
1 teaspoon vanilla extract
1 tablespoon white vinegar
3 large eggs
1 (1-ounce) bottle liquid red food coloring

2½ cups all-purpose flour
2 tablespoons unsweetened cocoa
1 teaspoon baking soda
½ teaspoon salt
1 cup buttermilk
Cream Cheese Frosting

• Beat butter at medium speed with an electric mixer until fluffy; gradually add sugar, vanilla, and vinegar, beating well. Add eggs, 1 at a time, beating until blended after each addition. Add food coloring, beating until combined.

• Combine flour and next 3 ingredients; add to butter mixture alternately with buttermilk, beginning and ending with flour mixture. Beat at low speed until blended after each addition. Pour into 2 greased and floured 9-inch cakepans.

• Bake at 350° for 20 to 22 minutes or until a wooden pick inserted in center comes out clean. Cool in pans on wire racks 5 minutes; remove from pans, and cool on wire racks.

• Spread Cream Cheese Frosting between layers and on tops and sides of cake. Store in refrigerator. Yield: 1 (2-layer) cake.

Cream Cheese Frosting

Prep: 5 min.

1 (8-ounce) package cream cheese, softened
½ cup butter or margarine, softened

1 (16-ounce) package powdered sugar
1½ teaspoons vanilla extract
1 cup chopped pecans

• Beat cream cheese and butter until creamy; gradually add sugar and vanilla, beating well. Stir in pecans. Yield: 3 cups.

Caramel-Glazed Pear Cake

Prep: 25 min.　**Cook:** 1 hr.　**Other:** 5 min.

Very ripe pears make this cake ultramoist.

4 ripe Bartlett pears, peeled and
　diced (about 3 cups)
1 tablespoon sugar
3 large eggs
2 cups sugar
1¼ cups vegetable oil
3 cups all-purpose flour

1 teaspoon salt
1 teaspoon baking soda
1½ cups pecans, coarsely
　chopped
2 teaspoons vanilla extract
Caramel Glaze

• Toss together pears and 1 tablespoon sugar; let stand 5 minutes.
• Beat eggs, 2 cups sugar, and oil at medium speed with an electric mixer until blended.
• Combine flour, salt, and baking soda, and add to egg mixture, beating at low speed until blended. Fold in pears, chopped pecans, and vanilla extract. Pour batter into a greased and floured 10-inch Bundt pan.
• Bake at 350° for 1 hour or until a long wooden pick inserted in center comes out clean. Remove from pan, and drizzle Caramel Glaze over warm cake. Yield: 1 (10-inch) cake.

Caramel Glaze

Prep: 5 min.　**Cook:** 8 min.

1 cup firmly packed brown
　sugar

½ cup butter
¼ cup evaporated milk

• Stir together all ingredients in a small saucepan over medium heat; bring to a boil, and cook, stirring constantly, 2½ minutes or until sugar dissolves. Yield: 1½ cups.

KITCHEN COMFORT
★ ★ ★ ★ ★

Cooks Chat

"Thank you, thank you, thank you! This recipe is great and simple. I made this for a 69-year-old's birthday, and it brought back fond memories for him. His mother used to make him a cake that was very close to this one."

"This is absolutely the best cake I have ever eaten!"

"Excellent flavor and moistness! I substituted 1 cup whole wheat flour for 1 cup all-purpose. My family agrees that this recipe is a keeper!"

Cooks Chat

"I made this as an after-theater dessert for friends. The recipe directions were well written and easy to understand. The two 15-year-olds who tasted it asked for second helpings. I don't think there could be any higher approval than that."

"This recipe is delicious. I will make this again just for the pound cake alone!"

Buttered Rum Pound Cake with Bananas Foster Sauce

Prep: 30 min.   **Cook:** 1 hr., 30 min.   **Other:** 4 hrs., 15 min.

1 cup butter, softened
2½ cups sugar
6 large eggs, separated
3 cups all-purpose flour
¼ teaspoon baking soda
1 (8-ounce) container sour cream

1 teaspoon vanilla extract
1 teaspoon lemon extract
½ cup sugar
Buttered Rum Glaze
Bananas Foster Sauce
Vanilla ice cream

• Beat butter at medium speed with a heavy-duty mixer until creamy. Add 2½ cups sugar, beating 4 to 5 minutes or until fluffy. Add egg yolks, 1 at a time, beating just until yellow disappears.
• Combine flour and baking soda; add to butter mixture alternately with sour cream, beginning and ending with flour mixture. Stir in extracts.

• Beat egg whites until foamy; gradually add ½ cup sugar, 1 table-spoon at a time, beating until stiff peaks form. Fold into batter. Pour batter into a greased and floured 10-inch tube pan.

• Bake at 325° for 1½ hours or until a long wooden pick inserted in center comes out clean. Cool in pan 10 to 15 minutes; remove from pan. Place on a serving plate. While warm, prick cake surface at 1-inch intervals with a wooden pick; pour warm Buttered Rum Glaze over cake. Let stand 4 hours or overnight before serving. Serve with Bananas Foster Sauce and vanilla ice cream. Yield: 1 (10-inch) cake.

Lemon Pound Cake: Add 2 tablespoons grated lemon rind to batter. Proceed with cake recipe as directed. Omit Buttered Rum Glaze and Bananas Foster Sauce.

Buttered Rum Glaze

Prep: 2 min.   **Cook:** 5 min.

6 tablespoons butter
3 tablespoons light rum
¾ cup sugar

3 tablespoons water
½ cup chopped pecans, toasted

• Combine first 4 ingredients in a small saucepan; bring to a boil. Boil, stirring constantly, 3 minutes. Remove from heat, and stir in pecans. Yield: 1¼ cups.

Bananas Foster Sauce

Prep: 5 min.   **Cook:** 8 min.

½ cup firmly packed brown sugar
¼ cup butter or margarine, melted

¼ teaspoon ground cinnamon
⅓ cup banana liqueur
4 bananas, peeled and sliced
⅓ cup light rum

• Combine first 4 ingredients in a large skillet; cook over medium heat, stirring constantly, until bubbly. Add bananas, and cook 2 to 3 minutes or until thoroughly heated. Remove from heat.

• Heat rum in a small saucepan over medium heat (do not boil). Quickly pour rum over banana mixture, and immediately ignite with a long match just above the liquid mixture to light the fumes (not the liquid itself). Let flames die down; serve immediately with Buttered Rum Pound Cake. Yield: 8 servings.

Cream Cheese Pound Cake

Prep: 15 min.   **Cook:** 1hr., 40 min.

1½ cups butter or margarine, softened
1 (8-ounce) package cream cheese, softened
3 cups sugar
6 large eggs
3 cups all-purpose flour
⅛ teaspoon salt
1 tablespoon vanilla extract

• Beat butter and cream cheese at medium speed with an electric mixer until creamy; gradually add sugar, beating well. Add eggs, 1 at a time, beating until combined.
• Combine flour and salt; gradually add to butter mixture, beating at low speed just until blended after each addition. Stir in vanilla. Pour batter into a greased and floured 10-inch Bundt pan.
• Bake at 300° for 1 hour and 40 minutes or until a long wooden pick inserted in center comes out clean. Cool in pan on a wire rack 10 to 15 minutes; remove from pan, and let cool completely on wire rack. Yield: 1 (10-inch) cake.

Mocha Cake

Prep: 25 min.   **Cook:** 55 min.   **Other:** 15 min.

2 cups sour cream
2 large eggs
1 (18.25-ounce) package chocolate cake mix
½ cup coffee liqueur
¼ cup vegetable oil
1 (12-ounce) package semi-sweet chocolate morsels
½ cup crushed toffee bits (optional)
Powdered sugar
1 pint whipping cream
¼ cup powdered sugar

• Stir together first 5 ingredients in a large bowl; blend well. Stir in morsels and, if desired, toffee bits. Pour batter into a greased and floured 10-inch Bundt pan.
• Bake at 350° for 50 to 55 minutes or until a long wooden pick inserted in center comes out clean. Cool in pan on a wire rack 10 to 15 minutes; remove from pan, and cool completely on wire rack. Sprinkle with powdered sugar.
• Beat whipping cream at medium speed with an electric mixer until foamy; gradually add ¼ cup powdered sugar, beating until soft peaks form. Serve with cake. Yield: 1 (10-inch) cake.

Note: For testing purposes only, we used Kahlúa coffee liqueur and Heath Bits O' Brickle Toffee Bits.

Praline-Pumpkin Torte

Prep: 15 min.   **Cook:** 35 min.

¾ cup brown sugar
⅓ cup butter or margarine
3 tablespoons whipping cream
¾ cup chopped pecans
4 large eggs
1⅔ cups granulated sugar
1 cup vegetable oil
1 (15-ounce) can pumpkin

¼ teaspoon vanilla extract
2 cups all-purpose flour
2 teaspoons baking powder
2 teaspoons pumpkin pie spice
1 teaspoon baking soda
1 teaspoon salt
Whipped Cream Topping
Chopped pecans

• Cook first 3 ingredients in a saucepan over low heat, stirring until brown sugar dissolves. Pour into 2 greased 9-inch round cakepans; sprinkle evenly with ¾ cup pecans. Cool.
• Beat eggs, 1⅔ cups granulated sugar, and oil at medium speed with an electric mixer. Add pumpkin and vanilla; beat well.
• Combine flour and next 4 ingredients; add to pumpkin mixture, beating until blended. Spoon batter evenly into prepared cakepans.
• Bake at 350° for 30 to 35 minutes or until a wooden pick inserted in center comes out clean. Cool cake layers in pans on wire racks 5 minutes; remove from pans, and cool on wire racks.
• Place 1 cake layer on a serving plate, praline side up; spread evenly with half of Whipped Cream Topping. Top with remaining layer, praline side up, and spread remaining Whipped Cream Topping over top of cake. Sprinkle cake with chopped pecans. Store in refrigerator. Yield: 1 (2-layer) torte.

Whipped Cream Topping

Prep: 5 min.

1¾ cups whipping cream
¼ cup powdered sugar

¼ teaspoon vanilla extract

• Beat cream until soft peaks form. Add sugar and vanilla, beating until blended. Yield: 3½ cups.

Cooks Chat

"Beautiful presentation, easy to make, and always gets a standing ovation! It's easier to slice if you chill the torte thoroughly (overnight is best). Delicious!"

"Amazing! We had this last year, and now it's a new tradition! The praline crunchy coating around the sides is wonderful. I froze the leftovers in small wedges. They make perfect single servings when thawed out a couple of months later."

Chocolate-Vanilla Holiday Torte

Cooks Chat

"This is a fantastic cake. I made it for our block party last Christmas, and people didn't want to cut it because it was 'too pretty to cut.' My wife had me make three more cakes—two for the hospital and one for church; the one for church was for an Easter bake sale, so I used pastel colors."

"This recipe is fantastic! I could never get the bow right, so I simply drizzled the cake with semisweet chocolate ganache. I won a 'Best in Show' award in a local cake competition with this recipe. My family adores it, too!"

"The bow was tricky, but the taste of this cake was unbelievable."

Prep: 40 min.   **Cook:** 2 hrs.   **Other:** 9 hrs., 30 min.

2 (8-ounce) packages semisweet chocolate baking squares, chopped
1 cup butter or margarine, cut into pieces
3 cups sugar, divided
8 large eggs
3 (8-ounce) packages cream cheese, softened
3 tablespoons all-purpose flour
3 large eggs
1 (8-ounce) container sour cream
4 (1-ounce) white chocolate baking squares, grated
1 tablespoon vanilla extract
White Chocolate Ganache
Burgundy food coloring paste
White Chocolate Ribbons and Bow
Garnish: silver ornaments

• Line 2 (9-inch) square cakepans with aluminum foil; grease foil. Cook semisweet chocolate and butter in a small saucepan over low heat, stirring until blended. Cool.
• Beat 2 cups sugar and 8 eggs at medium speed with an electric mixer 3 minutes or until foamy. Gradually add chocolate mixture, beating at low speed until blended. Pour into 1 prepared pan.
• Bake at 325° for 1 hour or until set. Cool on a wire rack. Cover; chill 8 hours. Remove from pan, discarding foil. Trim edges, if necessary.
• Beat cream cheese at medium speed with an electric mixer until creamy. Add remaining 1 cup sugar and flour, beating well. Add remaining 3 eggs, 1 at a time, beating just until blended after each addition. Stir in sour cream, white chocolate, and vanilla. Pour into remaining prepared pan.
• Bake at 325° for 1 hour. Turn oven off. Leave cake layer in oven, with oven door partially opened, 30 minutes. Remove cake from oven; cool in pan on a wire rack. Cover cake, and chill 8 hours. Remove from pan, discarding foil.
• Reserve 1 cup White Chocolate Ganache. Place chocolate layer, bottom side up, on a serving plate. Spread with ½ cup White Chocolate Ganache, and top with white chocolate layer, bottom side up. Spread top and sides of cake with remaining ganache.
• Stir desired amount of food coloring paste into reserved 1 cup ganache. Insert metal tip No. 2 into a large decorating bag; fill with ganache. Pipe lace design (continuous string of frosting without touching) on top and sides of cake.
• Arrange 2 (17- x 2½-inch) White Chocolate Ribbons on cake. Form bow with 1 (13- x 2½-inch) strip; arrange 2 (4- x 2½-inch) strips and 2 (3- x 2½-inch) strips for bow ends. Place 1 (2½- x 1-inch) strip in center of bow for knot.
• Store cake in refrigerator. Remove from refrigerator, and let stand at room temperature 1 hour before serving. Garnish, if desired. Yield: 1 (9-inch) torte.

White Chocolate Ganache

Prep: 5 min.　**Other:** 45 min.

2 (12-ounce) packages white 　 1 cup whipping cream
　　chocolate morsels

• Heat chocolate morsels and cream in a heavy saucepan over low heat, stirring often, until chocolate melts. Chill 45 minutes or until thickened. Beat at medium speed with an electric mixer until spreading consistency. Yield: 5 cups.

White Chocolate Ribbons and Bow

Prep: 1 hr.

6 ounces vanilla bark coating 　 Burgundy food coloring paste
3½ tablespoons light corn
　　syrup

• Melt coating in a small saucepan over low heat. Remove from heat; stir in corn syrup and desired amount of food coloring paste. Cover; chill 1 hour.
• Knead mixture until the consistency of dough. (Kneading with warm hands keeps mixture soft; letting it stand on a cool surface hardens it.)
• Roll bark coating mixture out onto a cool surface to ⅛-inch thickness. Using a fluted pastry wheel, cut into 2 (17- x 2½-inch) ribbons. Cut remaining mixture into 1 (13- x 2½-inch) strip, 2 (4- x 2½-inch) strips, 2 (3- x 2½-inch) strips, and 1 (2½- x 1-inch) strip. Yield: enough for 2 ribbons and 1 bow.

Cooks Chat

"This easy-to-understand recipe was perfect for Mardi Gras, and the cake turned out to be great!"

"This is the best king cake I've ever had, store-bought or homemade. I am a native New Orleanian, and this beats them all! I made one exactly as the instructions suggested, and then I made another with cream cheese instead of butter in the middle with the brown sugar."

"I've made this recipe many times and have added canned almond paste each time with excellent results. Everyone hopes they get the piece with the baby inside."

King Cake

Prep: 50 min.　**Cook:** 15 min.　**Other:** 1 hr., 25 min.

This treat's a fitting end to any traditional Mardi Gras celebration.

¼ cup butter or margarine
1 (16-ounce) container sour cream
⅓ cup sugar
1 teaspoon salt
2 (¼-ounce) envelopes active dry yeast
1 tablespoon sugar
½ cup warm water (100° to 110°)

2 large eggs
6 to 6½ cups all-purpose flour, divided
½ cup sugar
1½ teaspoons ground cinnamon
⅓ cup butter or margarine, softened
Colored Frostings
Colored Sugars

• Cook first 4 ingredients in a saucepan over low heat, stirring often, until butter melts. Cool mixture to 100° to 110°.
• Dissolve yeast and 1 tablespoon sugar in ½ cup warm water in a large bowl; let stand 5 minutes. Add butter mixture, eggs, and 2 cups flour; beat at medium speed with an electric mixer 2 minutes or until smooth. Gradually stir in enough remaining flour to make a soft dough.

• Turn dough onto a lightly floured surface; knead until smooth and elastic, about 10 minutes. Place in a well-greased bowl, turning to grease top. Cover and let rise in a warm place (85°), free from drafts, 1 hour or until doubled in bulk.
• Stir together ½ cup sugar and cinnamon; set aside.
• Punch dough down; divide in half. Turn 1 portion out onto a lightly floured surface; roll to a 28- x 10-inch rectangle. Spread half each of cinnamon mixture and softened butter on dough. Roll dough, jellyroll fashion, starting at long side. Place dough roll, seam side down, on a lightly greased baking sheet. Bring ends together to form an oval ring, moistening and pinching edges together to seal. Repeat with remaining dough, cinnamon mixture, and butter.
• Cover and let rise in a warm place, free from drafts, 20 minutes or until doubled in bulk.
• Bake at 375° for 15 minutes or until golden. Decorate with bands of Colored Frostings; sprinkle with Colored Sugars. Yield: 2 cakes.

Note: Once the cakes have cooled, randomly insert a plastic baby doll, if desired, before frosting. Legend has it that whoever gets the piece with the baby has good luck.

Colored Frostings

Prep: 15 min.

3 cups powdered sugar
3 tablespoons butter, melted
3 to 6 tablespoons milk
¼ teaspoon vanilla extract

1 to 2 drops each of green, yellow, red, and blue liquid food coloring

• Stir together powdered sugar and melted butter. Add milk to reach desired consistency for drizzling; stir in vanilla. Divide frosting into 3 batches, tinting 1 green, 1 yellow, and combining red and blue food coloring for purple frosting. Yield: about 1½ cups.

Colored Sugars

Prep: 20 min.

1½ cups sugar, divided
1 to 2 drops each of green, yellow, red, and blue liquid food coloring

• Place ½ cup sugar and 1 drop of green food coloring in a jar or zip-top plastic bag; seal. Shake vigorously to evenly mix color with sugar. Repeat procedure with ½ cup sugar and 1 drop yellow food coloring. For purple, combine 1 drop red and 1 drop blue food coloring before adding to remaining ½ cup sugar. Yield: ½ cup of each colored sugar.

Festive Piña Colada Cheesecake

Prep: 15 min.   **Cook:** 1 hr., 15 min.   **Other:** 8 hrs.

6 tablespoons unsalted butter, melted
1¾ cups graham cracker crumbs
¾ cup chopped pecans, toasted
1 tablespoon sugar
3 (8-ounce) packages cream cheese, softened
½ cup sugar
5 large eggs
1 (8-ounce) can crushed pineapple, drained
1 cup cream of coconut
1 cup sour cream
⅓ cup light rum
4 teaspoons coconut extract
Glaze
Garnishes: whipped cream and toasted coconut

• Stir together first 4 ingredients, and press into bottom and 1½ inches up sides of a lightly greased 10-inch springform pan.
• Beat cream cheese and ½ cup sugar at medium speed with an electric mixer 3 minutes or until fluffy. Add eggs, 1 at a time, beating well after each addition. Add pineapple and next 4 ingredients, beating until blended. Pour mixture into crust.
• Bake at 325° for 1 hour and 15 minutes or until center is almost set. Cool on a wire rack. Spread Glaze over top of cheesecake, and cover and chill at least 8 hours. Store in refrigerator. Garnish, if desired. Yield: 1 (10-inch) cake.

Glaze

Prep: 5 min.   **Cook:** 5 min.

1 tablespoon cornstarch
1 tablespoon water
1 (8-ounce) can crushed pineapple
¼ cup sugar
2 tablespoons lemon juice

• Stir together cornstarch and 1 tablespoon water until smooth. Combine cornstarch mixture, crushed pineapple, ¼ cup sugar, and lemon juice in a saucepan over medium heat; cook, stirring constantly, 5 minutes or until mixture is thickened and bubbly. Remove from heat; let cool completely. Yield: 1 cup.

Pecan Praline Cheesecake

Prep: 30 min.   **Cook:** 1 hr., 10 min.   **Other:** 9 hrs.

1½ cups crushed gingersnaps
    (about 24 cookies)
½ cup butter or margarine,
    melted and divided
3 (8-ounce) packages cream
    cheese, softened
1 cup granulated sugar
6 tablespoons all-purpose flour,
    divided

3 large eggs
1 teaspoon vanilla extract
¼ teaspoon salt
¼ cup firmly packed light
    brown sugar
½ cup chopped pecans, toasted
15 caramels (optional)
2 tablespoons heavy whipping
    cream (optional)

• Stir together gingersnaps and ¼ cup melted butter; press mixture into bottom and 2 inches up sides of a 9-inch springform pan.
• Beat cream cheese, granulated sugar, and 2 tablespoons flour at medium speed with an electric mixer 2 minutes. Add eggs, vanilla, and salt; beat 3 minutes. Pour batter into prepared crust. Set aside.
• Stir together brown sugar, pecans, remaining ¼ cup flour, and remaining ¼ cup melted butter until crumbly. Sprinkle around edge of cream cheese mixture.
• Bake at 300° for 1 hour and 10 minutes or until center is firm. Turn off oven. Leave cheesecake in oven 30 minutes. Remove cheesecake from oven; cool in pan on a wire rack 30 minutes. Cover and chill 8 hours. Drizzle caramel topping on edge of chilled cheesecake, if desired. To make caramel topping, place caramels and whipping cream in a 1-cup microwave-safe bowl. Microwave at HIGH 30 seconds to 1 minute, stirring halfway through cooking time, until melted. Store in refrigerator. Yield: 1 (9-inch) cheesecake.

Note: Substitute commercial caramel ice-cream topping for caramel topping, if desired.

Cooks Chat

"What an incredible dessert! This is one of the best cheesecake recipes I've ever made. The amount of time it takes to make it as opposed to the finished result is extremely equitable, and it looks so delicious, too. I'm 16 years old, and I love to bake. This was not a difficult recipe, nor did it call for too many ingredients. To get the drizzled-down-the-sides look with the caramel, I used Smucker's caramel topping and poured it on just before serving. It was a huge success!"

"This recipe is great! I made it for Thanksgiving, and it was gone before any other dessert!"

Lemon-Blueberry Cream Pie

Prep: 25 min.   **Cook:** 8 min.   **Other:** 2 hrs.

1⅔ cups graham cracker
   crumbs
¼ cup granulated sugar
⅓ cup butter or margarine,
   melted
1 (8-ounce) package cream
   cheese, softened
1 (14-ounce) can sweetened
   condensed milk
¼ cup powdered sugar

1 (3.4-ounce) package lemon
   instant pudding mix
2 teaspoons grated lemon rind
½ cup fresh lemon juice
1 pint fresh blueberries
2 tablespoons blueberry
   preserves
1 cup whipping cream
Garnishes: lemon slices, fresh
   blueberries

• Stir together first 3 ingredients; press evenly in bottom and up
sides of a 9-inch pieplate.
• Bake piecrust at 350° for 8 minutes; remove piecrust to a wire
rack, and cool completely.
• Beat cheese, milk, and powdered sugar at medium speed with
an electric mixer until creamy. Add pudding mix, rind, and juice;
beat until blended. Spread half of lemon mixture evenly into
prepared crust.
• Stir together blueberries and preserves; spread evenly over lemon
mixture. Spread remaining lemon mixture over blueberry mixture;
cover and chill 2 hours or until set.
• Beat whipping cream with an electric mixer until soft peaks form,
and spread around outer edge of pie, forming a 3-inch border. Store
in refrigerator. Garnish, if desired. Yield: 1 (9-inch) pie.

Cooks Chat

*"Wow! What a crowd-pleaser! I've
made this for three events this week.
Everyone loved it. Beautiful and
refreshing!"*

*"I have made this recipe twice now,
and everyone loved it. It makes a
very pretty presentation and is quite
impressive."*

*"I served this at a party I hosted.
My guests raved about it! It was the
most popular item on the table, and
everyone wanted the recipe!"*

Fudge Pie

Prep: 12 min.   **Cook:** 40 min.

¾ cup butter or margarine
3 (1-ounce) unsweetened
    chocolate baking squares
3 large eggs
1½ cups sugar
¾ cup all-purpose flour

1 teaspoon vanilla extract
¾ cup chopped pecans,
    toasted and divided
Toppings: vanilla ice cream and
    chocolate syrup

• Cook butter and chocolate in a small saucepan over low heat, stirring often until melted.
• Beat eggs at medium speed with an electric mixer 5 minutes. Gradually add sugar, beating until blended. Gradually add chocolate mixture, flour, and vanilla, beating until blended. Stir in ½ cup pecans.
• Pour mixture into a lightly greased 9-inch pieplate.
• Bake at 350° for 35 to 40 minutes or until center is firm. Cool. Top each serving with vanilla ice cream and chocolate syrup; sprinkle with remaining chopped pecans. Yield: 1 (9-inch) pie.

Key Lime Pie

Prep: 20 min.   **Cook:** 38 min.   **Other:** 8 hrs.

1¼ cups graham cracker
    crumbs
¼ cup firmly packed light
    brown sugar
⅓ cup butter or margarine,
    melted

2 (14-ounce) cans sweetened
    condensed milk
1 cup fresh Key lime juice*
2 egg whites
¼ teaspoon cream of tartar
2 tablespoons granulated sugar

• Combine first 3 ingredients; press into a 9-inch pieplate. Bake piecrust at 350° for 10 minutes or until lightly browned; cool.
• Stir together sweetened condensed milk and lime juice until blended. Pour into prepared crust. Set aside.
• Beat egg whites and cream of tartar at high speed with an electric mixer just until foamy.
• Add granulated sugar gradually, 1 tablespoon at a time, beating until soft peaks form and sugar dissolves (2 to 4 minutes). Spread meringue over filling.
• Bake at 325° for 25 to 28 minutes. Chill 8 hours. Store in refrigerator. Yield: 1 (9 inch) pie.

*Substitute bottled Key lime juice for fresh juice, if desired.

Fudge Pie

Fresh Blackberry Pie

Prep: 30 min.   **Cook:** 17 min.   **Other:** 10 hrs., 30 min.

Though this pie should be assembled and served the same day, you can get a head start by combining the berries and sugar and chilling them the night before.

1½ cups fresh blackberries
1¼ cups sugar, divided
½ (15-ounce) package
    refrigerated piecrusts
3 tablespoons cornstarch
1¼ cups water
½ teaspoon vanilla extract

1 (3-ounce) package raspberry
    gelatin
4 drops blue liquid food
    coloring
Sweetened whipped cream
    (optional)

• Gently toss berries and ¼ cup sugar in a large bowl; cover and chill 8 hours. Drain.
• Fit piecrust into a 9-inch pieplate according to package directions; fold edges under, and crimp. Prick bottom and sides of piecrust with a fork.
• Bake at 450° for 7 to 9 minutes or until lightly browned.
• Stir together cornstarch and remaining 1 cup sugar in a small saucepan; slowly whisk in 1¼ cups water and vanilla. Cook over medium heat, whisking constantly, 7 to 8 minutes or until mixture thickens.
• Stir together raspberry gelatin and blue liquid food coloring in a small bowl; whisk into the warm cornstarch mixture.
• Spoon blackberries into piecrust. Pour glaze evenly over berries, pressing down gently with a spoon to be sure all berries are coated. Chill 2½ hours. Serve with whipped cream, if desired. Yield: 1 (9-inch) pie.

Fudgy Chocolate Malt-Peppermint Pie

Cooks Chat

"With a 17-year-old chocoholic son who has several chocoholic friends, this is definitely a new tradition in my house! The 'locusts' loved it, and so did I. Easy to make, creamy, and decadently smooth. This makes a sumptuous finale to any dinner. Try it with espresso afterward for a special treat."

Prep: 45 min.   **Cook:** 40 min.   **Other:** 8 hrs.

½ cup butter or margarine
2 (1-ounce) unsweetened
   chocolate baking squares
1 (1-ounce) semisweet
   chocolate baking square
1 cup granulated sugar
2 large eggs
1 teaspoon vanilla extract
¼ cup all-purpose flour
¼ cup chocolate malt mix

¼ teaspoon salt
¼ teaspoon ground cinnamon
1 cup coarsely chopped pecans
1 pint peppermint ice cream,
   softened
1 cup whipping cream
¼ cup powdered sugar
¼ cup crushed peppermint
   candy

• Melt first 3 ingredients in a heavy saucepan over low heat, stirring occasionally until smooth. Remove from heat; cool.

Fudgy Chocolate Malt-Peppermint Pie

- Beat chocolate mixture and granulated sugar at medium speed with an electric mixer until blended. Add eggs and vanilla, beating until smooth. Add flour and next 3 ingredients, beating until blended. Stir in pecans. Pour into a lightly greased 9-inch pieplate.
- Bake at 325° for 40 minutes. Remove from oven; cool completely on wire rack.
- Press down center of crust gently. Spread ice cream over crust. Cover and freeze 8 hours.
- Beat whipping cream and powdered sugar at medium speed with electric mixer until soft peaks form. Spread over ice cream. Sprinkle with crushed candy. Store in freezer. Yield: 1 (9-inch) pie.

Note: For testing purposes only, we used Ovaltine Chocolate Malt Mix.

Coconut Cream Pie

Prep: 25 min.   **Cook:** 8 min.   **Other:** 2 hrs.

Look for cream of coconut near the piña colada and margarita mixes.

1⅔ cups graham cracker crumbs
¼ cup sugar
⅓ cup butter or margarine, melted
1 (8-ounce) package cream cheese, softened
1 cup cream of coconut
1 (3.4-ounce) package cheesecake instant pudding mix
1 (6-ounce) package frozen sweetened flaked coconut, thawed
1 (8-ounce) container frozen whipped topping, thawed
1 cup whipping cream
Garnish: sweetened flaked coconut

- Stir together first 3 ingredients; press mixture evenly in bottom and up sides of a 9-inch pieplate.
- Bake at 350° for 8 minutes; remove to a wire rack, and cool completely.
- Beat cheese and cream of coconut at medium speed with an electric mixer until smooth. Add pudding mix, beating until blended.
- Stir in coconut; fold in whipped topping. Spread cheese mixture evenly into prepared crust; cover and chill 2 hours or until set.
- Beat whipping cream with an electric mixer until soft peaks form, and spread evenly over top of pie. Garnish, if desired. Store in refrigerator. Yield: 1 (9-inch) pie.

Note: For testing purposes only, we used Jell-O Instant Pudding Cheesecake Flavor.

SOUTHERN CLASSIC
★★★★★

Cooks Chat

"This is so good that it should be illegal! Best of all, it is easy and very impressive for company. I like to garnish with some toasted coconut."

"What a yummy pie! I'd give it 6 stars if that was a choice. Coconut pie has always been my husband's favorite, and he said that this is the best I have made in 50 years of marriage. I followed the recipe exactly, except for the piecrust. I made a plain crust from scratch because I don't like the sweetness of graham cracker crust."

"My version was a no-bake recipe, since I made this with a ready-to-use crust. It was extremely easy to make. It tasted very light and delicious. You can just top with Cool Whip instead of whipping cream to save time. This is a pie everyone will love."

Mystery Pecan Pie

Prep: 15 min.   **Cook:** 55 min.

Taste pecan pie and cheesecake together in this recipe, and the only mystery will be "Where'd it all go?"

1 (15-ounce) package refrigerated piecrusts
1 (8-ounce) package cream cheese, softened
4 large eggs
¾ cup sugar, divided

2 teaspoons vanilla extract, divided
¼ teaspoon salt
1 cup chopped pecans
1 cup light corn syrup

• Unroll and stack 2 piecrusts; gently roll or press together. Fit into a 9-inch pieplate according to package directions; fold edges under, and crimp.
• Beat cream cheese, 1 egg, ½ cup sugar, 1 teaspoon vanilla, and salt at medium speed with an electric mixer until smooth. Pour into piecrust. Sprinkle with pecans.
• Stir together corn syrup, remaining 3 eggs, remaining ¼ cup sugar, and remaining 1 teaspoon vanilla; pour mixture over pecans.
• Bake at 350° for 50 to 55 minutes or until set. Yield: 1 (9-inch) pie.

Granny Smith Apple Pie

Prep: 30 min.   **Cook:** 50 min.

1½ (15-ounce) packages refrigerated piecrusts, divided
6 medium Granny Smith apples, peeled and sliced
1½ tablespoons lemon juice

¾ cup brown sugar
½ cup granulated sugar
⅓ cup all-purpose flour
1 teaspoon ground cinnamon
½ teaspoon ground nutmeg

• Unroll and stack 2 piecrusts; gently roll or press together. Fit into a 9-inch deep-dish pieplate.
• Toss together apple and lemon juice in a large bowl. Combine brown sugar and next 4 ingredients; sprinkle over apple mixture, and toss to coat. Spoon into prepared piecrust.
• Unroll remaining piecrust; place over filling. Fold edges under, and crimp; cut slits in top for steam to escape.
• Bake at 450° for 15 minutes. Reduce oven temperature to 350°, and bake 35 more minutes. Yield: 1 (9-inch) pie.

Simmie's Pecan Pie

Prep: 5 min.   **Cook:** 1 hr.

3 large eggs
¾ cup sugar
1 cup dark corn syrup
3 tablespoons butter or
    margarine, melted

⅛ teaspoon salt
1 teaspoon vanilla extract
1½ cups chopped pecans
1 unbaked 9-inch pastry shell

• Stir together eggs and sugar until blended. Stir in corn syrup and next 3 ingredients. Stir in chopped pecans. Pour mixture into pastry shell. Place pie on a baking sheet.
• Bake at 400° on lower oven rack for 15 minutes. Reduce oven temperature to 325°, and bake 40 to 45 more minutes, shielding with aluminum foil to prevent excessive browning, if necessary. Yield: 1 (9-inch) pie.

Giant Oatmeal-Spice Cookies

Prep: 20 min.   **Cook:** 14 min. per batch

If you like these cookies spicier, increase the ginger, allspice, and cloves.

1½ cups all-purpose flour
1 teaspoon ground cinnamon
½ teaspoon salt
½ teaspoon baking soda
½ teaspoon ground ginger
¼ teaspoon ground allspice
⅛ teaspoon ground cloves
1 cup butter or margarine,
    softened

1 (16-ounce) package dark
    brown sugar
2 large eggs
1 teaspoon vanilla extract
3 cups quick-cooking oats
1 cup chopped pecans, toasted
½ cup raisins (optional)

• Stir together first 7 ingredients.
• Beat butter and sugar at medium speed with an electric mixer until fluffy. Add eggs and vanilla, beating until blended. Gradually add flour mixture, beating at low speed until blended.
• Stir in oats, chopped pecans, and if desired, raisins.
• Drop dough by ¼ cupfuls onto lightly greased baking sheets; lightly press down dough.
• Bake, in batches, at 350° for 12 to 14 minutes (cookies should not be brown around the edges, and centers will not look quite done). Cool slightly on baking sheets. Remove to wire racks; cool completely. Yield: about 2½ dozen.

Cooks Chat

"Absolutely wonderful. My adult kids ate them up! Hard to believe that they don't even contain flour. They stayed soft and chewy."

Chewy Red, White, and Blue Cookies

Prep: 35 min.   **Cook:** 15 min. per batch

You can find red, white, and blue candies at supermarkets and discount stores before the Fourth of July.

1 cup firmly packed light
    brown sugar
1 cup granulated sugar
½ cup butter or margarine,
    softened
3 large eggs
1½ cups creamy peanut butter
1 teaspoon vanilla extract

1 teaspoon light corn syrup
4½ cups uncooked regular oats
1 cup (6 ounces) semisweet
    chocolate morsels
1 cup (6 ounces) red, white,
    and blue candy-coated
    chocolate pieces
2 teaspoons baking soda

• Beat sugars and butter at low speed with an electric mixer until creamy. Add eggs and next 3 ingredients, beating until combined. Stir in oats and remaining ingredients.
• Drop by tablespoonfuls onto ungreased baking sheets.
• Bake, in batches, at 350° for 15 minutes. Remove to wire racks to cool. Yield: 5 dozen.

Note: For testing purposes only, we used red, white, and blue M&M's.

White Chocolate Chip-Oatmeal Cookies

Prep: 15 min.　**Cook:** 12 min. per batch

1 cup butter or margarine,
　softened
1 cup firmly packed light
　brown sugar
1 cup granulated sugar
2 large eggs
2 teaspoons vanilla extract
3 cups all-purpose flour

1 teaspoon baking soda
1 teaspoon baking powder
1 teaspoon salt
1½ cups uncooked regular oats
2 cups (12 ounces) white
　chocolate morsels
1 cup coarsely chopped pecans

Cooks Chat

"I'm in college, and I bribe people with these cookies all the time! Everyone loves them!"

"These cookies were terrific! I will definitely make them again."

• Beat butter at medium speed with an electric mixer until creamy; gradually add sugars, beating well. Add eggs, 1 at a time, beating just until yellow disappears after each addition. Stir in vanilla.
• Combine flour and next 3 ingredients; gradually add to butter mixture, beating until blended. Stir in oats, morsels, and pecans. Drop by tablespoonfuls onto greased baking sheets.
• Bake at 350° for 12 minutes. Cool on baking sheets 3 minutes; remove to wire racks to cool completely. Yield: about 5 dozen.

Sweetheart Jamwiches

Prep: 45 min.　**Cook:** 17 min.

1 (15-ounce) package
　refrigerated piecrusts
1 egg white, lightly beaten
2 tablespoons granulated sugar
1 (3-ounce) package cream
　cheese, softened
¼ cup powdered sugar
2 tablespoons butter, softened

½ teaspoon almond extract
½ (10-ounce) jar seedless
　raspberry preserves or
　strawberry jam
½ cup (3 ounces) white
　chocolate morsels
1 tablespoon butter
Red sparkling sugar (optional)

• Unroll piecrusts on a lightly floured surface. Cut with a 2-inch heart-shaped cookie cutter. Reroll remaining dough, and repeat procedure (there should be a total of 46 pastry hearts). Brush 1 side of each pastry heart with egg white, and sprinkle evenly with granulated sugar. Place pastry hearts on 2 ungreased baking sheets.
• Bake at 400° for 7 to 8 minutes or until lightly browned. Remove hearts to wire racks, and let cool.
• Stir together cream cheese, powdered sugar, 2 tablespoons butter, and almond extract until blended.
• Spread cream cheese mixture evenly on unsugared sides of half the hearts; spread about ½ teaspoon preserves over mixture on each heart. Top with remaining hearts, unsugared sides down.
• Microwave white chocolate morsels and 1 tablespoon butter in a glass bowl at HIGH 1 minute or until melted. Stir until smooth. Place mixture in a small zip-top freezer bag; seal bag. Snip a tiny hole in 1 corner of bag, and drizzle over tarts. Let cool completely; sprinkle with red sparkling sugar, if desired. Place in candy boxes, if desired. Yield: 23 tarts.

Cooks Chat

"These are delicious and really good as a light desert."

"Great cookies! Make sure to let the jam cool completely before cutting the cookies. You can also try filling the indentations with melted semisweet chocolate—very tasty!"

"This recipe will be a new family favorite. It was excellent!"

Raspberry Shortbread

Prep: 15 min.   **Cook:** 40 min.

1 cup butter, softened
⅔ cup granulated sugar
2½ cups all-purpose flour
1 (10-ounce) jar seedless
    raspberry jam, divided

1½ cups powdered sugar
3½ tablespoons water
½ teaspoon almond extract

• Beat butter and granulated sugar at medium speed with an electric mixer until light and fluffy. Gradually add flour, beating at low speed until blended. Divide dough into 6 equal portions; roll each portion into a 12- x 1-inch strip. Place strips on lightly greased baking sheets.
• Make a ½-inch-wide x ¼-inch-deep indentation down the center of each strip using the handle of a wooden spoon. Spoon half of jam evenly into indentations.
• Bake at 350° for 15 minutes. Remove from oven; spoon remaining jam into indentations. Bake 5 more minutes or until lightly browned.
• Whisk together powdered sugar, water, and extract; drizzle over warm shortbread. Cut each strip diagonally into 1-inch slices. Cool in pans on wire racks. Yield: 6 dozen.

Cooks Chat

"Oh my gosh! These are too good to share with the family. Hide them in your pillowcase or somewhere safe and eat them when everyone's asleep."

"If I wasn't dieting, I would most definitely eat these cookies all day long. They can be eaten at any time of the day or at any time of the year! I served pumpkin pie with these, and no one touched the pie. They loved the cookies! The only advice I have for you is to eat slowly and savor the yummy goodness!"

Pecan Pie Cookies

Prep: 30 min.   **Cook:** 16 min. per batch   **Other:** 1 hr., 35 min.

1 cup butter or margarine,
    softened
½ cup granulated sugar
½ cup dark corn syrup
2 large eggs, separated

2½ cups all-purpose flour
¼ cup butter or margarine
½ cup powdered sugar
3 tablespoons dark corn syrup
¾ cup finely chopped pecans

• Beat 1 cup butter and granulated sugar at medium speed with an electric mixer until light and fluffy. Add ½ cup corn syrup and egg yolks, beating well. Gradually stir in flour; cover and chill 1 hour.
• Melt ¼ cup butter in a heavy saucepan over medium heat; stir in powdered sugar and 3 tablespoons corn syrup. Cook, stirring often, until mixture boils. Remove from heat. Stir in pecans; chill 30 minutes. Shape mixture by ½ teaspoonfuls into ¼-inch balls; set aside.
• Shape cookie dough into 1-inch balls; place 2 inches apart on lightly greased baking sheets. Beat egg whites until foamy; brush on dough balls.

• Bake at 375° for 6 minutes. Remove from oven, and place a pecan ball in center of each cookie. Bake 8 to 10 more minutes or until lightly browned. Cool 5 minutes on baking pans; remove to wire racks to cool completely. Freeze up to 1 month, if desired. Yield: 4½ dozen.

Lemon Icebox Cookies

Prep: 20 min.　**Cook:** 14 min. per batch　**Other:** 8 hrs.

You can freeze this simple dough up to 2 months.

1 cup butter, softened	1 teaspoon grated lemon rind
1 cup granulated sugar	2 tablespoons fresh lemon juice
1 cup firmly packed light brown sugar	3½ cups all-purpose flour
	1 teaspoon baking soda
2 large eggs	½ teaspoon salt

• Beat butter and sugars at medium speed with an electric mixer until fluffy. Add eggs, 1 at a time, beating well after each addition. Add grated lemon rind and lemon juice, beating until blended.
• Combine flour, baking soda, and salt; gradually add to butter mixture, beating just until blended.
• Divide dough into 3 equal portions; roll each portion on wax paper into a 12-inch log. Cover and chill 8 hours.
• Cut each log into ½-inch slices (about 28 slices), and place on lightly greased baking sheets.
• Bake at 350° for 12 to 14 minutes or until edges are lightly browned. Remove to wire racks to cool. Store cookies in an airtight container, or freeze, if desired. Yield: 7 dozen.

Lemon-Coconut Cookies: Add 1 cup toasted coconut; proceed with recipe as directed.

Lemon-Almond Cookies: Add 1 cup sliced almonds, toasted; proceed with recipe as directed.

Lemon-Poppy Seed Cookies: Add 2 teaspoons poppy seeds; proceed with recipe as directed.

Lemon-Pecan Cookies: Add 1 cup finely chopped pecans, toasted; proceed with recipe as directed.

FREEZER FRIENDLY
★★★★★

Cooks Chat

"These cookies make very tasty treats for anyone. These are very easy to make, too. Yum, yum, yum! Try them—you'll like them!"

"My grandmother loved these cookies and said they reminded her of her mother's cookies."

Basic Brownies

Prep: 10 min. **Cook:** 45 min.

1 cup butter or margarine
4 (1-ounce) squares
    unsweetened chocolate
    baking squares
4 large eggs
2 cups sugar
2 cups all-purpose flour
½ teaspoon salt
1 teaspoon vanilla extract
1½ cups chopped walnuts or
    pecans (optional)
Crème De Menthe Frosting
    (optional)
Chocolate Glaze (optional)

• Microwave butter and chocolate squares in a 1-quart microwave-safe bowl at HIGH 2 minutes or until both are melted, stirring mixture once.
• Beat eggs at medium speed with an electric mixer; gradually add sugar, beating well.
• Add flour, salt, and vanilla, beating well. Stir in chocolate mixture, and, if desired, chopped walnuts. Pour batter into a lightly greased 13- x 9-inch pan.
• Bake at 325° for 40 to 45 minutes. Cool in pan on a wire rack. Spread with frosting, if desired, and cut into squares. Drizzle with glaze, if desired. Yield: 2½ dozen.

Raspberry Brownies: Fold 1 cup fresh raspberries into Basic Brownies batter; pour into pan. Melt ½ cup raspberry jam; drizzle over batter, and swirl with a knife. Bake as directed. Sprinkle with sifted powdered sugar; cut into squares. Garnish with fresh raspberries and raspberry leaves, if desired.

Note: For added interest, stir 1 cup of any of the following ingredients into Basic Brownie batter: butterscotch, peanut butter, semisweet, or white chocolate morsels; candy-coated chocolate pieces; chopped candy bars or caramels; toffee bits; or dried cherries. Bake as directed.

Crème De Menthe Frosting

Prep: 8 min.

½ cup butter or margarine,
    softened
4 cups sifted powdered sugar
3 to 4 tablespoons half-and-half
3 tablespoons green crème de
    menthe

• Beat butter at medium speed with an electric mixer until fluffy; gradually add powdered sugar, half-and-half, and crème de menthe, beating until frosting is smooth. Yield: 3 cups.

Chocolate Glaze

Prep: 2 min.

1 cup (6 ounces) semisweet
   chocolate morsels

3 tablespoons butter or
   margarine

• Microwave chocolate and butter in a 1-quart microwave-safe
bowl at HIGH 1½ minutes or until melted, stirring once. Yield:
⅔ cup.

Double-Cherry Cheesecake Cobbler

Prep: 15 min.   **Cook:** 35 min.   **Other:** 15 min.

1 (8-ounce) package cream
   cheese, softened
⅓ cup sugar
⅓ cup all-purpose flour
1 large egg
1 teaspoon vanilla extract
¼ teaspoon almond extract

1 (15-ounce) can dark sweet
   cherries, drained
1 (21-ounce) can cherry pie
   filling
¼ cup butter, melted and
   divided
20 vanilla wafers, crushed

• Beat cream cheese, sugar, and flour at low speed with an electric
mixer; add egg and extracts, beating until smooth. Set aside.
• Stir together cherries, cherry pie filling, and 2 tablespoons melted
butter in a large saucepan, and cook over medium heat, stirring
often, 5 minutes or until thoroughly heated. Spoon hot cherry
mixture into a lightly greased 9-inch deep-dish pieplate. Spoon
cream cheese mixture evenly over hot cherries.
• Combine crushed vanilla wafers and remaining 2 tablespoons
melted butter. Sprinkle evenly over cream cheese mixture.
• Bake at 350° for 30 minutes or until golden brown and set. Let
stand 15 minutes before serving. Yield: 8 servings.

KITCHEN COMFORT
★★★★★

Cooks Chat

*"This is a great recipe. The cheese-
cake mixture was delicious. The
almond extract really complements
the cherry taste. I made this for a
friend who was on bed rest for preg-
nancy a couple of weeks ago, and
she enjoyed it. I'll make this again."*

*"Wonderful dessert. My family loved
this dish, and it will be in my recipe
box forever. Quick and easy to fix."*

*"We absolutely loved the flavor of
this cobbler, and it was very easy
to make."*

Blackberry Cobbler

Prep: 10 min.   **Cook:** 45 min.

1⅓ cups sugar
½ cup all-purpose flour
½ cup butter or margarine, melted
2 teaspoons vanilla extract
2 (14-ounce) bags frozen blackberries, unthawed

½ (15-ounce) package refrigerated piecrusts
1 tablespoon sugar
Vanilla ice cream (optional)
Sugared Piecrust Sticks (optional)

• Stir together first 4 ingredients in a large bowl. Gently stir in blackberries until sugar mixture is crumbly. Spoon fruit mixture into a lightly greased 11- x 7-inch baking dish.
• Cut 1 piecrust into ½-inch-wide strips; arrange strips diagonally over blackberry mixture. Sprinkle top with 1 tablespoon sugar.
• Bake at 425° for 45 minutes or until crust is golden brown and center is bubbly. Serve with ice cream and Sugared Piecrust Sticks, if desired. Yield: 6 to 8 servings.

Sugared Piecrust Sticks

Prep: 10 min.   **Cook:** 8 min.

1 refrigerated piecrust, cut into
    ½-inch-thick strips

1 tablespoon sugar

• Sprinkle strips with sugar; place on a lightly greased baking sheet. Bake at 425° for 6 to 8 minutes or until golden brown. Yield: 6 to 8 servings.

Apple-Gingerbread Cobbler

Prep: 15 min.   **Cook:** 40 min.

1 (14-ounce) package
    gingerbread mix, divided
¾ cup water
¼ cup firmly packed light
    brown sugar

½ cup butter, divided
½ cup chopped pecans
2 (21-ounce) cans apple pie
    filling
Vanilla ice cream

• Stir together 2 cups gingerbread mix and ¾ cup water until smooth; set mixture aside.
• Stir together remaining gingerbread mix and brown sugar; cut in ¼ cup butter until mixture is crumbly. Stir in pecans; set aside.
• Combine apple pie filling and remaining ¼ cup butter in a large saucepan, and cook, stirring often, 5 minutes over medium heat or until thoroughly heated.
• Spoon hot apple mixture evenly into a lightly greased 11- x 7-inch baking dish. Spoon gingerbread and water mixture evenly over hot apple mixture; sprinkle with pecan mixture.
• Bake at 375° for 30 to 35 minutes or until set. Serve cobbler with vanilla ice cream. Yield: 8 servings.

KIDS LOVE IT

Cooks Chat

"I made this recipe over the holidays, and it was a hit! I got nothing but wonderful compliments, and I even shared the recipe with my relatives. It is sort of rich, so this recipe works well after a not-so-heavy supper."

"This was unique and easy. Good for quick entertaining, while not being too ordinary. I gave some leftovers to my neighbor. It was a huge hit."

"This recipe was easy to make, and everyone in my family loved it. It was good even without the ice cream."

Cooks Chat

"Wonderful dessert—absolutely delicious! My guests raved for weeks. This is easy and can be made ahead of time—perfect for a small dinner party."

Chocolate Mousse Loaf with Raspberry Puree

Prep: 40 min. **Cook:** 10 min. **Other:** 8 hrs.

This sweet finale can be made a day ahead and chilled until time to serve.

2 cups whipping cream, divided
2 (8-ounce) packages semisweet
    chocolate baking squares
½ cup light corn syrup
½ cup butter or margarine
¼ cup sifted powdered sugar

1 teaspoon vanilla extract
1 (10-ounce) package frozen
    raspberries, thawed
Garnishes: fresh mint sprigs,
    fresh raspberries

• Line a 9- x 5-inch loafpan with plastic wrap, extending edges of wrap over sides of pan; set aside.
• Combine ½ cup whipping cream, chocolate squares, corn syrup, and butter in a heavy saucepan; cook, stirring constantly, over low heat until chocolate melts. Cool.
• Beat remaining 1½ cups whipping cream, powdered sugar, and vanilla at high speed with an electric mixer until stiff peaks form; fold into chocolate mixture. Pour into prepared pan, and chill at least 8 hours.
• Process raspberries in a blender or food processor until smooth, stopping once to scrape down sides. Pour puree through a fine wire-mesh strainer, if desired, pressing with the back of a spoon; discard seeds. Chill.
• Invert mousse loaf onto a serving platter, and remove plastic wrap. Slice loaf, and serve with raspberry puree. Garnish, if desired. Store in refrigerator. Yield: 16 servings.

Brownie Trifle

Prep: 1 hr., 20 min.   **Other:** 2 hrs.

For a change, assemble this trifle in a 3-quart bowl. Measure the size of your bowl with water; it should hold at least 12 cups. Assemble the brownie pieces, cream cheese mixture, caramel topping, and pudding in several layers when using a deep bowl.

2 (21-ounce) packages chewy fudge brownie mix
1 (8-ounce) package cream cheese, softened
1 (7-ounce) jar marshmallow cream
2 (8-ounce) containers frozen whipped topping, thawed and divided
3 cups fat-free milk
2 (3.3-ounce) packages instant white chocolate pudding
1 (12¼-ounce) jar caramel topping

• Prepare each brownie mix according to package directions for chewy brownies in a 13- x 9-inch pan. Cool and break into large pieces.
• Beat cream cheese at medium speed with an electric mixer until creamy; beat in marshmallow cream. Stir in 1 container of whipped topping; set mixture aside.
• Stir together milk and white chocolate pudding mix, stirring until thickened. Stir in remaining container of whipped topping.
• Crumble half of brownie pieces in an even layer in bottom of a 13- x 9-inch baking dish. Pour cream cheese mixture evenly over brownies; drizzle evenly with caramel topping. Pour pudding mixture evenly over caramel topping; crumble remaining brownie pieces over top. Cover and chill 2 hours. Store in refrigerator. Yield: 15 servings.

Note: For testing purposes only, we used Duncan Hines Chewy Fudge Brownie Mix and Smucker's Caramel Topping.

KIDS LOVE IT

Cooks Chat

"This dessert was delicious! I made the recipe exactly as described for a family gathering, and it was quite popular. I put it in a small crystal punch bowl, and it was a beautiful addition to our table."

"Very yummy. Great for a big party. You do need a very big bowl for this recipe. If you are making this for a smaller group, you can easily cut the recipe in half."

"This was a huge neighborhood potluck success—it was gone in 10 minutes. I actually caught someone running his fingers around the empty dish. Very yummy! A keeper."

Chocolate Cookie Pudding

Prep: 15 min.   **Other:** 5 min.

1 (5.9-ounce) package chocolate instant pudding mix
2 cups milk
1 (3-ounce) package cream cheese, softened
1 (8-ounce) container frozen whipped topping, thawed

16 double-stuffed cream-filled chocolate sandwich cookies, crushed (about 2 cups)
¾ cup chopped pecans, toasted

• Whisk together chocolate instant pudding mix and 2 cups milk for 2 minutes. Cover pudding, and chill 5 minutes.
• Stir together cream cheese and whipped topping, blending well.
• Place 1 cup crushed cookies evenly on bottom of an 8-cup bowl. Spread half of cream cheese mixture over crushed cookies; sprinkle with half of pecans. Spread all of pudding evenly over top; spread remaining cream cheese mixture evenly over pudding. Sprinkle with remaining cookies and pecans. Chill until ready to serve. Yield: 6 to 8 servings.

Note: For testing purposes only, we used Oreo Double Stuf for double-stuffed cream-filled chocolate sandwich cookies.

Chocolate-Peanut Butter Cookie Pudding: Crush 16 peanut butter cream-filled chocolate sandwich cookies. Substitute ¼ cup creamy peanut butter for cream cheese and 1 cup chopped dry roasted peanuts for pecans. Proceed as directed.

Note: For testing purposes only, we used Double Delight Oreo Peanut Butter & Chocolate for sandwich cookies.

Old-Fashioned Bread Pudding

Prep: 15 min.   **Cook:** 45 min.

One spoonful will tell you why this received our highest rating.

1 (16-ounce) day-old French
   bread loaf, cubed
2 (12-ounce) cans evaporated
   milk
1 cup water
6 large eggs, lightly beaten
1 (8-ounce) can crushed
   pineapple, drained

1 large Red Delicious apple,
   grated
1½ cups sugar
1 cup raisins
5 tablespoons vanilla extract
¼ cup butter or margarine, cut
   up and softened
Bourbon Sauce

• Combine first 3 ingredients; stir in eggs, blending well. Stir in pineapple and next 4 ingredients. Stir in butter, blending well. Pour mixture into a greased 13- x 9-inch baking dish.
• Bake at 350° for 35 to 45 minutes or until set. Serve with Bourbon Sauce. Yield: 8 servings.

Bourbon Sauce

Prep: 2 min.   **Cook:** 13 min.

3 tablespoons butter or
   margarine
1 tablespoon all-purpose flour
½ cup sugar

1 cup whipping cream
2 tablespoons bourbon
1 tablespoon vanilla extract
1 teaspoon nutmeg

• Melt butter in a small saucepan; whisk in flour, and cook 5 minutes. Stir in sugar and whipping cream; cook 3 minutes. Stir in bourbon, vanilla, and nutmeg, and simmer 5 minutes. Yield: 1½ cups.

PARTY PLEASER
★ ★ ★ ★ ★

Cooks Chat

"There are not enough stars for this recipe. This is the very best bread pudding I've ever had. It stayed so moist. I made a rum sauce instead of the Bourbon Sauce. Excellent! The apple and pineapple definitely added to the flavor."

"Loved this recipe! Reminded me of my grandmother's bread pudding. This is a keeper for sure!"

"My family loves this dessert. We usually have it for Christmas, but I also make it on cold, rainy days just to make them special. Sometimes I add a handful of shredded coconut or chopped pecans. We like it best warm, but it's good at any temperature."

Chocolate Bread Pudding with Whiskey Sauce

Prep: 50 min.   **Cook:** 1 hr., 45 min.   **Other:** 1 hr.

¼ cup unsalted butter
7 cups French bread cubes
2 cups whipping cream
1 cup milk
8 (1-ounce) bittersweet
    chocolate baking squares,
    chopped

5 egg yolks, lightly beaten
⅔ cup firmly packed light
    brown sugar
1 teaspoon vanilla extract
Whiskey Sauce
Garnish: chocolate shavings

• Melt butter in a large heavy skillet over medium heat. Add bread cubes, and cook, stirring constantly, 3 minutes or until golden. Transfer to a lightly greased 13- x 9-inch baking dish.
• Bring whipping cream and milk to a boil over medium heat in skillet. Remove from heat, and whisk in chocolate until smooth. Whisk in egg yolks, brown sugar, and vanilla. Pour over bread cubes; let stand 30 minutes. Cover with foil; cut 6 small holes in foil to allow steam to escape.
• Place baking dish in a roasting pan. Add hot water to pan to a depth of 1½ inches.
• Bake at 325° for 1 hour and 45 minutes or until set. Remove bread pudding from water. Cool 30 minutes on a wire rack. Serve warm with Whiskey Sauce. Garnish, if desired. Yield: 8 to 10 servings.

Whiskey Sauce

Prep: 10 min.   **Cook:** 5 min.

1½ cups milk
½ cup butter or margarine
1 cup sugar

3 tablespoons cornstarch
¼ cup water
½ cup bourbon

• Cook first 3 ingredients in a heavy saucepan over low heat, stirring often, until butter melts and sugar dissolves.
• Combine cornstarch and ¼ cup water, stirring until smooth. Add to butter mixture; stir in bourbon. Bring to a boil over medium heat, stirring constantly; boil, stirring constantly, 1 minute. Yield: 2¾ cups.

Mrs. Floyd's Divinity

Prep: 30 min.   **Cook:** 20 min.

2½ cups sugar
½ cup water
½ cup light corn syrup
¼ teaspoon salt

2 egg whites
1 teaspoon vanilla extract
1 cup chopped pecans, toasted
Garnish: toasted pecan halves

• Cook first 4 ingredients in a heavy 2-quart saucepan over low heat until sugar dissolves and a candy thermometer registers 248° (about 15 minutes). Remove syrup mixture from heat.
• Beat egg whites at high speed with an electric mixer until stiff peaks form. Pour half of hot syrup in a thin stream over egg whites, beating constantly at high speed, about 5 minutes.
• Cook remaining half of syrup over medium heat, stirring occasionally, until a candy thermometer registers 272° (about 4 to 5 minutes). Slowly pour hot syrup and vanilla extract over egg white mixture, beating constantly at high speed until mixture holds its shape (about 6 to 8 minutes). Stir in 1 cup chopped pecans.
• Drop mixture quickly by rounded teaspoonfuls onto lightly greased wax paper. Garnish, if desired. Cool. Yield: 4 dozen (1¾ pounds).

FOR THE HOLIDAYS
★★★★★

Cooks Chat

"I have just one word to describe this divinity—awesome! I made it last night, and everyone loved it!"

"Superb! Delicious! A great candy!"

"When spooning, work quickly because this mixture sets up fast. For a yummy variation, try adding mint instead of vanilla flavoring."

Pecan Toffee

Prep: 10 min.   **Cook:** 15 min.   **Other:** 30 min.

1½ cups chopped pecans, divided
1 cup sugar
1 cup butter, softened

⅓ cup water
5 (1.55-ounce) milk chocolate bars, broken into small pieces

• Line a 15- x 10-inch jellyroll pan with heavy-duty aluminum foil; lightly grease foil. Sprinkle with 1 cup pecans to within 1 inch of edges.
• Bring sugar, butter, and ⅓ cup water to a boil in a heavy saucepan over medium heat, stirring constantly. Cook over medium-high heat, stirring constantly, 12 minutes or until a candy thermometer registers 310° (hard crack stage). Pour over pecans in pan; sprinkle with chocolate pieces. Let stand 30 seconds.
• Sprinkle with remaining ½ cup pecans. Chill 30 minutes. Break up toffee using a mallet or rolling pin. Store in an airtight container. Yield: 1¾ pounds.

Soft-and-Chewy Caramels

Prep: 5 min.   **Cook:** 20 min.   **Other:** 3 hrs.

These rich candies are more tender than their store-bought cousins.

1 cup butter
1 (16-ounce) package light brown sugar

1 (14-ounce) can sweetened condensed milk
1 cup light corn syrup

• Line an 8-inch square baking pan with foil, extending foil over edges of pan. Generously coat foil with cooking spray; set aside.
• Melt 1 cup butter in a 3-quart saucepan over low heat. Stir in brown sugar, condensed milk, and corn syrup until smooth. Bring mixture to a boil. Cook over medium heat, stirring often, until a candy thermometer registers 235° (soft ball stage).
• Remove mixture from heat; stir by hand 1 minute or until mixture is smooth and no longer bubbling. Quickly pour mixture into prepared pan; let stand 3 hours or until cool.
• Lift foil and caramel out of pan. Cut caramels into 1-inch pieces with a buttered knife. Wrap each piece with plastic wrap. Yield: 64 pieces.

Pecan Toffee

Cooks Chat

"Very easy to make! Everyone loved these! I won't chop the pecans as small the next time, though. Very yummy!"

Pralines

Prep: 20 min.   **Cook:** 12 min.   **Other:** 30 min.

3 cups firmly packed light
   brown sugar
1 cup whipping cream
2 tablespoons light corn syrup

¼ teaspoon salt
¼ cup butter or margarine
2 cups chopped pecans
1 teaspoon vanilla extract

• Bring first 4 ingredients to a boil in a 3-quart saucepan over medium heat, stirring mixture constantly. Cook mixture, stirring occasionally, 6 to 8 minutes, or until a candy thermometer registers 236° (soft ball stage).
• Remove mixture from heat, and add butter (do not stir). Let stand until candy thermometer reaches 150°. Stir in pecans and vanilla, using a wooden spoon; stir constantly until candy begins to thicken.
• Drop by heaping teaspoonfuls, working rapidly, onto wax paper. Let stand until firm. Yield: 2½ dozen.

Cooks Chat

"Fantastic! Everyone loved this! I added walnuts because our family likes nuts. The fudge was very creamy, and it stayed creamy. I'll make this again!"

Microwave Chocolate Fudge

Prep: 5 min.   **Cook:** 5 min.   **Other:** 8 hrs.

3 cups (18 ounces) milk
   chocolate morsels
1 (14-ounce) can sweetened
   condensed milk

¼ cup butter or margarine, cut
   into pieces

• Combine all ingredients in a 2-quart glass bowl. Microwave chocolate mixture at MEDIUM (50% power) 5 minutes, stirring at 1½-minute intervals. Pour into a greased 8-inch square dish. Cover and chill 8 hours; cut into 1½-inch squares. Store in refrigerator. Yield: 3 dozen.

Cracker Candy

Prep: 13 min.   **Cook:** 8 min.   **Other:** 3 min.

2½ cups miniature round
   buttery crackers*
¾ cup butter
¾ cup firmly packed brown
   sugar

2 cups milk chocolate morsels
Chopped pecans (optional)
Rainbow candy sprinkles
   (optional)

• Place crackers in a lightly greased aluminum foil-lined
13- x 9-inch pan.
• Bring butter and brown sugar to a boil in a medium saucepan,
stirring constantly; cook, stirring often, 3 minutes. Pour mixture
over crackers.
• Bake at 350° for 5 minutes. Turn oven off. Sprinkle crackers with
chocolate morsels, and let stand in oven 3 minutes or until chocolate melts. Spread melted chocolate evenly over crackers. Top with
pecans or candy sprinkles, if desired. Cool and break into pieces.
Store in refrigerator. Yield: 10 servings.

*For testing purposes only, we used Mini Ritz crackers. If minia-
ture round buttery crackers aren't available in your area, substitute
2 sleeves regular round buttery crackers, broken in half.

Cooks Chat

*"Wonderfully simple! Great for
last-minute events. I substituted
Keebler Club crackers, and I only
used ½ cup butter. I popped mine
into the freezer when finished for a
quick, hard set. This tasted very
much like English toffee."*

Buckeye Balls

Prep: 1 hr.   **Other:** 10 min.

1 (16-ounce) jar creamy peanut
   butter
1 cup butter or margarine,
   softened
1½ (16-ounce) packages
   powdered sugar

2 cups (12 ounces) semisweet
   chocolate morsels
2 tablespoons shortening

• Beat peanut butter and butter at medium speed with an electric
mixer until blended. Gradually add powdered sugar, beating until
blended.
• Shape into 1-inch balls; chill 10 minutes or until firm.
• Microwave chocolate and shortening in a 2-quart glass bowl at
HIGH 1½ minutes or until melted, stirring twice.
• Dip each ball in chocolate mixture until partially coated; place on
wax paper to harden. Store in an airtight container. Yield: 7 dozen.

Cooks Chat

*"I have been looking everywhere for
this recipe. I am so glad I have
found it! This recipe is very good.
You will love it. I have never had
such a wonderful combo of chocolate and peanut butter."*

*"I got this recipe from my mother-
in-law about 12 years ago. Though I
never knew the actual name of them,
my family has requested that I make
these every year. That should tell
you something. Everyone who tries
them absolutely loves them."*

Cordial Cherries

Prep: 10 min.   **Cook:** 10 min.   **Other:** 8 hrs.

Brandy-soaked cherries can be left in the freezer for up to 2 days before you dip them into the chocolate.

Cooks Chat

"These were so easy and delicious, and they made a great presentation! I made half of them with semisweet chocolate chips and half with milk chocolate. I will definitely make these again. They would make a great gift!"

"These were so easy to make and were a huge hit for Valentine's Day. My husband loved them. You have to work quickly with the chocolate because it starts to harden before you are able to get through the whole jar of cherries. Great hostess gift."

1 (10-ounce) jar maraschino cherries with stems
½ cup brandy (optional)

1 (8-ounce) package semisweet chocolate baking squares, chopped

• Drain maraschino cherries, and return to jar. Pour brandy, if desired, into jar; cover with a lid, and freeze 8 hours. Drain cherries, and pat dry, reserving brandy for another use.
• Melt two-thirds of chocolate baking squares in a saucepan over medium heat, stirring until a candy thermometer reaches 115°. Remove from heat; add remaining chocolate, and stir until candy thermometer reaches 89° and chocolate is smooth.
• Dip cherries quickly into melted chocolate, coating well. Place cherries on wax paper, stem sides up, and cool. Yield: 2½ dozen.

Butterscotch Drops

Prep: 15 min.

1 (6-ounce) package
    butterscotch morsels*
1 cup dry-roasted peanuts

1 cup shoestring potato sticks,
    broken into pieces

• Melt morsels in a saucepan over low heat. Stir in peanuts and potato sticks. Drop by teaspoonfuls onto wax paper, and cool completely. Yield: 2½ dozen.

*Substitute 1 (6-ounce) package peanut butter morsels for butterscotch morsels, if desired.

Cooks Chat

"Unbelievable recipe! It took me all of 15 minutes from start to finish. Most of all, these were delicious. I used peanut butter chips instead of butterscotch. The combination sounded weird, but it worked very well. I only hope they last until tomorrow night when I have to take them to a cookie exchange."

Cinnamon-Chocolate Chip Ice-Cream Balls

Prep: 25 min.   **Other:** 2 hrs.

1½ cups cinnamon-sugar
    whole wheat-and-rice
    cereal, crushed
½ cup semisweet chocolate
    mini-morsels

1 cup finely chopped pecans
    (optional)
½ gallon ice cream
Caramel syrup

• Combine crushed cereal, morsels, and, if desired, pecans in a large bowl.
• Scoop out ice cream, and shape into 6 (3-inch) balls.
• Roll balls in cereal mixture, coating evenly. Place in a 9-inch square pan; freeze 2 hours or until firm. Drizzle with caramel syrup before serving. Yield: 6 servings.

Note: For testing purposes only, we used Cinnamon Toast Crunch cereal.

Cooks Chat

"This is a good treat for kids."

"I tried this recipe about 2 years ago, and my friends, family, and loved ones all ask for it over and over again! It's a good one to try!"

"I made this for my family, and they loved it. I drizzled chocolate syrup on the plate before placing the balls on top and adding the caramel. The mini-morsels were a good addition."

Mocha Ice Cream

Prep: 45 min.   **Cook:** 15 min.   **Other:** 3 hrs.

1 (8-ounce) package semisweet
   chocolate baking squares,
   coarsely chopped
¼ cup strong brewed coffee
2 cups whipping cream
1 cup half-and-half

¾ cup sugar, divided
3 tablespoons instant coffee
   granules
4 egg yolks
Assorted cookies (optional)

• Microwave chocolate in a 1-quart microwave-safe bowl at HIGH
1½ minutes or until melted, stirring twice; stir in brewed coffee.
Set chocolate mixture aside.
• Bring whipping cream, half-and-half, ½ cup sugar, and coffee
granules to a boil in a heavy saucepan over medium-high heat,
stirring until sugar and coffee dissolve.
• Beat yolks and remaining ¼ cup sugar at high speed with an
electric mixer until thick and pale. With mixer at low speed, gradually pour hot cream mixture into yolk mixture; return to saucepan.
• Cook over medium heat, stirring constantly, 6 to 8 minutes or
until mixture thickens and coats a spoon. Remove from heat; stir in
chocolate mixture. Cover and chill 2 hours.
• Pour chilled mixture into freezer container of a 5-quart hand-
turned or electric ice-cream maker. Freeze according to manufacturer's instructions.
• Pack freezer with additional ice and rock salt, and let stand
1 hour. Serve ice cream with cookies, if desired. Yield: 5 cups.

PARTY PLEASER
★ ★ ★ ★ ★

Cooks Chat

*"We love homemade ice cream, and
this is a really good recipe. I serve
this chocolaty treat at special occasions. Most of the time, I add sliced
almonds."*

Summertime Peach Ice Cream

Prep: 30 min.   **Other:** 1 hr., 30 min.

Soft, ripe fruit lends the smoothest texture and most pronounced flavor to this refreshing dessert.

Cooks Chat

"Peachy keen! Fab! Yummy! Easy! What else is left to say? Try it!"

"This is the best peach ice cream I've ever tasted, and it's so easy to make! No cooking or eggs! I've made this recipe for large gatherings many times already, and it has always been a huge hit with everyone. It's a real winner!"

"This is a simple no-cook recipe that is smooth, creamy, and has a really good flavor. I think it tasted even better the second day. It would be just as good with strawberries or raspberries instead of the peaches."

4 cups peeled, diced fresh
    peaches (about 8 small ripe
    peaches)
1 cup sugar
1 (12-ounce) can evaporated
    milk
1 (3.4-ounce) package vanilla
    instant pudding mix
1 (14-ounce) can sweetened
    condensed milk
4 cups half-and-half
Garnish: fresh mint sprigs

- Combine peaches and sugar, and let stand 1 hour.
- Process peach mixture in a food processor until smooth, stopping to scrape down sides.
- Stir together evaporated milk and pudding mix in a large bowl; stir in peach puree, condensed milk, and half-and-half.
- Pour mixture into freezer container of a 4-quart hand-turned or electric ice-cream maker. Freeze according to manufacturer's instructions. Spoon into an airtight container, and freeze until firm. Garnish, if desired. Yield: 2 quarts.

Watermelon Sorbet

Prep: 15 min.   **Cook:** 5 min.   **Other:** 3 hrs.

3 cups water
1 cup sugar
4 cups seeded, chopped
    watermelon

¼ cup lime juice

Cooks Chat

"We have tried all of these variations, and they are delicious and so easy to prepare. We use a blender and freeze in small containers."

"This dessert can also be made with mangos, blueberries, or peaches. I'm planning to make a sugar-free version with a substitute sweetener."

• Bring 3 cups water and sugar just to a boil in a medium saucepan over high heat, stirring until sugar dissolves. Remove from heat, and cool.
• Process sugar syrup and watermelon, in batches, in a blender until smooth. Stir in lime juice. Cover and chill 2 hours.
• Pour mixture into freezer container of a 1-gallon ice-cream maker. Freeze according to manufacturer's instructions. Yield: about ½ gallon.

Grapefruit Sorbet: Substitute 3 cups fresh grapefruit juice and 1 teaspoon chopped fresh mint for watermelon and lime juice. Proceed as directed.

Pineapple Sorbet: Substitute 2 cups chopped pineapple for watermelon and lime juice. Strain and discard pulp after processing mixture in blender, if desired. Proceed as directed.

Lemon Sorbet: Substitute ½ cup fresh lemon juice and 2 teaspoons grated lemon rind for watermelon and lime juice. Proceed as directed.

Orange Sorbet: Substitute 3 cups fresh orange juice and 2 teaspoons grated orange rind for watermelon and lime juice. Proceed as directed.

Strawberry Sorbet: Substitute 5 cups fresh or frozen strawberries and 2 tablespoons lemon juice for watermelon and lime juice. Proceed as directed.

Cantaloupe Sorbet: Substitute 4 cups chopped cantaloupe for watermelon and lime juice. Proceed as directed.

Cherry Sorbet: Substitute 1 (6-ounce) can frozen lemonade concentrate, prepared, and 1 (16-ounce) jar maraschino cherries for watermelon and lime juice. Strain and discard pulp after processing mixture in blender, if desired. Proceed as directed.

Raspberry Sorbet: Substitute 5 cups fresh or frozen raspberries for watermelon and lime juice. Proceed as directed.

Index

SOUTHERN CLASSIC
★ ★ ★ ★ ★

PARTY PLEASER
★★★★★

Cooks Chat

"An instant hit at my gathering! The perfect dessert—light and tasty. I had several requests for the recipe. These are so simple to make—they take just minutes to assemble! I added ¼ teaspoon orange essence to the orange curd, and the tartlets were luscious. Perfect for a quick dessert."

Creamy Citrus Tartlets

Prep: 30 min.   **Other:** 1 hr.

Look for orange and lemon curds on the grocery aisle with the jams and jellies.

2 (2.1-ounce) packages frozen
   mini phyllo pastry shells
1 cup whipping cream, divided
⅓ cup orange curd*

½ teaspoon almond extract,
   divided
⅓ cup lemon curd*
Garnish: fresh mint leaves

• Bake pastry shells according to package directions; cool completely.
• Beat ½ cup whipping cream, orange curd, and ¼ teaspoon almond extract at medium speed with an electric mixer until thickened and soft peaks form. Spoon the mixture evenly into half of pastry shells.
• Beat lemon curd, remaining cream, and remaining extract at medium speed with an electric mixer until thickened and soft peaks form. Spoon into remaining shells. Chill tartlets 1 hour. Garnish, if desired. Yield: 30 tartlets.

*Substitute strawberry curd for orange or lemon curd, if desired.

Note: For testing purposes only, we used Dickinson's Orange Curd and Lemon Curd.

Spiced Apples

Prep: 10 min.   **Cook:** 20 min.

½ cup butter or margarine
8 large Granny Smith apples,
    peeled, cored, and sliced
1½ cups sugar

1½ teaspoons ground
    cinnamon
½ teaspoon ground nutmeg

• Melt butter in a large skillet over medium-high heat; add apples and remaining ingredients. Sauté 15 to 20 minutes or until apples are tender. Yield: 8 servings.

Cooks Chat

"Easy to make. Kids love these apples served hot with a scoop of ice cream. These make the house smell wonderful. I have even put the mixture in tart shells. Try this recipe—you'll like it! The dessert is quite rich, so a little goes a long way. Each time I make it, I cut down on the butter a bit."

Mixed Fruit
with Sour Cream Sauce

Prep: 15 min.   **Cook:** 5 min.   **Other:** 1 hr.

⅓ cup granulated sugar
1 cup water
6 fresh mint leaves
1 (8-ounce) can pineapple
    chunks in juice, drained

1 banana, sliced
1 Granny Smith apple, chopped
1 cup seedless green grapes
1 cup sliced strawberries
Sour Cream Sauce

• Bring first 3 ingredients to a boil in a saucepan, and cook, stirring constantly, 4 to 5 minutes or until sugar mixture reaches a syrup consistency. Discard mint leaves, and cool sugar syrup completely.
• Combine pineapple, banana, apple, grapes, and strawberries in a large bowl. Pour syrup over fruit mixture; toss gently. Cover and chill at least 1 hour. Serve with Sour Cream Sauce. Yield: 4 servings.

Cooks Chat

"My family could not get enough of this healthy, refreshing, delicious dessert. Bring it on! It has been requested for cookouts and birthdays by all. Yum!"

Sour Cream Sauce

Prep: 10 min.

⅓ cup butter or margarine,
    softened
1 cup powdered sugar

½ cup sour cream
½ teaspoon lemon juice
¼ teaspoon vanilla extract

• Beat butter and powdered sugar at medium speed with an electric mixer until smooth. Add sour cream, lemon juice, and vanilla, beating until mixture is creamy. Cover and chill until ready to serve or up to 8 hours. Yield: about 1¾ cups.

Index